Please return this book on or before the date shown above. To renew go to www.essex.gov.uk/libraries, ring 0345 603 7628 or go to any Essex library.

Essex County Council

FAMILY HISTORY FROM PEN & SWORD

Tracing Secret Service Ancestors

Tracing Your Air Force Ancestors

Tracing Your Ancestors

Tracing Your Ancestors from 1066 to 1837

Tracing Your Ancestors Through Death Records

Tracing Your Ancestors Through Family Photographs

Tracing Your Ancestors Using the Census

Tracing Your Ancestors' Childhood

Tracing Your Ancestors' Parish Records

Tracing Your Aristocratic Ancestors

Tracing Your Army Ancestors – 2nd Edition

Tracing Your Birmingham Ancestors

Tracing Your Black Country Ancestors

Tracing Your British Indian Ancestors

Tracing Your Canal Ancestors

Tracing Your Channel Islands Ancestors

Tracing Your Coalmining Ancestors

Tracing Your Criminal Ancestors

Tracing Your East Anglian Ancestors

Tracing Your East End Ancestors

Tracing Your Edinburgh Ancestors

Tracing Your First World War Ancestors

Tracing Your Great War Ancestors: The Gallipoli Campaign

Tracing Your Great War Ancestors: The Somme

Tracing Your Great War Ancestors: Ypres

Tracing Your Huguenot Ancestors

Tracing Your Jewish Ancestors

Tracing Your Labour Movement Ancestors

Tracing Your Lancashire Ancestors

Tracing Your Leeds Ancestors

Tracing Your Legal Ancestors

Tracing Your Liverpool Ancestors

Tracing Your London Ancestors

Tracing Your Medical Ancestors

Tracing Your Merchant Navy Ancestors

Tracing Your Naval Ancestors

Tracing Your Northern Ancestors

Tracing Your Pauper Ancestors

Tracing Your Police Ancestors

Tracing Your Prisoner of War Ancestors: The First World War

Tracing Your Railway Ancestors

Tracing Your Royal Marine Ancestors

Tracing Your Rural Ancestors

Tracing Your Scottish Ancestors

Tracing Your Second World War Ancestors

Tracing Your Servant Ancestors

Tracing Your Service Women Ancestors

Tracing Your Shipbuilding Ancestors

Tracing Your Tank Ancestors

Tracing Your Textile Ancestors

Tracing Your Trade and Craftsmen Ancestors

Tracing Your Welsh Ancestors

Tracing Your West Country Ancestors

Tracing Your Yorkshire Ancestors

TRACING HISTORY THROUGH TITLE DEEDS

A Guide for Family and Local Historians

N.W. Alcock

Published in association with
The National Archives

Pen & Sword
FAMILY HISTORY

First published in Great Britain in 2017
PEN & SWORD FAMILY HISTORY
an imprint of
Pen & Sword Books Ltd
47 Church Street
Barnsley, South Yorkshire, S70 2AS

The National Archives logo device is a trade mark of
The National Archives and is used under licence

Copyright © N.W. Alcock, 2017

ISBN 978 1 52670 345 3

The right of N.W. Alcock to be identified as Author
of the Work has been asserted by him in accordance
with the Copyright, Designs and Patents Act 1988.

A CIP catalogue record for this book is
available from the British Library.

All rights reserved. No part of this book may be reproduced or
transmitted in any form or by any means, electronic or mechanical
including photocopying, recording or by any information storage
and retrieval system, without permission from the Publisher in writing.

Typeset in Palatino and Optima by CHIC GRAPHICS

Printed and bound in England by
CPI Group (UK), Croydon, CR0 4YY

Pen & Sword Books Ltd incorporates the imprints of Pen & Sword Airworld,
Archaeology, Atlas, Aviation, Battleground, Discovery, Family History, Fiction,
History, Maritime, Military, Military Classics, Politics, Select, Social History, True
Crime, Frontline Books, Leo Cooper, Remember When, Seaforth Publishing, The
Praetorian Press, Wharncliffe Local History, Wharncliffe Transport.
Wharncliffe True Crime and White Owl.

For a complete list of Pen & Sword titles please contact
PEN & SWORD BOOKS LTD
47 Church Street, Barnsley, South Yorkshire, S70 2AS, England
E-mail: enquiries@pen-and-sword.co.uk
Website: www.pen-and-sword.co.uk

* * *

Jacket captions: (a) Top left: Lease of a lease and release of 1692 (TNA, E 330/31; see Illus. 4.4); (b) Top right: Plan of a house in Botolph Lane, London, from a deed of 1785 (see Illus. 2.9); (c) Bottom left: Dial House, Knowle, Warwickshire, traced back to its building in 1651 through court rolls (see p. 34); (d) Bottom right: Lease of a house and malt-kiln in Coventry in 1340 (TNA, E40/8153, see Illus. 2.10).

CONTENTS

List of Illustrations ... viii
List of Tables ... x
Preface ... xi
Abbreviations ... xii
Image Credits ... xii

Chapter 1: Introduction ... 1
    Deeds as History ... 3

Chapter 2: Why ... 10
    Deeds for People ... 10
        Post-medieval Evidence ... 11
        Medieval Evidence ... 17
        People in the Community ... 19
        People in Copyhold Deeds and Manor
            Court Rolls ... 22
    Deeds for Places and for Houses ... 24
        Land ... 24
        Houses ... 31
    Large-scale Studies of Deeds ... 40

Chapter 3: Where ... 45
    What to Look For ... 46
        The Local Historian's Objectives ... 46
        The Family Historian's Objectives ... 47
    Where to Look ... 48
        Local Collections ... 48
        Out-county Records ... 48
        National Collections ... 49
        The National Archives ... 51
        Enrolled and Registered Deeds ... 59
        Private Copies of Deeds ... 66
        The Land Registry ... 67

Deeds in Private Hands	69
Dispersed Deeds	71
On the Trail	75
New Ways to Find Deeds	76

Chapter 4: How — 81
- Tenure — 82
- Post-medieval Deeds — 83
  - Introduction — 83
    - Studying a Deed Bundle — 83
    - Shapes and Patterns — 88
  - Types of Post-Medieval Deeds — 94
    - Lease and Counterpart Lease; Assignment of Lease — 95
    - Lease and Release — 99
    - Mortgage — 109
    - Bond — 112
    - Settlements — 114
    - Fines and Recoveries — 118
    - Letters Patent — 125
    - Bargain-and-Sale; Feoffment — 127
    - Quitclaim — 130
    - Perpetual Lease — 130
    - Copies of Court Roll — 131
    - Miscellaneous Post-Medieval Deeds — 132
  - The Contents of Deed Bundles — 133
- Medieval Deeds — 135
  - Introduction — 135
    - Dating — 136
    - Shapes and Patterns — 137
    - Clauses — 138
  - Types of Medieval Deeds — 143
    - Gifts and Grants — 143
    - Quitclaims — 147
    - Leases — 147
    - Fines — 148
    - Other Medieval Deeds — 149

Contents

Manorial Court Rolls and Copies of Court Roll	151
Copies of Court Roll	153
Manorial Customs	158
Medieval Copies of Court Roll	160
Appendix 1: Flowchart to Identify Deed Types	165
Appendix 2: Sample Deed Record Sheet	168
Appendix 3: Post-medieval Letter Forms	170
Appendix 4: Texts of Typical Deeds	171
Further Resources and Select Bibliography	190
Glossary of Deed Terms	195
Index of Subjects	200
Index of People and Places	210

LIST OF ILLUSTRATIONS

1.1	Letter from Thomas á Becket, Archbishop of Canterbury.	4
1.2	Early thirteenth-century lease of a house in Coventry.	5
1.3	Copper plaque on the gate-arch of Cooling Castle.	6
1.4	Deeds for an annuity from 1505 to 1757.	7
1.5	Sixteenth- to eighteenth-century wooden deed boxes.	8
1.6	A family settlement for the Marquess of Hertford.	8
2.1	Family tree of Benjamin Woodcock of Coventry.	12
2.2	Ancestry of Ann Edwards of Sherborne, Warwickshire.	13
2.3	Family links between the Wymond and Austin families in early fourteenth-century Coventry.	19
2.4	Social relationships in Coventry, 1680–1700.	21
2.5	Family tree for the Fisher family of Temple Balsall, Warwickshire.	23
2.6	Plan of Avin's Yard, Atherstone, Warwickshire.	26
2.7	Nineteenth-century property boundaries in part of central Coventry.	27
2.8	Medieval tenement boundaries in part of central Coventry.	28
2.9	Plan of a courtyard house in Botolph Lane, London.	33
2.10	Fourteenth-century lease of property in Coventry.	35
2.11	The development of a Coventry court.	38
2.12	Successive plans of a Coventry factory.	39
4.1	A nineteenth-century deed endorsement.	84
4.2	Endorsements on a seventeenth-century Coventry deed.	85
4.3	Eighteenth-century printed blank deed form for a mortgage.	91
4.4	The lease of a lease and release for a house in Derby.	99
4.5	Terrier of open-field land at Thurlaston, Warwickshire.	106
4.6	A bond to keep the covenants in an indenture.	113
4.7	The left- and right-hand indentures of a fine.	120

List of Illustrations

4.8	Exemplification of a recovery.	123
4.9	Example of letters patent.	126
4.10	Endorsement of Chancery enrolment.	129
4.11	A medieval gift (conveyance).	140
4.12	A medieval letter of attorney.	150
4.13	Eighteenth-century copy of court roll.	153
4.14	Memorandum for enrolment on a manor court roll.	157
4.15	Instructions for a manor court steward to carry out a Common Recovery.	159
4.16	Fifteenth-century copy of court roll.	160

LIST OF TABLES

3.1	Deed classes in The National Archives.	51
3.2	Deeds enrolled in the royal courts.	60
4.1	Calendar table for the Commonwealth period.	88
4.2	Types and shapes of post-medieval deeds.	89
4.3	Clauses of post-medieval indentures.	90
4.4	Post-medieval indentures: summary of principal clauses.	94
4.5	Conditions in post-medieval leases.	98
4.6	Shapes of medieval deeds.	138
4.7	Initial words and 'action' clauses of medieval deeds.	139
4.8	Abuttals of a Coventry house.	145

PREFACE

This book has a new title and a new publisher, but it is otherwise a direct successor to my previous book, *Old Title Deeds*. It has the same intention: to explain the significance of title deeds for the study of local and family history, and more generally for wider aspects of history. The period since the second edition of *Old Title Deeds* has seen an explosion in the use of personal computers, laptops and tablets, and of digital photography. With this has come important development in the availability of online catalogues at many record offices. All these changes are mentioned where appropriate. However, the essentials of the study of title deeds – like the deeds themselves – are unchanged, so this book tells the same story as its predecessor, though with changes of emphasis and detail.

Working with title deeds has required uncountable hours spent in record offices, where I have received never-failing assistance from the staff. They are far too numerous to name individually, but I hope they will accept my thanks collectively. Mark Booth kindly checked the transcripts of medieval texts. J.B. Post originally advised me on the deed resources of The National Archives, and Sean Cunningham has also given me useful information. My thanks also go to Rupert Harding and Alison Miles of Pen & Sword and Timothy Cross of The National Archives for smoothing the publication of the volume. Permission to reproduce the deeds used in the illustrations is gratefully acknowledged. Additional information and comments will gladly be received for incorporation in future editions.

Nat Alcock
Leamington Spa, October 2017

ABBREVIATIONS

CHC Coventry History Centre
SCLA Shakespeare Centre Library and Archive, Stratford-upon-Avon
TNA The National Archives
WCRO Warwickshire County Record Office

IMAGE CREDITS

Author (2.1, 2.11, 2.12, 2.2, 2.3, 2.4, 2.5, 2.7, 2.8, 4.15); British Records Association (2.9); The National Archives logo and images (1.1, 2.10, 4.4, 4.6, 4.7 (part), 4.8, 4.10, 4.13, 4.16) © Crown copyright, 2017; Warwickshire County Record Office (1.2, 1.4, 1.5, 1.6, 2.6, 4.1, 4.14, 4.2, 4.3, 4.5, 4.9, 4.7 (part), 4.11, 4.12); Glyn Baker, *Creative Commons*, Cooling_Castle_Inscription_-_geograph. org. uk_-_169842.jpg (1.3).

Chapter 1

INTRODUCTION

Deeds can be the ugly ducklings of the record office – bedraggled, dirty and ignored – but it is the purpose of this book to show how they may be used to create, if not a family of swans, at least a well-constructed historical study. They are by far the most numerous but the least used source of historical evidence, surviving in their thousands in collection after collection in record offices, libraries and muniment rooms up and down the country, and even overseas. Their neglect has been partly because they can be difficult to understand, written in technical language and often in Latin. It is also because the information they contain can be summarised in a few lines, and therefore seems insignificant. This overlooks the possibility of writing the history of a community by correlating the evidence of a group of deeds. For family history in particular, they are a generally neglected resource, even though one single deed may supply crucial links in a sequence of family relationships.

The book is primarily intended for people without extensive historical training, and therefore concentrates especially on the two branches of history where 'amateurs' most often begin their historical research – local history and family history. Of course, people with a great deal of skill are also working in these areas, and they have probably learnt most of the information presented here in the same way as the author, simply by working with deeds. I hope that they and other 'professionals' may find something interesting here as well.

The scope of the book is defined by the three questions it sets out to answer: **Why** should local and family historians use deeds, and what sort of historical information can they expect and hope to obtain? **Where** should they look for deeds and what should the deeds concern? **How** can their evidence be extracted? The last is the most important question, and occupies the largest of the three main chapters of the book. It examines post-medieval deeds first because these are easier to decipher than the medieval ones or the copies of court roll covered in the second and third sections. In each, the different types of deeds likely to be encountered are analysed clause by clause, to show how the parts containing important information can be separated from the legal jargon and repetition. The technical problems, such as methods of dating, that may perplex the less experienced are also covered. This chapter is essentially practical rather than theoretical, and avoids exhaustive legal detail.

The second chapter is intended as a guide to locating deeds relating to particular people and places. In this task, initial failure may well *not* mean that the evidence does not exist, because local deeds can be scattered throughout the country, and even abroad. This chapter also looks at the clues that a bundle of deeds itself may give, and how these may help in the discovery of related evidence.

The first chapter tries to remedy the neglect of deeds by historians, by demonstrating some of their uses. It reviews the information that can be found in deeds, and how they illuminate historical evidence for a wide range of topics divided broadly into the history of people and families and the history of places and houses. It also includes a brief discussion of what can be achieved by computer analysis of large groups of deeds.

The appendices provide a chart for identifying the different types of deed, a form that can be used for recording and abstracting deeds, an illustration of post-medieval letter forms and the texts of the various deeds illustrated. Suggestions for further reading are provided, and a glossary includes brief explanations of the principal terms relating to deeds.

The book deals specifically with English and Welsh deeds, which are identical in form. Deeds relating to Ireland follow the same patterns, with occasional idiosyncrasies in wording or layout. In Scotland, however, land tenure depended on Roman law, and title deeds have a completely different form which is beyond the scope of this book.[1]

Introduction

The majority of the examples I give relate to the Midlands, especially Warwickshire, and in particular most of the urban ones are drawn from Coventry. The deeds from one area are virtually identical to those from any other, and so I have chosen those within my own knowledge, rather than searching for them elsewhere. The Coventry deeds have been encountered in the course of a detailed study of the city that has been in progress for a number of years. As this city combines great medieval prosperity, eighteenth-century growth and nineteenth-century industrialisation, with excellent survival of deeds from the twelfth century onwards, their evidence as a whole probably exceeds that from most cities; of course, other places provide their own particular insights.[2]

Apart from the two editions of my own book, *Old Title Deeds* referred to in the preface (and now out of print), the only previous aids for historians working with deeds are the short books by J. Cornwall and A.A. Dibben, and a more recent guide by Tim Wormleighton (see Further Resources, below). Both are useful, but their scale prevents them from including more than the most straightforward analysis. A couple of articles in local publications are also often referred to (by A.G. Foster and R.B. Pugh); both these are helpful in explaining conveyancing practice, but go no further. Textbooks by eminent lawyers describe the land law through the centuries. It is amazingly difficult to match the content of a specific deed with their descriptions of its function, and such prominent features as the dower trustee (see p. 101) find no mention in their pages. The most useful guide to understanding the legal niceties of deeds might be one of the many eighteenth-century text books on conveyancing (e.g. Gilbert Horsman, *Precedents in Conveyancing* (3rd edn, 1768) or an attorney's *vade-mecum* of the eighteenth or nineteenth centuries, such as F.C. Jones, *Attorney's Pocketbook* (1841), but readers are unlikely to have easy access to these. I hope the present book will help to fill the gap between all these publications.

DEEDS AS HISTORY

One aspect of old deeds that can be overlooked in their detailed examination is their fascination as historical objects, beyond their

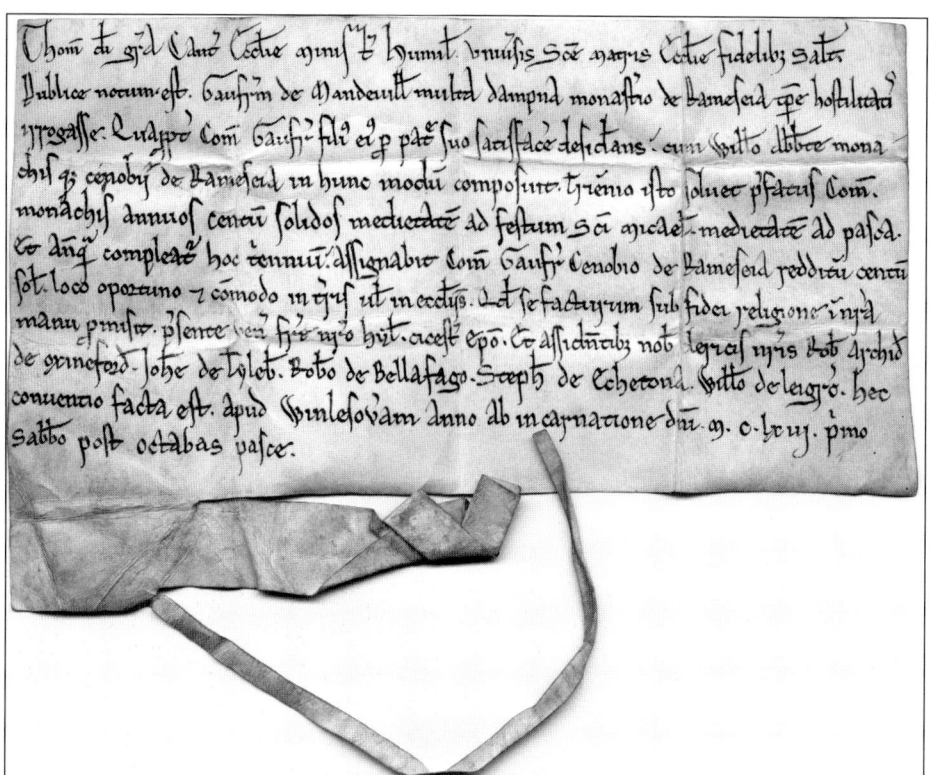

1.1 Letter from Thomas (á Becket), Archbishop of Canterbury concerning payments to be made to Ramsey Abbey by Earl Geoffrey, son of Geoffrey de Mandeville, dated the first Saturday after the octave of Easter (6 April), 1163. Note the two tags, the second of which would have been used to close the letter (see p. 138). For a translation, see D.C. Douglas and G.W. Greenaway (eds), *English Historical Documents. Vol. 2 1042–1189* (1996), item 167 (p. 929). (TNA, E 40/14414)

significance as historical evidence. The only way most of us will see a twelfth- or thirteenth-century manuscript outside a showcase is in the form of a deed. The first, which can be called up by any visitor to TNA, is a letter sent by Thomas á Becket as Archbishop of Canterbury, in the year 1163, that would certainly have been handled and sealed by him (Illus. 1.1). The second is the lease dating from 1223 of a house in Coventry, 'beside the water', in the street known as 'between the bridges', which we can identify as the later 1–2 Burges (Illus. 1.2). This is one of the earliest known deeds for a small property that includes a date (at least by implication). Because the lease was for a specified period, it had to state exactly when it started: The feast of the birth of St John the Baptist, the third after

Introduction

the Translation of St Thomas Martyr (i.e. St Thomas á Becket, when his tomb in Canterbury Cathedral was opened and his relics moved (translated) to a grander shrine on 7 July 1220). Deeds at this social level were not routinely dated until about 1300, and the unusual way this date is specified shows that the standard procedure of dating by the year of the king's reign (p. 87) had not yet evolved. Similarly, another early thirteenth-century deed is dated to the second Michaelmas after the first fire at Worcester Cathedral, which happened on 17 April 1202 (TNA, DL 25/221).

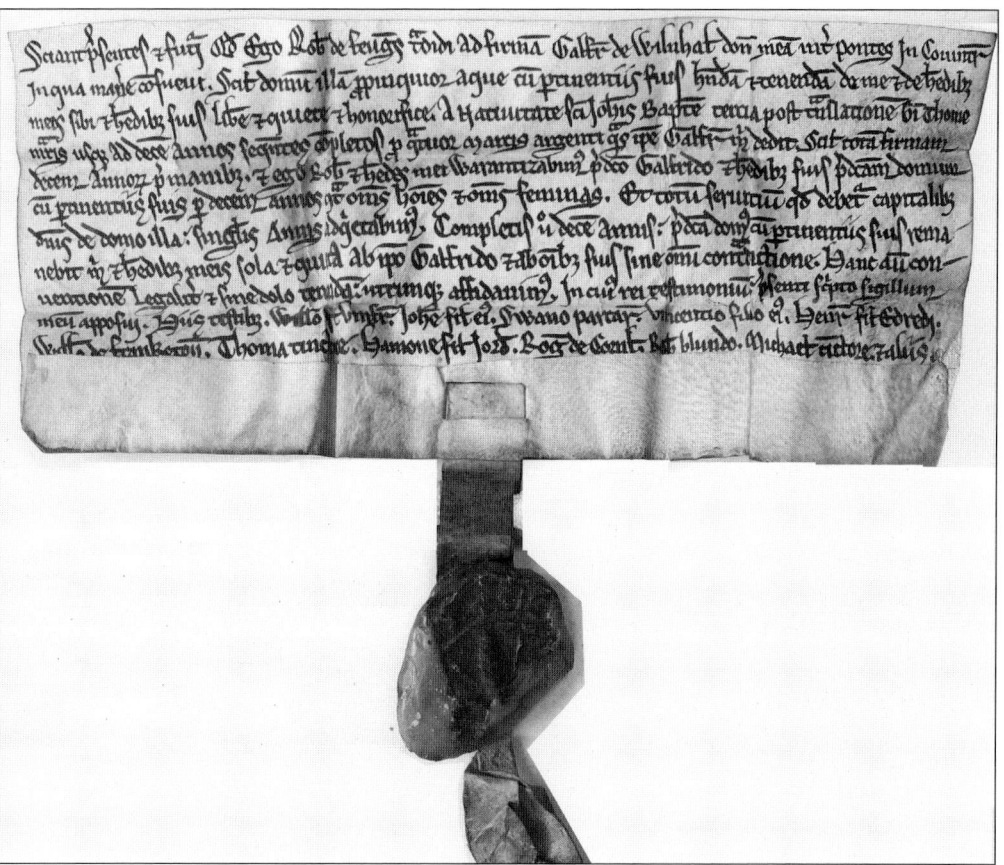

1.2 Lease of a Coventry house for ten years from 24 June 1223. For the text and translation, see p. 171. (WCRO, DR564/205)

1.3 Copper plaque on the gate-arch of Cooling Castle, Kent (c. 1380). The text reads: *Knouwyth that beth and schul be / That I am mad in help of the cuntre / In knowying of whyche thing / Thys is charter and wytnessing.*

Deeds also had great, almost magical, significance for their medieval owners – they might be placed on the altar of a church or monastery to associate the gift they recorded with the saint to whom it was given. Knives or other objects (even including a gold ring) were also sometimes attached to them to enhance their significance.[3] Perhaps even more remarkable is the creation of a deed of title as a plaque on the gatehouse of Cooling Castle (Illus. 1.3).[4] The text starts with an English equivalent of the standard Latin phrase, *Sciant presentes et future*, and instead of witnesses' names, the castle itself seems to be witnessing the charter.

The historian's eye should not necessarily glaze over even when faced by a pile of post-medieval deeds. Take, for example, an eighteenth-century deed in Warwick Record Office (Illus. 1.4). When opened, it contained a complete series of small deeds as clean and perfect as the day they were written. They started with the original

Introduction

grant in 1505 of an annuity (annual payment) by the owner of the manor of Burton Dassett, Warwickshire, which was transferred from family to family until all the deeds were folded up together in 1757. Although the record office staff had examined them, they had left them in the original arrangement, so that we can handle the same

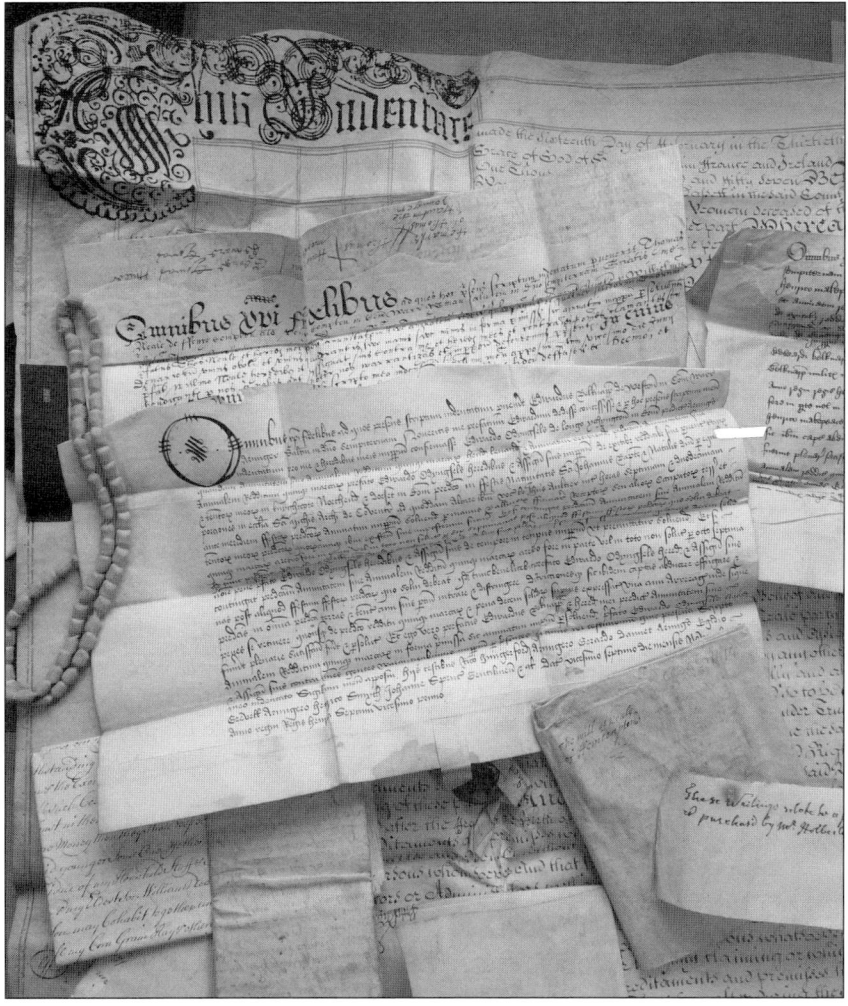

1.4 Deeds for an annuity of 24*s*. 6*d*. payable from the manor of Burton Dassett, Warwickshire. The earlier deeds for the annuity back to its original grant in 1505 (top) were found folded into the 1757 deed. (WCRO, CR457/6)

1.5 Sixteenth- to eighteenth-century wooden deed boxes.

1.6 A family settlement for the Marquess of Hertford.

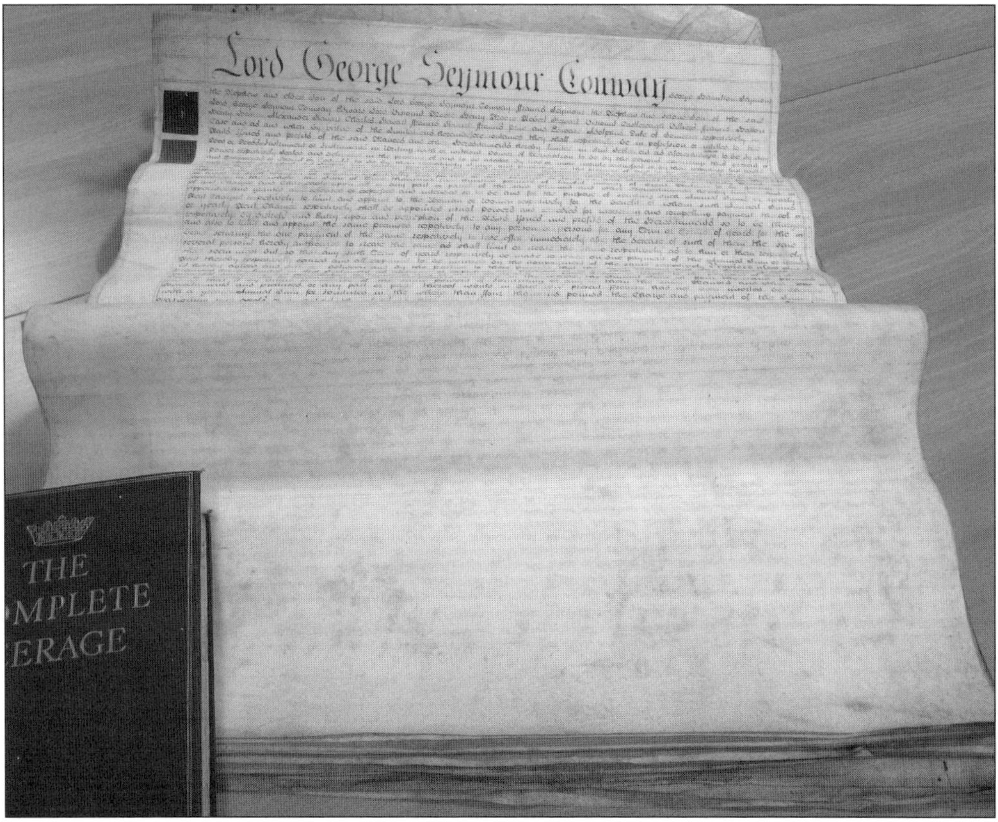

Introduction

prized and valuable possession as did the members of the Makepeace and Neale families.

Occasionally special containers, usually wooden boxes, were made for deeds, like the examples from Lapworth church shown in Illus. 1.5. To visit a farm, be shown the seventeenth-century deed box and open it to find the deeds still inside, as I have done once, is truly to touch history (despite the feeling that the deeds might be safer in the record office). Even the driest of eighteenth-century family settlements, such as that of 1802 for the Conway family (Marquesses of Hertford) of Ragley Hall, Warwickshire (Illus. 1.6), evokes images of Georgian mansions surrounded by parkland and tenant farms, all of which are described in its hundred sheets of parchment. A deed like this needs considerable athleticism and great patience to disentangle, but its record of the patriarch, his wife and children parallels on parchment the canvas of the Gainsboroughs in his hall.

Notes

1. The most significant difference between Scotland and England as far as property is concerned is that systematic registration of sales began as early as the sixteenth century in Scotland and is generally complete from the seventeenth century onwards. No simple guide to Scottish deeds has been produced, but a useful introduction is given by R.F. Dell, 'Some differences between Scottish and English Archives', *J. Society of Archivists*, 3 (1968), 386–97. Another useful source is Peter Gouldesbrough, *Formulary of Old Scots Documents* (Stair Society, Vol. 36, 1985), which gives examples of Scottish legal forms; it also includes 'Essay on Early Scottish Conveyancing' by Gordon Donaldson.
2. For example, seventeenth-century industrial housing is not significant in Coventry, but deed evidence has been effectively used in Frome, Somerset: see R. Leech, *Early Industrial Housing: The Trinity Area of Frome* (HMSO, 1981).
3. M.T. Clanchy, *From Memory to Written Record* (Blackwell, 1993), pp. 38, 156, 258.
4. Discussed in C.M. Cervone, *Poetics of the Incarnation: Middle English Writing and the Leap of Love* (University of Pennsylvania Press, 2012), pp. 94–5.

Chapter 2

WHY

The two main sections of this chapter are divided according to subject. The first involves the use of deeds as evidence for people, particularly the concern of the family historian, and the second their evidence for places and for houses and buildings, which are linked rather more to the local historian and those compiling house histories. However, the applications of deeds, and their relevance to different types of history inevitably overlap from one section to the other. A final section looks briefly at how large groups of deeds can be analysed by computer to discover their historical evidence.

DEEDS FOR PEOPLE
The principal task for the family historian is to establish relationships – to link one person to another, father to son, husband to wife and so on. This information is also of value to the local historian in working out the social networks in the community, the descent and succession of property, and the strength of links to neighbouring or distant communities as shown by migrations and marriages. Typically, the evidence comes from parish registers and wills, but is complicated and confused by the recurrence of names from one generation to another and from one family to another. Deeds are particularly helpful in resolving these ambiguities because they give explicit details of relationships. Also, they link the individuals or the families to the property concerned, which serves as a marker to distinguish one family from another. The type of information that can be discovered varies considerably depending on the period concerned, and this section starts with the later evidence.

Post-medieval Evidence
Family Relationships in Deeds
Deeds contain evidence of family relationships, to an extent that may not always be appreciated. At a rough estimate, from the eighteenth century onwards, one in every three or four conveyances of property includes some genealogical information (with rather less in leases and mortgages). Such evidence is less frequent in earlier deeds, but it can be even more important because of the lack of other sources; almost invariably deeds will also identify the occupation or social status of the individuals mentioned.[1] Finding the deeds relating to a particular family is often more difficult than finding register entries or wills and, of course, there is no guarantee that the evidence actually exists. Success depends partly on what indexes are available, partly on persistence and partly on luck – first that the information was recorded in deeds and second that they have survived and can be located; all this is examined in detail in the next chapter. However, the amount of family information in deeds is so great that overall the chances of its discovery are much better than they might seem at first sight.

Family relationships were included in deeds so that there could be no doubt of the continuity of ownership from one deed to another. Generally, this involved demonstrating that the person or people selling the property were fully entitled to do so. If the owner had bought it himself, no problem arose, but it was not usually considered sufficient just to state that he had been in undisputed possession for many years (in contrast to the present day, when a period of twelve years' ownership is all that has to be proved). Thus one common statement in deeds is that the seller's father (or grandfather as the case may be) had held the property. If it had been bequeathed by will so much the better. This gave a particularly strong proof of ownership and was often used as a starting point in establishing title. Another situation in which deeds include particularly good information on family relationships is the inheritance of a property by a number of co-owners. This could arise through someone dying *intestate* (without making a will), leaving only daughters who would by common law inherit equally.

Occasionally, property was left by will in equal shares, say, to all the testator's grandchildren. In either case one owner could only sell his share, so we find deeds for an 'undivided fifth' of a house. Alternatively, if the property was sold complete, everyone who owned a share had to be a party to the transaction. As an example, deeds for the sale of 49 St John's Street, Coventry in 1902 give the complete descent to that date of Benjamin Woodcock of Coventry, mason, who died in 1777 (Illus. 2.1). This is an extreme case (though not unique) because often the practical inconveniences of co-ownership led either to the property being sold fairly soon, or to one owner buying out the shares of the others.

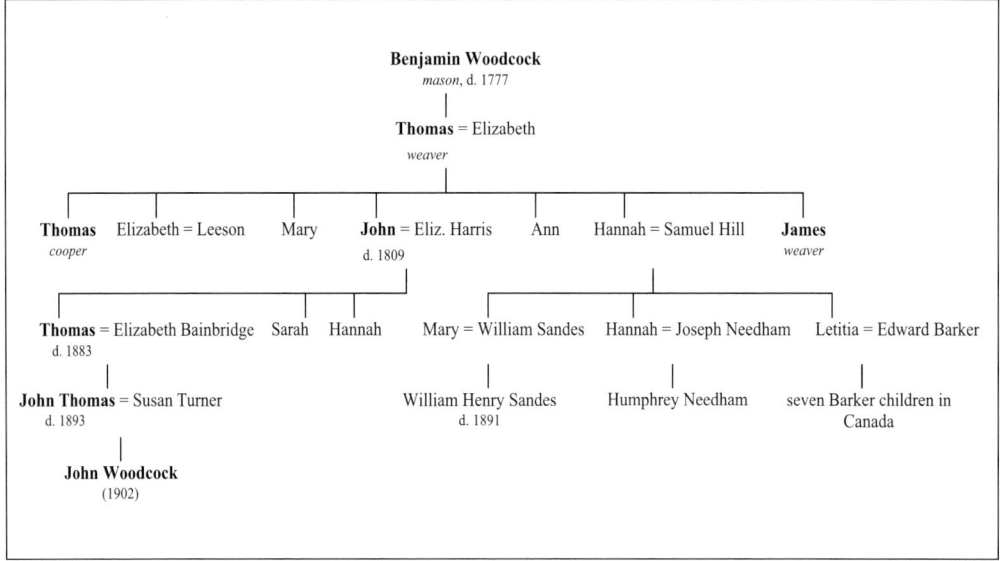

2.1 Woodcock family tree, 1777–1902. Bold type indicates the direct male descendants of Benjamin Woodcock of Coventry. This tree is based only on the information in the deeds, so dates are rather sparse. (Coventry City Council, Deeds 1229, for 49 St John's Street, Coventry)

The family links recorded for one party in a marriage settlement of 1776 relating to land in Hill Morton, Warwickshire (WCRO,

Why

CR449/1/62/a/3) seem almost excessively complicated. The husband is described as:

> William Yerrow of Burton Dassett, Warwickshire, gentleman & Ann his wife, late Ann Edwards, spinster, only child & heir of John Edwards late of Sherborne, Warwickshire, yeoman who was only son & heir of William Edwards late of Sherborne, yeoman, deceased & Mary his wife, who was only child & heir of William Smith formerly of Hill Morton, Warwickshire, weaver, and Mary his wife, formerly Mary Shakespeare, spinster.

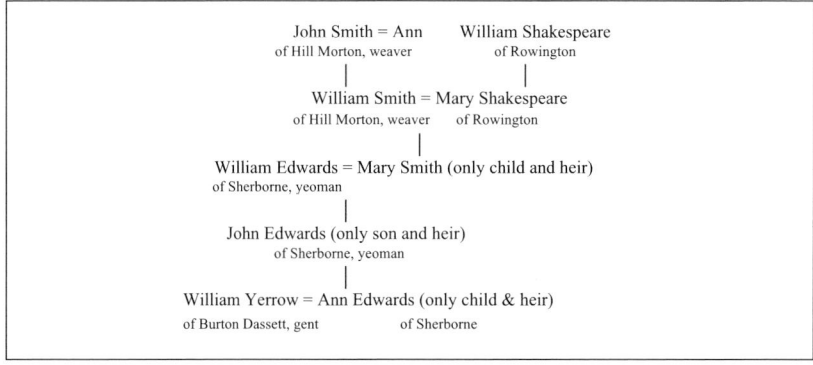

2.2 Ancestry of Ann Edwards of Sherborne, Warwickshire, wife of William Yerrow, from a marriage settlement of 1776. (WCRO CR449/1/62/a/3)

The whole connection becomes a bit clearer if converted to a family tree (Illus. 2.2).[2]

In general, the tracking down and the legal confirmation of heirs must have given lawyers much profit. Complete bundles of title deeds very often contain evidence of their work in the form of baptism, marriage and burial certificates extracted from registers, or sworn statements setting out relationships; actual family trees are quite common, though they usually only cover three or four generations. The earliest pedigree I have ever seen is from the late fifteenth century; it was drawn up to explain the descent of a Coventry property from the 1420s through an extremely complicated series of marriages and remarriages. It is now part of a group of family papers, but comparison to the related deeds shows that they originally belonged together. Regrettably the fate of these slips of paper is often to be thrown away as of no value if the deed bundles are broken up and the deeds themselves sold.

It may seem that the use of deeds to establish family relationships is unnecessary, because the parish registers can provide the evidence more easily. Often this may be so, but family historians will know that registers are not without their difficulties, even allowing for the many which have not survived. It only needs a slight problem to break a line – a trifling accident like a man dying intestate away from home, or idleness like that of Edward Agborow, vicar of Stoneleigh, Warwickshire, who from 1679 to his death in 1691 did not touch his registers. Deeds may well provide the means to bridge such gaps. They may also show that people are not always who they seem. In 1719, William Parker (I) of Oxhill, Warwickshire died, leaving his farm in the village to his son William (II). In 1797 William Parker (III) in his turn bequeathed the same property to his son William (IV). Even without any extra evidence, it seems clear that William (III) must either be William (II) himself or his son. Unfortunately, the obvious is not correct. In a deed of 1766, William (II), identified as the son of William (I) and described as of Stratford-upon-Avon, sells his Oxhill inheritance to another William Parker (perhaps a cousin, though this is not stated), and it is this William who died in 1797 (SCLA, ER3/4491-4).

Marriage and Family Settlements

One particular type of deed, the settlement, is directly concerned with families and their relationships. The marriage settlement was drawn up before (or sometimes shortly after) marriage. It gives the names, occupations and places of residence of husband and wife, generally with details of their parents. Trustees are included, who are either friends or members of the two families involved. The property they hold on behalf of the married couple is, of course, described, and it is not uncommon to find details of the parents' own marriage settlement twenty or thirty years earlier (with their parents' and relatives' names).

Family settlements were usually drawn up once every generation, perhaps when the eldest son came of age.[3] They give details of the family as it existed at that moment, listing the property or money that was earmarked for each child. They also often include information on the preceding settlement. The people involved in big family settlements (Illus. 1.6) were almost always substantial landowners, gentry at the very least, but marriage settlements are also found for people of very modest status, perhaps owning just a cottage.

MIGRATION AND EMIGRATION

Deeds can also be very helpful in identifying migrants and emigrants if they owned or inherited property. Many deeds give the names of people living in London, who have inherited distant property that they are disposing of. Thus, in 1687–8, Sir Richard Newdigate of Arbury, Warwickshire bought two cottages in the adjacent village of Chilvers Coton. The respective sellers had both moved to London and their relationships would be very difficult to confirm without the deed evidence (WCRO, CR136/C971; C978):

(a) (1) Thomas White of London, shoemaker, son of Bartholemew White, late of Chilvers Coton, shoemaker, deceased (son & heir of Leonard White of Chilvers Coton, deceased)
and (2) Thomas White of Chilvers Coton, mason (son of William White, of Chilvers Coton, mason, deceased) and Elizabeth his wife.
 [How the two Thomases were related is not stated]
(b) John Perry of London, plasterer (eldest son & heir of John Perry of Chilvers Coton, husbandman, grandson of John Perry of Attleborough, yeoman).

Similarly, the William Parker (I) of Oxhill, mentioned above, had bought his Oxhill property in 1690 from Ann Parker, widow and her son Richard Parker, gardener, both of Chelsea; Ann's husband had lived in Oxhill.

The Bond family originating in Kingsbury, Warwickshire is perhaps exceptional, both because of the number of members and its geographical spread, as documented in the sale of a cottage in 1819 (WCRO, CR153/11/138). The joint owners of a cottage in the nearby village of Wilnecote were recorded as:

> Richard Bond of Whateley
> William Bond of Kingsbury, farmer and maltster
> John Bond of Nuneaton, surgeon
> Joseph Bond of Polesworth, surgeon
> Richard and William Bond (*again*, as administrators of Abraham Bond of Kingsbury, farmer)
> John Mills of Little Aston, Staffs, farmer & Sarah his wife (who before her marriage with the said John Mills was called Sarah Bond, spinster)
> John Daffern of Treaford, Aston, farmer & Catherine (Bond) his wife
> Peter Williamson Quinvill, late of Knutsford, Cheshire, now of Manchester & Mary (Bond) his wife
> Charles Gleddall of South Kirby, Yorks & Ann (Bond) his wife
> Sarah Bond, mother of Abraham [who had been bequeathed the share of Thomas Bond, a deceased brother].

Although, surprisingly, the deed only identifies the family members as joint owners, in fact they were the children (and the widow) of William Bond of Kingsbury, who had died in 1785, leaving his property jointly to them.

Individual movements may also be documented. A Thomas Whateley bought property in Glascote, Tamworth, Staffordshire in 1777, but when he mortgaged it in 1798, he was of Sheperdshill in Buxted, Sussex; in 1810 he had moved to Possingworth in Waldron in the same county and finally, when he sold the property in 1814, he was living in Coity, Llanvigan (Llanfeugan), Breconshire (WCRO, CR228/5/8-12).[4] As another example, in 1760, one Anthony Bezely, formerly of Stratford-upon-Avon, was then 'a private man in Sir Charles Howard's Regiment of Dragoon Guards' (WCRO, CR643/14).

Migrants could, of course, have moved much further. Thus, a fairly recent deed for a house in Kenilworth, Warwickshire (in private hands) shows a typical example of emigrants owning property. It was being sold by the children of the deceased owner, William Skutt of Turua, Auckland, New Zealand, and Henry Skutt of Mint Spring, Virginia, USA.

Sometimes we get unusual detail about migrants. A Kenilworth, Warwickshire deed bundle (SCLA, DR18/10/10/776) contains a sad letter of 1774 from John Ireland, a soldier serving with the East India Company, explaining that his fellow recruit William Riley, who had inherited a farm in the parish, had died of cholera. The hazards of life overseas, and the difficulties of communication, are sometimes explicitly recognised in wills, in bequests (not usually of property) to 'my son John who is beyond the seas, if he shall return'.

Looked at in reverse, finding a deed relating to a particular emigrant will probably be even more difficult than finding parish register entries, but when found one can be very confident that the right person has been identified. It is relevant to remember that statements in deeds were made with legal care, so that their accuracy could be defended in a law court if necessary; inconsistencies are found in such matters as the spelling of Christian names and surnames, but deeds are generally of a better standard than registers. Children in a family are usually only mentioned if they survive to adulthood, but these are the most important for genealogy, and the entries in a register for those who died young may be a source of confusion rather than clarification.

Medieval Evidence
In the medieval period, it is usually fairly easy to establish the pedigree for someone of 'manorial' status, who held at least one manor (preferably directly from the Crown, so that *inquisitions post mortem* can be used).[5] Indeed, minor gentry living on their single manor and owning perhaps a farm or two elsewhere, were probably the most stable families in medieval society, sometimes showing little change for 200 or 300 years. Below that social level, migration, changing family names and the lack of sources make the tracing of

family relationships extremely difficult. A long series of medieval manor court rolls undoubtedly gives the best evidence, but these are extremely rare.[6] Title deeds are far more common, though we can be certain that nothing like a complete set ever survives. Quite large (sometimes very large) groups do exist for many places, and these provide evidence about a vast number of families. It is necessary, though, to remember that title deeds never existed for some property and some people. In principle, deeds relate only to land owned by free men, held by free tenure, rather than by unfree villeins, transfers of whose land were recorded in the manor court. This limitation is not as severe as might be supposed, partly because it was not always respected.[7] Furthermore, most manors contained some free holdings and some had hardly anything else.[8] However, town property, held by *burgage tenure*, would always be transferred by deed.

Two or three individual deeds are all that is needed to reveal a short family tree, but one that can be very complex; indeed, the complexity is often the reason for the information having been recorded. Illus. 2.3 shows a short medieval family tree from Coventry, which has a particular value for local history in demonstrating that property belonging to a William Wymond passed to Robert Bonhomme (in his wife's right), which explains why a lane called Wymond Lane was later known as Bonhomme Lane. The descent to John Bonhomme is not directly mentioned in the deeds, but is deduced because in 1359 he received a rent of 6s. that was formerly paid to William Wymond. Such indirect evidence often has to be used for lack of anything better, though its dangers are obvious.

Similar correlations may also help circumvent the worst problems of medieval family history, changing names and migration. For both, it is vital to look not only at the actual owners of property, but at people holding adjoining tenements. An example given later (p. 145) shows how a series of fluctuating references identify four names (Robert de London, Robert de Kenilworth, Robert le Keu and Robert Coki – the cook) as one individual. Similarly, if a property is recorded as belonging to someone from elsewhere, this probably resulted from migration, as people living outside a community hardly ever bought property within it. The exact relationship to a previous

Why

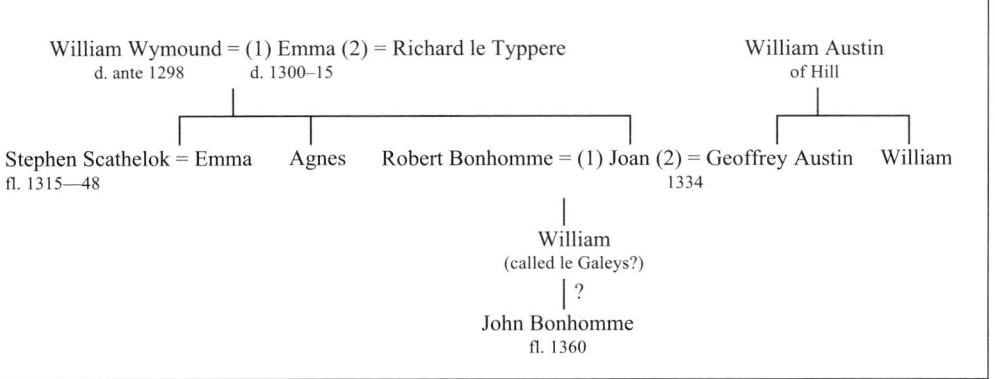

2.3 Family links between the Wymond, Austin and Bonhomme families in early fourteenth-century Coventry. (From N.W. Alcock, 'The Catesbys in Coventry: a medieval estate and its archives', *Midland History*, XV (1990), 1–36)

resident owner may not be straightforward, but could for example involve inheritance by a sister who had married an outsider.

In working out such problems, the medieval rules of inheritance can sometimes be of help. Although freehold property could be bought and sold, before 1540 land that had been inherited could not be left by will, but descended according to fixed rules. Almost always, inheritance went to the eldest son, though occasionally it followed local custom, either *Borough English* (descent to the youngest son), or *gavelkind* (equal division between sons). Daughters were next in line after sons, always sharing equally, followed by brothers in order and sisters (divided). If more distant relatives had to be found, the result was often a law suit between people with roughly equal claims. A widow had the right to one-third of the property (her 'dower') but for life only, so that if the son sold it with her agreement, she would renounce her right in a *quitclaim* (p. 143). If she herself made a *gift* (p. 143), then she had certainly inherited the property herself, rather than holding it as her dower.

People in the Community

Deeds contain most information about the owners of property, but this is not as serious a limitation as might be feared, as many people of humble status owned a little land, such as a cottage and field. By contrast, wealthy yeoman families might rent their farm for generation after generation, perhaps with a series of three-life leases which gave reasonably secure tenure (p. 96). Fortunately, leases of this particular type are excellent sources of family information and have a good chance of being preserved among the records of the estate owning the farm. In any case, people with money to invest would often buy land, even if they rented their own farm.

Many people other than the buyer and seller are mentioned in deeds. Some are important – trustees for one or another party, mortgagees, people relinquishing a possible claim. Others slip in almost accidentally – occupiers of houses, owners of adjoining property, witnesses. In the medieval period, witnesses were not random, but were chosen first from people of importance in the community, and secondly from near neighbours who could confirm the boundaries and details of the property. The final witness was usually the clerk or scribe who drew up the deed. Thus, almost everybody in the community, down to the occupier of an eighteenth- or nineteenth-century slum cottage, was likely to be recorded in deeds on one occasion or another. The limitation to adult males and widows does not apply as strongly to deeds as to many other documentary sources. Wives were often named with their husbands as buyers or sellers, as well as occurring in marriage settlements, while children, young and old, are found in three-life leases (p. 96) and in family settlements.

Viewed as sources of information about an individual, deeds contribute many small items, and some larger ones. One of the most significant is the acquisition of property, perhaps enlarging a main farm, buying houses for their rental value or to develop their sites, or perhaps only at second hand, through mortgages. Although a will may list property (though not invariably), deeds are essential to show how an estate was built up, and at what cost, and whether there were disposals as well as acquisitions. Were the purchases within the owner's community, or was he investing elsewhere, either by choice or because nothing was available locally? As the reverse of this, was

Why

property in a village or town passing through the hands of people primarily from inside or outside the community?

The network of relationships – family, friendship, business association and professional service – makes up a vital part of the individual character of a village or town, but is the most difficult to identify and describe. It is revealed in the specific links in deeds: buyers with sellers, business men with their partners, mortgagors with mortgagees, trustees with those whose property they hold in trust. These links (supplemented with evidence from other sources) can be drawn out on paper, perhaps with heavier and lighter lines joining the names according to the strength of the connection, to

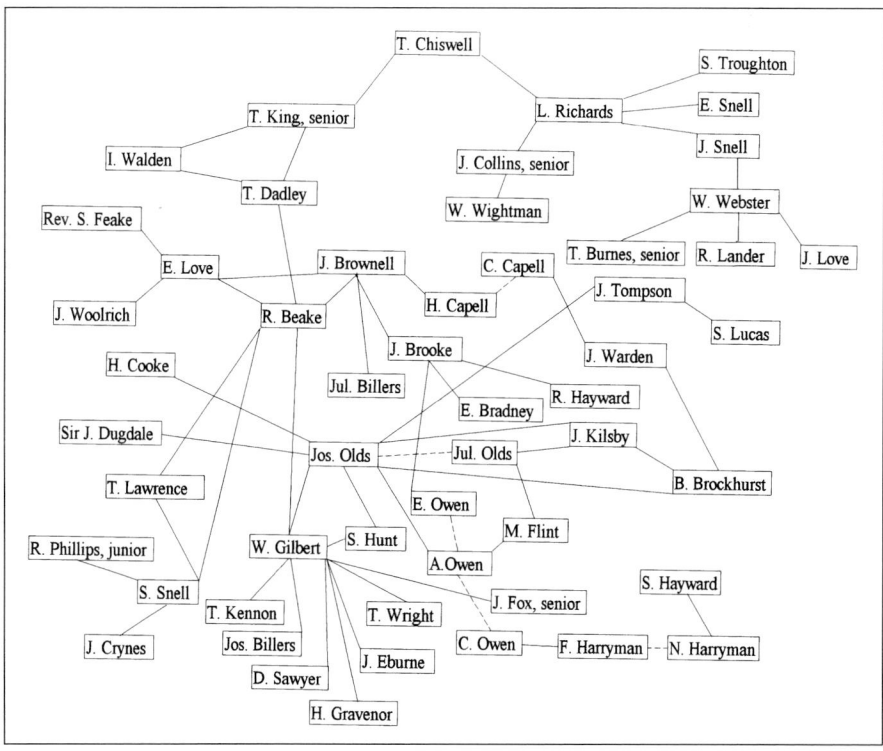

2.4 Social relationships in Coventry, 1680–1700. Solid lines indicate links derived from probate records; dashed lines indicate family relationships. (From unpublished work by J. Hunt)

show the community as a working organism (Illus. 2.4). Such diagrams are complicated, but effectively reflect the character of a village or town. In particular, they can reveal any sub-groups it contains, corresponding to political, social or religious alignments. For individuals, the most important feature of deeds in comparison to other evidence is that they relate to people in the fullness of life, not only at the turning points of birth, marriage and death. For the family historian, the activities recorded in deeds build up rounded portraits of the names on the family tree, identifying their friends, and even allowing insights into their character and into their approach to life and business. This surely must be the aim of anyone seriously interested in chronicling the history of a family. For the local historian, this same rounding out of individuals who are otherwise just names on a tax list, or passing members of a town's administration, enables their roles to be assessed, perhaps picking out those people who were key figures in the growth of the community, or in its decline. In this way, deeds add a human dimension to the description of places and happenings.

People in Copyhold Deeds and Manor Court Rolls
If you find that the people you are researching are recorded in a copyhold deed (holding property by copy of court roll (p. 131)) or that they lived on a manor for which court rolls survive (fortunately the case in the post-medieval period for very many places in England), then you should be able to discover a considerable amount about the family. This is particularly true if they held copyhold property (even if only a cottage or a few strips in the open fields), but the standard entries in the rolls will also help to provide a rounded view of their place in village society. They may have transgressed against village orders, overstocked the common lands or left dung heaps in the street – or they may have served as jurors on the court, as constables, ale tasters or other village officials. Property deeds for copyhold land (copies of court roll) are often found in deed bundles, but the original court rolls can be particularly helpful, as they may well contain additional information.

The value of court rolls was highlighted through tracing a family called Fisher, living in Barston, Warwickshire. The principal problem was that the parish contained a whole *shoal* of Fishers. No less than six owned property in 1734 and received allocations in the enclosure award of that year, and one single court book for 1727–49 has thirty-one Fisher items, while the parish registers contain innumerable possibly relevant entries. My study started with Ann Fisher, spinster, the owner of a Barston house in 1818, who was then living in Cheltenham. Following her family back through the court books readily produced her family tree (Illus. 2.5), starting with George Fisher, who built the family house, and his son Thomas who died well before his father. Ann was the last of the direct line, dying in 1828, and left her property to her nieces, Lucy and Anna Moland, who lived in Cheadle, Staffordshire. Most importantly, because the court entries were linked by the property descriptions (and often included the date of the previous entry), it was extremely likely that the tree was correct; it was then easy to add information from the parish registers.

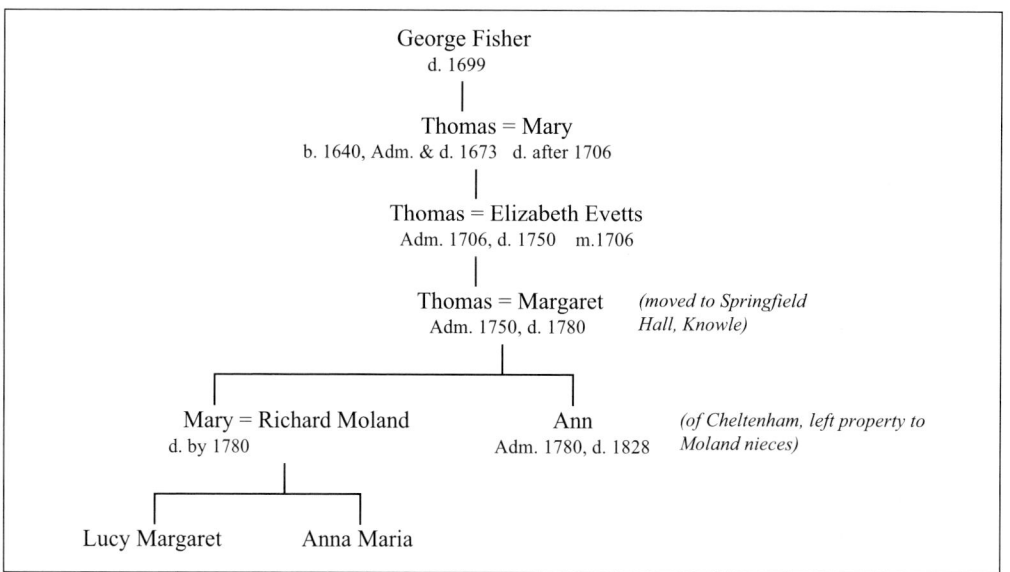

2.5 Family tree of one of several Fisher families in Temple Balsall, 1640–1828; Adm = *admitted to property*. (From court rolls for Temple Balsall, Warwickshire (WCRO, CR112) and parish registers for Barston, Warwickshire)

DEEDS FOR PLACES AND FOR HOUSES
Land
By their nature, deeds are a fundamental source for the history of land. Documents such as Land Tax lists and church or poor rates identify landowners by name, but only deeds show precisely what their property consisted of in land, buildings and other rights, who was the real owner of a given property and whether it was freehold, copyhold, held on a three-life lease, part of a marriage settlement or mortgaged to the last blade of grass. For agrarian history, deeds can be used to reconstruct the patterns of farms and their fields and to follow their development by working back from the earliest available detailed map. Changes in farm size relate directly to the social structure of a community, and to the balance between wealth and poverty. Alterations in fields can be evidence for changing patterns of husbandry, such as a conversion from arable to stock farming. Deeds also give direct evidence for this and other aspects of agricultural practice, such as the draining or cultivation of marshes and moors.[9]

Understanding and mapping enclosed fields is easy compared to dealing with an open-field system, the most complex element in the English agrarian landscape. Most deeds only describe open-field farms in outline, listing the number of yardlands or virgates (standard units of land measurement, nominally representing 32 acres, though their actual size varied considerably from place to place). These deeds therefore illustrate the regularity (or usually the reverse) of the division of the open fields between different properties. Occasionally, deeds include *Terriers*, lists of the component strips of the holding, generally with the names of the owners of adjoining strips (the abuttals) (Illus. 4.5).[10] The mass of information they give about the open-field system, with the names of fields and furlongs, and the distribution of strips among them, throws light on cultivation systems and the organisation of holdings. The abuttals should name a large number of villagers, but if most strips have the same neighbours, this is a strong indication of a regular strip layout, perhaps of the 'solskifte' or 'sun-sequence' type (in which the sequence of owners of strips repeated that of the houses in the village street); this has been found in some northern villages.[11] Post-medieval deeds, and especially leases, also illuminate agricultural practice in other ways, including requirements to spread manure or to pay extra rent if more than a certain area is ploughed. Both these and medieval leases may also demand special rents, e.g. in corn, fish or poultry, or special services, such as help with the harvest, or the carriage of stone, coal or crops (see Table 4.5, p. 98).

A notable example of the application of deed evidence to rural history is the study by W.G. Hoskins of Wigston Magna, Leicestershire in *The Midland Peasant* (Leicester University Press, 1961), which uses the deeds relating to the endowment of a sixteenth-century hospital as its principal medieval source.

LAND OWNERSHIP

The purchasers and vendors, landlords and tenants, named in a series of deeds reveal the nature of local land ownership, whether it was widely dispersed or concentrated in a few hands, and how this changed with time. They also show the social status of the property owners, and whether they were local people or outsiders looking for an investment. For urban property, the relationship between town and country is particularly significant. Did rural landowners buy urban property and vice versa, or did the two lead separate lives? As an illustration, in the seventeenth and eighteenth centuries, it was not uncommon for people from Coventry to buy farms in nearby villages; sometimes this was for very practical reasons, as shown by a lease of 1629 for a farm 3 miles away, which reserved the right for the owner to use the house 'at all such time as there shall be any infection of the plague in Coventry' (CHC, BA/C/17/14/1). The reverse, of country people owning Coventry property, was almost unknown, apart from the successful townsfolk who retired to the country; even these tended to sell their town property quite soon. Hugh Capell, mercer (mayor of Coventry in 1698) moved to Sutton-under-Brailes in south Warwickshire, where he died in 1704. His daughter disposed of his Coventry house and shop in 1739 (CHC, CCA/2/3/187).

TOWNS

Deeds illustrate urban history in a wide variety of ways, from street and house layouts, to building dates and financial arrangements.[12] For topographical evidence, urban deeds are even more valuable than rural ones, because the unit of property (the single house site or tenement) is much smaller than a farm, and needs more precise identification, akin to that for an individual open-field strip; the deed normally names the street and the abuttals (the adjacent owners). In the nineteenth century, large-scale plans of individual tenements were often drawn on deeds, and Illus. 2.6 shows the plan of a burgage plot in Atherstone, Warwickshire, taken from the court books for the manor. It was crowded with about twenty-five small cottages, for each of which the tenant's name is provided, and the various workshops and stables, and the pump and 'dust hole' and the three privies are also drawn.

These tenement plans can be used to reconstruct the overall tenement layout for part or all of a town, and Illus. 2.7 shows such a reconstruction for a small area in central Coventry, based on deed plans, drawn out onto a nineeenth-century map. Urban boundaries were often extremely stable, so that the early layout may be worked out by combining later plans with the evidence of a series of deeds running back into the medieval period (the process of *Map Regression*). This has been achieved for a few places, e.g. Oxford, and should be possible for many more.[13] By using the fifty-three surviving medieval deeds for this area, together with evidence from the Register of Coventry Priory, the medieval layout can be reconstructed

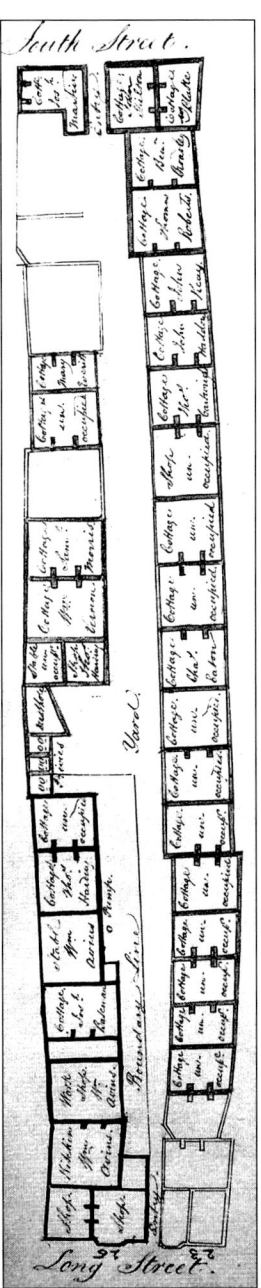

2.6 Plan of Avin's Yard, Atherstone, Warwickshire in 1848, drawn to identify its division between two owners, from the court book for the Manor of Atherstone. (WCRO, L2/8, p. 424)

Why

(Illus. 2.8).[14] It reveals, for example, three rows of shops for specialist trades, the fishmongers, the shoemakers (*corvisers*) and the cooks, which disappeared in the seventeenth century. The remarkably irregular pattern contrasts with the sequence of long equal-sized burgage plots that are more typical of medieval towns (and indeed appear elsewhere in Coventry); the layout probably arose from the subdivision of a few large properties.

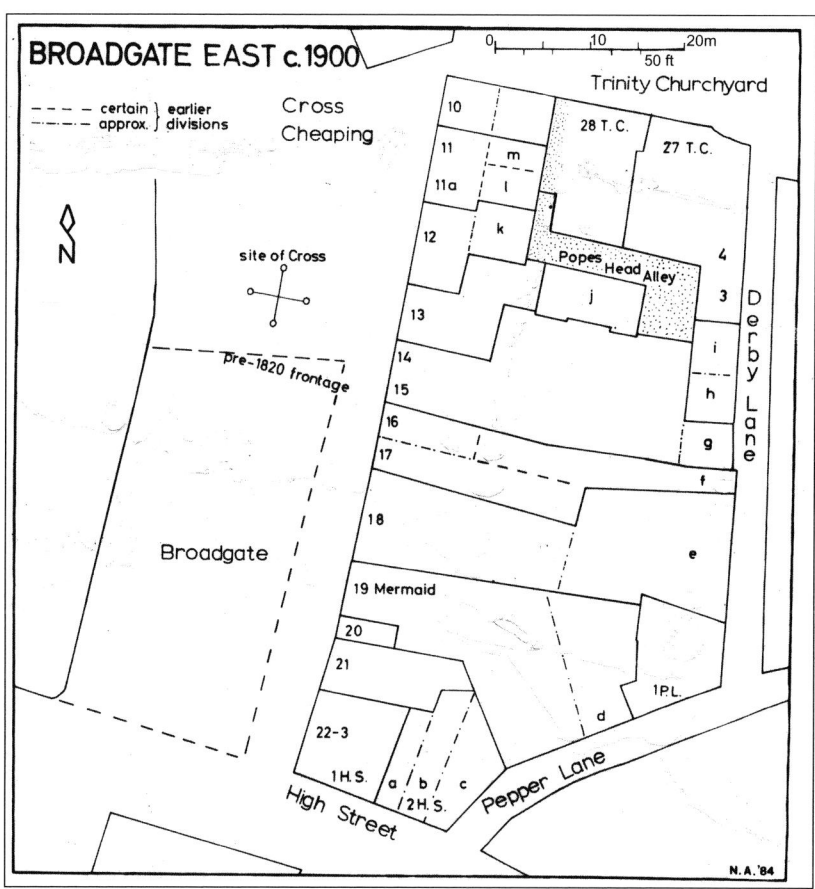

2.7 Nineteenth-century property boundaries for a part of central Coventry. Dashed lines show alterations recorded in deeds. (Illus 2.7 and 2.8 are redrawn from N.W. Alcock, 'Documentary Records', in Margaret Rylatt and Michael A. Stokes, *The Excavations at Broadgate East, Coventry, 1974–5* (Coventry Museums, 1996))

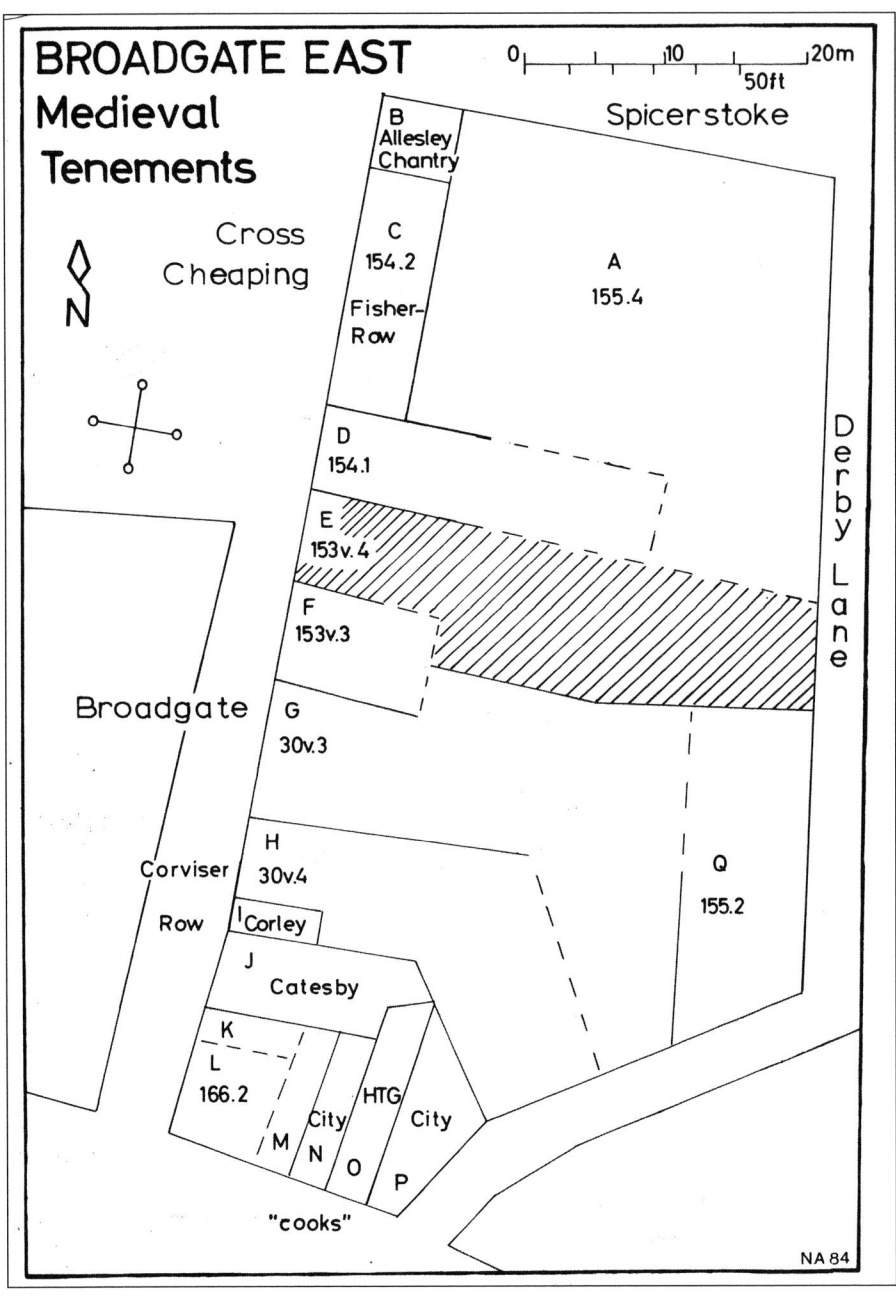

2.8 Medieval tenement boundaries (with some owners) in the same area as Illus. 2.7, based on fifty-three original deeds and evidence from the Coventry Priory Register (references 154.2, etc.); the Priory owned the shaded tenement, but collected rents from eight others. The names of some other tenement owners are given. HTG = Guild of the Holy Trinity.

Such plans, and the precise location of the property described in particular deeds, throw light on the town's topographical development, and on the social character of its different parts.[15] The location of occupiers, whether owners or tenants, is also very useful in relation to other evidence, particularly probate records. For example, it allows probate inventories to be linked to standing buildings, and the correlation of prosperity with locality.

Finance

The economic implications of deeds are sometimes concealed, with no better information given than that a sale was 'for good consideration'. However, after about 1600 the money involved is usually stated explicitly, and changes in value can be followed. This naturally has to be done with care, taking account of such factors as alterations in the precise size of the property. It is also important to make certain that the figure cited is the full value, not reduced by a mortgage (and indeed that the deed records a sale and not a mortgage). In towns, where the value of the buildings makes up a higher proportion of the total than for most rural property, their state of repair was obviously very important in setting the price. This cannot usually be discovered directly, though deeds may note that the premises or part of them were 'in decay' or 'ruinous'. The prices themselves sometimes suggest this by showing a sudden increase when other property values remain constant, implying a substantial addition or a rebuilding.

The results of these comparisons can be surprising. Thus, two houses built in the elegant Clarendon Crescent in Leamington Spa, Warwickshire in 1832–4 cost £1,150 and £1,350. Thereafter, their value declined steadily, reaching a low point in 1898 (£550 and £405 respectively). Only in the 1950s did they again fetch as much as when they were built.[16] The expectation that house values always increase was no more valid in the 1850s than in the 2000s.

Another aspect of finance in relation to property is its use as security for loans. From the seventeenth century onwards, lawyers developed forms of mortgage deed that were relatively safe, both for the lender (mortgagee), that he would recover his money, and for the borrower (mortgagor), that he would not be unjustly dispossessed. These deeds are very numerous among title deeds. Not only were many purchases followed by mortgages, but frequently while a mortgage continued, it would be transferred from one lender to another (and sometimes from one owner to the next).

Before about 1600, mortgages had a very different character. Receiving interest for a loan was prohibited as 'usury' until 1571, and instead the lender would take possession of the property and collect the rents, etc. Furthermore, failure to repay the loan by the specified date led to the permanent forfeiture of the property, though in practice, this danger might be reduced by choosing a friend or relative as mortgagee.[17] Curiously, the use of mortgages in the sixteenth century seems to have been very irregular. Thus in Devon they were not uncommon, but in the Midlands they seem hardly to have existed.[18] In contrast, a sample of late sixteenth-century wills from Wales contain numerous references to mortgages that were unlikely to be redeemed.[19]

Through the seventeenth and eighteenth centuries, when a single house or small farm was involved, mortgagees can be expected to be local people: well-to-do yeoman farmers, and particularly in towns local craftsmen (including in eighteenth-century Coventry, bakers, hatters, weavers and smiths); widows were also prominent, probably because they had money at their disposal, left them by their husbands. The mortgagees lending large sums on the security of big landed estates often seem to have been Londoners, but have no other obvious factors in common.

The pattern began to change by the beginning of the nineteenth century in towns at least, with the involvement of more people of what might be described as professional classes – attorneys (solicitors), bankers (first as individuals and then representing their banks) and those simply described as 'gentleman' or 'esquire' (i.e. people of some status though not necessarily of independent means). Later in the century, building societies began to take a part. They had their roots in true 'building associations', putting up houses for their members. These started on a small and informal scale like the 'Hare and Squirrel' Coventry Union Building Society, founded in 1821 and meeting monthly in the public house of that name. They later extended their activities to lending on the security of existing houses. The timescale of these changes probably varied very much from community to community, if indeed the pattern was the same everywhere. It has been found that the nineteenth-century development of the London suburbs was substantially financed with investment from the trustees of family and marriage settlements.[20] Preliminary work on provincial towns suggests that such investment was much less important outside the capital.

Houses

The most important value of deeds for those interested in individual houses is probably their use in establishing the sequence of owners and occupiers, which will unlock the information in sources like census and probate records. Often, though, the first problem is that of finding the right deeds, and for that reason the next chapter suggests that you may often need to look at whatever deeds can be found for the relevant place, to sort out which may be relevant. Manor court books and rolls are particularly helpful in creating this sequence of ownership – but only if the house of interest was copyhold rather than freehold.

DATES AND DESCRIPTIONS OF HOUSES IN DEEDS

The age of houses is often of special interest to local historians. Deeds may give excellent dating evidence, but this cannot be guaranteed, and the chances of success depend very much on the type of house and its location, and on the period concerned. Information from deeds earlier than 1600 about building dates is very rare, and the correlation of surviving buildings with the early deeds for them is also difficult. Unfortunately, this excludes many of the houses that are hardest to date in other ways. For medieval manor houses, or those of similar status, it is often supposed that a house is more likely to be rebuilt after a change of ownership than at another time, and deed evidence can be used to give more precision to an approximate architectural date. The argument is obviously not a strong one!

Deeds for a house built on a fresh site, created by dividing one cottage into two, or by converting farm buildings, are often more informative. If they can be followed back, the earliest ones should describe a field or barn, while the next refers to a messuage (i.e. a house). The deeds often add the name of the builder, to help confirm the legal identity of the earlier and later descriptions. A particularly interesting deed from Stoneleigh, Warwickshire provides a rare example of a medieval building date. On 10 September 1490, the rector of the next village granted to the Abbey of Stoneleigh a new-built house of two bays and a fulling mill on a plot of land, so that its rent could pay for an *obit* (prayers for his soul) (SCLA, DR10/996). The plot was called 'Robcroft', and it can be identified from later documents; as it lies well away from the rest of the village, the late medieval two-bay house that still stands there is clearly the one built by the rector.[21]

Eighteenth- and nineteenth-century deeds for houses in towns are much more likely to include either descriptions of buildings or information about rebuilding (statements like 'new-built in brick by . . .'), presumably because the structures made up a major part of the value; care is needed, however, as 'new-built' can continue to be used for a century or more in successive documents. Periods when building work was most frequent suggest times of local prosperity.[22] Deeds (and leases in particular) may include schedules of fixtures in rooms, covering such things as doors, shelves, brewing vats and window glass. In one Coventry house the windows of the best chamber contained '21 panes of wrought [*stained*] glass with the months of the year' (specified in the leases). A deed of 1660 for a mercer's house and shop lists the shop fittings in detail, complementing the descriptions of contents found in probate inventories.[23] When a large house in Leamington Spa, Warwickshire, was let furnished in 1834, the lease included an enormous schedule of all the contents in its thirty rooms, down to the tin-ware candlesticks in the housemaid's closet.[24]

Leases of 1785 and 1806 for a 'capital messuage & buildings in Botolph Lane' in the city of London show how a large courtyard house (built shortly after the Great Fire) had become warehouses

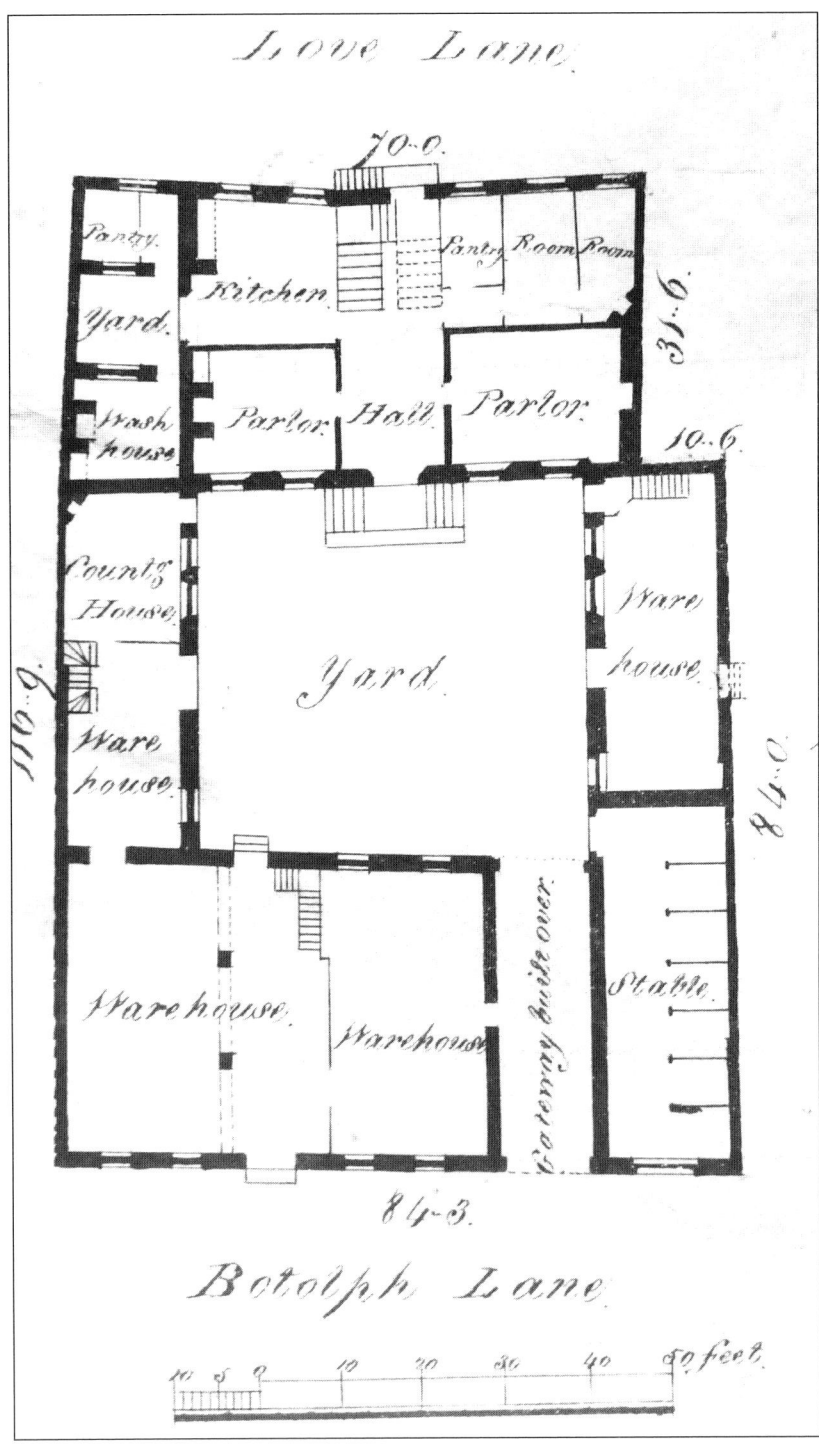

2.9 Plan of a courtyard house in Botolph Lane, London, from a lease of 1806. See also front cover, top left, for the plan on the 1785 lease. (British Records Association, Acc.2951, now London Metropolitan Archives, B15/122)

used by Stevenson, Howson and Fenn, wholesale grocers. The leases include plans of the premises, and the earlier one also has a schedule of fittings in the buildings (Illus. 2.9).[25]

An example of what can be achieved relatively easily for a house held by copyhold tenure comes from Dial House, Knowle, Warwickshire (front of book jacket, bottom right). The first step was to identify the owner as Sarah Dester, from the enclosure map for Knowle of 1820, who was awarded 10 acres, in lieu of her copyhold estate in the parish. Fortunately, an almost complete run of court rolls and books survive for the manor, and her admission in 1804 on the death of her husband William could be identified from the index in the earliest court book (1788 on). The later history, up to its enfranchisement in 1859, could also be followed through the court books. William's admission came in 1794 when he and Sarah (Tallis) were bequeathed the farm by their kinsman Edward Tallis. Tracing back through the annual rolls reveals that the Tallis family had bought it in 1699 from one Catesby Oadham. The latter's grandfather Matthew had in turn inherited the farm in 1647, and married one Anne Catesby in 1648. Tree-ring dating showed that the house was built in 1651, thus by Matthew – a new house for his new wife, very much up to the minute with its close-studding and oriel windows.

Frustratingly, sometimes even if deeds survive, they cannot give all the answers one would like, as happened for a very interesting medieval house in Long Marston, Warwickshire (formerly Gloucestershire). The house can be identified on a map of 1776, and traced back to 1725 and forward to the present day, through deeds and other records. The will of Robert Cooper of 1725 bequeathed to three relatives: (a) a house and three yardlands; (b) a house and four yardlands in his own occupation; (c) a house and two yardlands; (d) a house and 2½ yardlands. The house of interest is undoubtedly one of these, but no evidence in the deeds can identify which – perhaps most likely his own house. The numerous preceding deeds (back to the 1560s) can't be linked to the four different properties individually.

Why

MEDIEVAL HOUSES

A number of deeds and also court roll entries relate to the division of houses, usually between a widow or elderly couple and their successors. Thus, in 1347, when her house passed to the husband of her daughter, Juliana Rokeby of Wootton Underwood, Buckinghamshire, widow, received the solar and 'celer' with the chimney, on the east side of the hall, with free access to it, presumably through the hall; this indicates that the house was quite substantial, and the presence of the chimney in the solar is particularly intriguing at this early date. Another early chimney is recorded in an agreement of 1385, for Joan Gamage of Littlemore, Oxfordshire, widow, to have a chamber with chimney next to the garden door of the messuage, with access through one door to the garden and through another door to the hall.[26]

Medieval deeds, especially leases, can also occasionally be very informative about the character and development of houses. Thus,

2.10 Lease in 1340 of property in Coventry to a tanner, including details of the buildings concerned. For the text and translation, see p. 173. (TNA, E40/8153)

the lease of a hall and solar to a tanner in 1340 (Illus. 2.10) describes the various buildings on what must have been a small industrial complex; as well as the house, it included a malt kiln with the characteristic (horse-)hair cloth, and a barkstore, and it also mentions the owner's workshop and stable, as well as conditions about maintaining the buildings.[27] The lessor, Geoffrey de Hulle, is the same as the Geoffrey Austin (Illus. 2.3) who married Joan Bonhomme, thus acquiring the property in Wymond Lane, part of which is being leased in this deed.

DEVELOPMENT: HOUSES

The outward growth of towns over green fields has been going on since at least the seventeenth century, and deeds give excellent evidence for this. Broadly speaking, two procedures were followed. The landowner might grant leases (e.g. for ninety-nine years), with a requirement for the tenant to build a house within a certain time, to certain specifications, or even to a set design. Here the archives of the landowner should be informative, and a proportion of the leases can also be expected to survive. Other property was developed as freeholdings. A field was divided into house sites which were sold individually. Each purchaser received an identical 'abstract of title' (a summary of previous ownership, see p. 93), and these duplicates give an excellent chance for one or more to exist. They reveal the history of the land for up to a hundred years before the final subdivision, as well as indicating the probable building date. Succeeding deeds illuminate the social character of the purchasers and their successors, as well as prices and their changes. The invisible control that was exercised by the pattern of land ownership can often be seen in maps, and may be explained by the deed evidence.

In Leeds, for example, M.W. Beresford examined nineteenth-century back-to-back housing. He showed how curiosities of the plan, such as odd half-rows, changes in orientation, etc. relate precisely to the ownership of the underlying fields.[28] My own house in Leamington Spa, Warwickshire, reveals one way in which such developments were financed. It was built on land belonging to the manor, and so its title deeds refer back to the sale by Queen Elizabeth in 1596. This particular field was acquired by an entrepreneur, Stephen Peasnall, in 1824 and his various mortgages are described. The actual builder, John Knibb, worked in quite a small way, and he never purchased the plot outright. Instead, he agreed with Peasnall to buy the plot at some time in the future (for £151). In 1830, he built the house, and Peasnall sold house and land for £570 (a price not exceeded until the 1950s!); Knibb received £419. The purchaser was an elderly spinster of independent means, typical of the inhabitants of the spa, who lived in the house until her death in 1854. Knibb also built the adjoining five houses, working out from the town centre, and by 1830 the inner three had been completed and were in private hands, but Peasnall still owned the remaining plots (WCRO, CR2155).

Another example concerns Chapel Street in Warwick, lying just outside the town wall, behind the houses lining the main street. Title deeds for a number of Chapel Street houses are in Warwickshire County Record Office, and one includes the vital abstract of title (WCRO, CR1237). This follows the ownership of a 1-acre field from 1723 when it was part of a local estate, through various sales and mortgages to 1797, when a cotton weaving factory was built on part of it. The factory only prospered briefly, because in 1819 the site was sold and laid out for housing (and each of the purchasers received his copy of the abstract).

As well as outward growth, in many towns, population pressure was relieved by converting yards and gardens into houses. Deeds are very illuminating for this process, one series of mortgages revealing, for example, 'a messuage now converted into two tenements', '... with three houses behind, new-built by ...', '... now containing twelve tenements'. In Coventry, they show that this infilling was initially a response to population growth in the eighteenth rather than the nineteenth century, with the first development in this court starting in the 1750s (Illus. 2.11). Similarly, the infill of the burgage plot in Atherstone, Warwickshire, shown in Illus. 2.6 was principally financed by mortgages taken out in 1777 and 1788.[29]

Tracing History Through Title Deeds

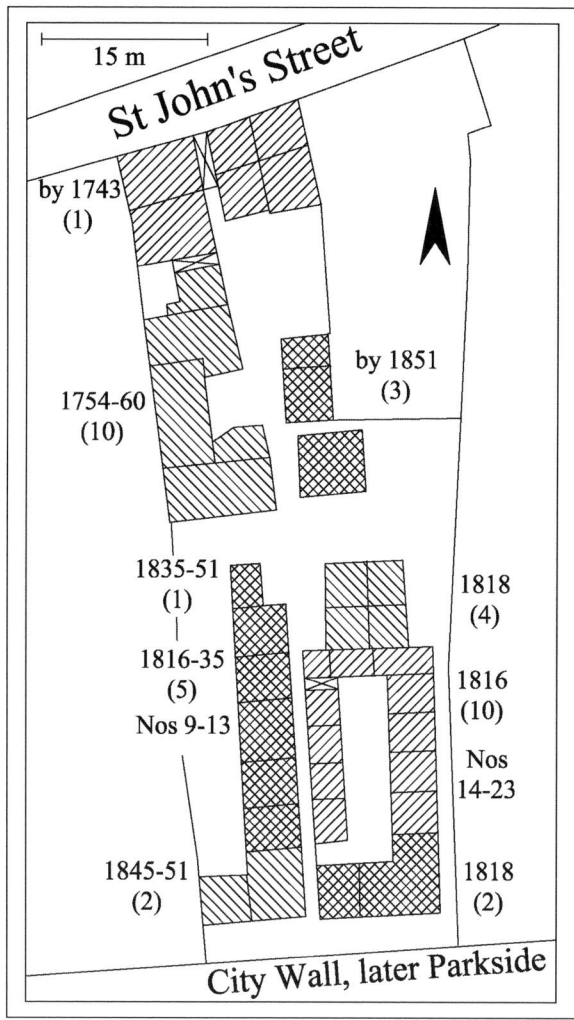

2.11 The development of a Coventry court: 46–7 St John's Street, Coventry, mainly based on an abstract of title of 1818. In 1754, the property consisted of a house facing St John's Street with a garden and orchard behind, stretching back to the city wall; the north-east corner of the original plot had been cut off at some much earlier date. Between 1754 and 1760, ten new houses were erected along the west side of the property. After this came a pause until 1816, when the property was sold off in five separate parts. The whole court was then filled in; by 1851 it contained at least thirty-seven houses, including four facing the new street, Parkside, on the line of the city wall. (CHC, PA491/83/6)

Why

DEVELOPMENT: INDUSTRY

Industrial development in the nineteenth century can be clearly illustrated from deeds. Factories frequently changed owners and tenants with the swings of industrial prosperity and depression, and mortgages were needed to raise working capital. Deed bundles may include documents relating to the general organisation and finance of the concern, such as partnership agreements and dissolutions, and debenture deeds (which guarantee the repayment of a loan to the company as a first charge on its assets). Occasionally, schedules of debts are given following a bankruptcy, or when a mortgage or sale took place for the benefit of creditors.

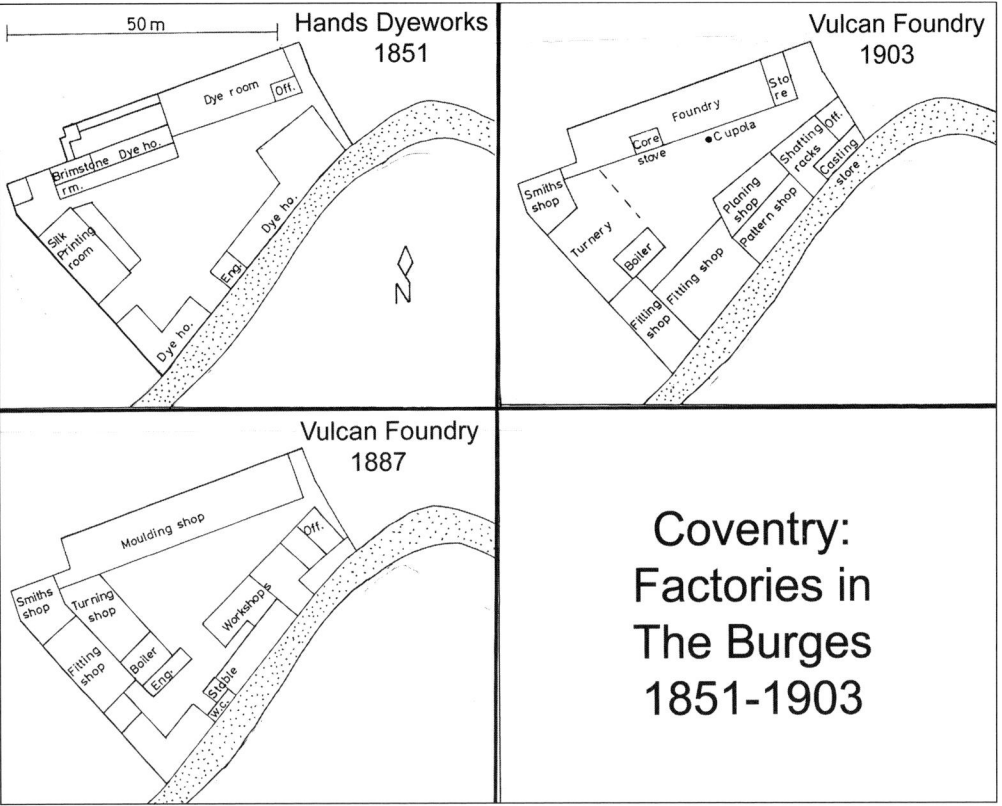

2.12 Successive plans of a Coventry factory, 1851–1903. In the medieval period, this large plot beside the River Sherborne (in the middle of the city) was not built over, probably because it flooded from time to time; it then carried tenters for stretching cloth, and in 1835 it was still a garden, with an enormous hot house. It was developed as a dye-works by Richard Hands, and in the 1880s became the Vulcan foundry. (Redrawn from N.W. Alcock, 'Coventry Streets: West Orchard and the Sherborne', *Trans Birmingham and Warws Archaeol. Soc*, 91 (1986), 83–116)

Buildings made up a major part of the value of an industrial site, and the deeds often include detailed descriptions of the factory. Large-scale plans are not uncommon, and one can find two or three successive plans for the same factory as it changed owners and uses (Illus. 2.12). Schedules of machinery and fittings may also be recorded.

LARGE-SCALE STUDIES OF DEEDS

With the many hundreds of deeds that may refer to a particular place, or be relevant to a particular investigation, using a computer for large-scale interpretation could be a great help – or it could swallow up time and effort to produce nothing at all. What follows is not intended to be a guide to what can be achieved. Rather, it suggests some questions that should be considered and identifies a few computer-based studies that have been successful. However, any large-scale study will involve considerable time and effort and may be something only to be undertaken with funding to support the research.

The first question has to be: what can the computer achieve that is impossible or impracticable by hand? Some tasks that might once have been undertaken by hand using file cards, such as compiling an index, will now start from a word-processed file, even though a simple text file is far from being convenient for indexing. For such tasks, the break-even point between computers and card indexes might represent a sample of about 100 deeds; since a simple medieval deed includes about 5 to 15 items of information (parties, places, dates, witnesses, etc.), this would correspond to about 1,000 separate data items.[30]

The most tedious part of a computer-based study is the *data capture*. Before starting on this, it is vital to decide just how the data should be organised, to minimise effort, to avoid duplication during input and to make the result as easy to use as possible. The simplest approach is to type the complete deed text, or an abstract, into a word-processing program – probably the best solution if you are planning to publish the deeds themselves. For more complex analyses involving the sorting and correlation of large amounts of data, the computer is essential. Among such procedures is statistical analysis, for example counting numbers of deeds of particular types or relating to particular places, or discovering whether two items (two people, say) tend to occur together (correlation analysis). Linked items can also be extracted and displayed, for example identifying all the references to a particular person, together with the place where they lived and the date of the item.[31] This can also help to distinguish different people of the same name and suggest the date of an undated medieval deed, by finding the occurrences of the people it names.

The question in any analysis of this sort is how the data should be structured. A particularly sophisticated application is in the DEEDS project, a large-scale study of medieval Essex deeds.[32] It involved the design of its own database, and the production of special programs to process the information. The data files had a very complex structure, but with most of the parts optional, so that the limitations of a rigid structure were avoided. The data were analysed by pattern-matching, to identify the probable dates of the individual charters. Another large-scale study is examining medieval deeds for the city of York, for which a database has been created of all the known deeds (about 5,000) for the period 1080–1530.[33] Applications of this database have involved 'mark-up' of the deed abstract to identify the different types of information it contains.

In another application, the names of individuals found in a group of 319 deeds dating from before 1350 and relating to the village of Wootton Underwood, Buckinghamshire were extracted into a database.[34] This highlighted the biggest problem with the names of people at this period: their enormous variability – not only their spelling but also in the application of completely different names to the same people. One of the lords of the manor, *William de Grenville*, had his surname spelt in at least ten ways (Grenevil, Grenevile, Grenevill, Grenevyle, Greneville, Grenvile, Grenvyle, Greynvil, Greynville, Greynvylle), and in addition was given as William Grenevylle and William *le* Grenevile as well as William *de* Grenville. Separating the surname and first name is the easiest way to proceed; the first name can usually be given a standard spelling, so that sorting on this name brings similar surnames together, and each individual can be separately identified. Then, the different surname spellings can be given standard forms and brought together to identify families.

In the Wootton Underwood study, the statistical procedure known as 'correspondence analysis' was then applied. The principal objective was to assign dates to the 148 undated deeds, by comparison to the 171 deeds which had dates, and the results were very successful, providing good indications of their dates, with an estimated error of no more than five years. It also proved possible to re-create some historical neighbourhood groups from the apparently unpromising deed witness lists.

Notes

1. This was required by the Statute of Additions of 1413, though indications of status remain relatively rare until the sixteenth century.
2. The first deed in the bundle is the 1689 marriage settlement of William Smith and Mary Shakespeare which provides the names of their parents.
3. For a full discussion of the interpretation of settlements and their significance for English landed estates, see B. English and J. Saville, *Strict Settlement: A Guide for Historians* (University of Hull, 1983).
4. Curiously, when first recorded his name was written Wheatley, but after 1798 was always Whately; the deeds make it clear that only one person is referred to.
5. The inquiries made by the Crown to establish the heir of the deceased, and what property he had held; they are at TNA.
6. Z. Razi, *Life, Marriage and Death in a Medieval Parish: Economy, Society and Demography in Halesowen, 1270–1400* (Cambridge University Press, 1980).
7. Discussed in C.N.L. Brooke and M.M. Postan (eds), 'Carte Nativorum', *Northamptonshire Records Society*, Vol. 20 (1960).
8. Especially woodland manors, where the land was cleared in the post-Conquest period, e.g. Tanworth-in-Arden, Warwickshire; see A.R.H. Baker and R.A. Butlin (eds), *Studies of Field Systems in the British Isles* (Cambridge University Press, 1973), pp. 226–7.
9. C. Clay's survey, 'Landlords and Estate Management in England' (in J. Thirsk (ed.), *The Agrarian History of England and Wales: Vol. 5, 1640–1750* (Cambridge University Press, 1985), Part II, p. 119) builds on a very wide range of evidence, principally from deeds, to draw a comprehensive picture of the development of estates and the correlation between types of tenure and farming practice in the seventeenth and eighteenth centuries. For map reconstruction, see for example

N.W. Alcock, 'Fields and Farms in an East Devon Parish', *Report and Transactions of the Devonshire Association* (hereafter *Trans Devonshire Assoc.*), 107 (1975), 93.

10. Terriers were most often included in deeds when an open-field holding was being divided, so that the purchaser knew precisely what he was buying.

11. See under *sun-division* in Baker and Butlin (eds), *Studies of Field Systems*.

12. For a survey see D. Keene, 'The Medieval Urban Environment in Documentary Records', *Archives*, 16 (1983), 137–44. An excellent short explanation of the use of deeds to study urban topography in Nottingham is given by S. Mastoris, *History in the Making* (City of Nottingham Museums, 1985), p. 11. An interesting case study by the same author using deed evidence back to the mid-fourteenth century is in S.P. Douglass, A.G. MacCormick and S.N. Mastoris, 'The old 'Flying Horse', Nottingham: a structural and documentary survey', *Trans Thoroton Soc*, Vol. 91 (1987), 115–25.

13. H.E. Salter, *Map of Medieval Oxford* (Oxford University Press, 1934).

14. P. Coss and Joan C. Lancaster Lewis (eds), *Coventry Priory Register* (Dugdale Society, 2013).

15. An excellent example on a very small scale is M. Prior, *Fisher Row: Fishermen, Bargemen and Canal Boatmen in Oxford: 1500–1900* (Clarendon Press, 1982).

16. N.W. Alcock, 'The Building of Clarendon Crescent: 1830–1840', *Warwickshire History*, 10 (6) (1998–9), 213–29.

17. Technically, there was no equity of redemption, by which the mortgagor could exercise a right to redeem his land, even though he had failed to pay his debt in time.

18. See J.E. Kew, 'Mortgages in Mid-Tudor Devonshire', *Trans Devonshire Ass.*, 99 (1967), 165. In the Midlands, references to mortgages in either deeds or wills seem to be almost non-existent at this period.

19. See for example National Library of Wales, Brecon Probate Copy Register I, p. 467 (Thomas ap Kydwgan, 1578); II, p. 629 (Hugh Price), 1588.

20. H. Dyos, *Exploring the Urban Past* (Cambridge University Press, 1982), p. 171.

21. See Nat Alcock and Dan Miles, *The Medieval Peasant House in Midland England* (Oxbow Books, 2013) (ref. STO-G).

22. See F. Sheppard, V. Belcher and P. Cottrell, 'The Middlesex and Yorkshire deeds registries and the study of building fluctuations', *London Journal*, Vol. 5 (2) (1979), 176–217.

23. Both these examples are included in N.W. Alcock, 'Documentary Records', in Margaret Rylatt and Michael A. Stokes, *The Excavations at Broadgate East, Coventry 1974–5* (Coventry Museums, 1996). The houses are respectively nos 19 and 14–15 Broadgate (Illus. 2.7).

24. Nat Alcock, 'Luxury lodging in Leamington Spa', *Warwickshire History*, 13 (5) (Summer 2007), 197–211.

25. The house was celebrated for containing exotic wall-paintings, which were saved when it was demolished in 1906. See N.W. Alcock and Mireille Galinou, 'The Beake House revealed', *London Topographical Record*, 29 (2006), 65–107.

26. Huntington Library, San Marino, California, STG Evidences, Box 23/22; see also N.W. Alcock, 'The medieval peasant at home', in C. Beattie, A. Maslakovic and S.R. Jones (eds), *The Medieval Household in Christian Europe, c. 850–c. 1550* (Brepols, 2003), and E. Clarke, 'Some aspects of social security in medieval England', *J. Family History*, 7 (1982), 307–20; for Littlemore, Corpus Christi College, Oxford, Cap. 8, Evid. 19, Fasc. 1 (information from Julian Munby).

27. *The Dictionary of Medieval Latin: Fascicule II: C Fascicule IIC* (British Academy, 1981), p. 337 under cilicium identifies this as a 'hair-cloth', characteristically used for drying malt.

28. M.W. Beresford, *Time and Place* (Hambledon Press, 1984), especially pp. 308–94.

29. N.W. Alcock, 'Housing the urban poor in 1800: courts in Atherstone and Coventry, Warwickshire', *Vernacular Architecture,* 36 (2005), 49–60.

30. See, for example, J. Blair and P. Riden, 'Computer-assisted analysis of medieval deeds', *Archives*, 15 (1982), 195–208.

31. J.L. Kordecki, 'Computer techniques and medieval land transfers: the DEEDS project', J. *Society of Archivists,* 7 (1984), 299–311.

32. See Kordecki, 'Computer techniques', and also the papers in Michael Gervers (ed.), *Dating Undated Medieval Charters* (The Boydell Press, 2000).

33. See Sarah Rees Jones, *York: The Making of a City 1068–1350* (OUP, 2013). The project is known as ChartEx (https://www.chartex.org/index.html).

34. F.D. Neiman and N.W. Alcock, 'Archaeological Seriation by Correspondence Analysis: An Application to Historical Documents', *History and Computing,* 7 (1995), 1–21. See also 'Archaeology' in *Encyclopaedia of Statistical Sciences* (Wiley, 1982), Vol. I (and the references given there), and C. Orton, *Mathematics in Archaeology* (Collins, 1980), pp. 47, 81. Seriation techniques have been used in archaeology, but to my knowledge this is the first application to historical studies.

Chapter 3

WHERE

Before deeds can be used as historical evidence, they have to be located. This chapter considers what to look for and where to look. Sometimes the deeds are easy to find, collected in the most obvious local record office, but they can be scattered – in other record offices, in national collections, in private hands or even in American, Australian or Canadian libraries. Some collections have detailed descriptions accessible online, or have been thoroughly indexed, but neither the online description nor the indexes may be easily accessed. It is important to be as thorough as possible, because the odd stray deed in an American library might be the vital link in locating a medieval street, or connecting two parts of a family tree. Some online catalogues cover more than one collection (see p. 77) but, unfortunately, checking all possible locations is hardly practical even for the most dedicated researcher. We can only hope that overarching searches will become more feasible in the future, perhaps through the energies of the growing army of family historians.

Traditionally in a record office, documents of interest were identified through the card index, and these are still important despite the growth of electronic resources. Place indexes list the deeds by the places to which they relate, usually with their dates. Less commonly, person indexes have been compiled, listing those named in deeds and other documents (though they rarely include minor people like former owners or witnesses), but these are often less helpful to researchers, since they usually omit the context in which the name occurs.

Most online catalogues take a quite different approach to finding relevant documents. Instead of an index, they comprise summaries or abstracts of individual documents (*Item level*) or of groups of documents (*Collection level* or *Series level*). These descriptions, particularly at item level, are much more helpful to the researcher, since they show not only the specific place or person name, but also the context. However, they also are unlikely to include all the names in the deeds, so it will still be necessary to look at the original document. Furthermore, they may well use idiosyncratic forms of names, that the computer search may not find, unlike a card index, where similar name forms will be brought together under one heading.

Ideally (though not yet realised as far as is known), the searchable database would combine the merits of both an index and a catalogue. It would be structured and browseable, so that groups of similar names appear together, while the corresponding descriptions appear in another window; place names should (optionally) be grouped by county, to bring together names likely to relate to each other. It should also be possible to examine the structure of the catalogue, to see the relationship between individual documents in the collection. This final aspect is in fact available in the most-used archive catalogue software, and it is always worthwhile to see how a particular document relates to others.

In what follows the targets for research are discussed, irrespective of whether your searches are undertaken using online catalogues or in a card index. The final section gives further details about some wide-ranging resources.

WHAT TO LOOK FOR
The Local Historian's Objectives
Obviously the local historian will look for deeds relating to the parish or town with which they are concerned. It is important not to be too precise in setting the limits. A simple precaution is to check for hamlets and subsidiary settlements, which are not always cross-referenced under the parish name; this is particularly relevant for medieval deeds. It can also be useful to range further afield, though the practicality of this strategy varies with the amount of material to be covered, and with its difficulty of access. Farms in one parish not uncommonly lap over into another (and the small component

sometimes escapes the indexer's attention), while individuals can have very scattered property holdings. Following up the latter line of enquiry is perhaps more important for the family historian.

When scanning lists of places, it is wise to collect even peripheral references, to avoid the need to repeat the search. Similarly, if a bundle of deeds has been located in some out-of-the-way library or solicitor's office, it is worthwhile recording it in as much detail as possible, even if it does not fit in immediately with the project under way. At a later stage you may well find such items assuming new significance.

The Family Historian's Objectives
The family historian has a more difficult task than the local historian in finding deed evidence. Virtually all deed collections are indexed principally by place, and personal indexes often fail to distinguish individuals of the same name. Unless the family name is extremely rare, a simple search by name will find a lot of irrelevant items, while probably missing vital ones. The first step has to be to place the family in its village or town, from parish registers, wills, census records, etc. Deeds can then fill in the family links, its prosperity and property ownership, its social background and relationships with neighbours.

Family historians therefore have almost the same requirement as local historians, to find deeds relating to a particular place, though the information they want from them is rather different. They may be able to concentrate on a specific period, though this may change with new information. Using online catalogues, they will be able to search for the family name in combination with the place name, and may well be able to home in on documents that are directly significant. It is important not to restrict the study, say, to deeds in which a member of the family is purchaser or seller, as important evidence may come from the names of tenants or owners of adjoining properties – and these names may well not be included in catalogue descriptions. Thus, like local historians, they may find it valuable to look at all the deeds relating to the place where the family lived at the appropriate date.

WHERE TO LOOK
Local Collections
The obvious place to start the search for title deeds is in the appropriate county record office. Frequently, though, these are not the only substantial collections of local records in the county. For example, in Nottinghamshire the University of Nottingham has major collections while the Shakespeare Centre Library and Archive, Stratford-upon-Avon, complements the Warwickshire County Record Office; the area of the West Midlands is also served by Coventry History Centre and the Library of Birmingham, Archives. The latter deserves special mention. It has been collecting records since 1866, though almost all its holdings were destroyed in 1879 (and lists of what was lost then make tantalising reading). Since then, however, it has acquired immense numbers of deeds and other records, not merely for Birmingham itself but for the three adjoining counties and many more scattered places.[1]

As a general principle, all the local record offices should be checked for parishes in a particular county, as there is rarely much logic to where collections have arrived. Record offices can be located by using the 'Find an Archive' section of the TNA Discovery catalogue, either by place or by an interactive map. This provides addresses, phone numbers, links to the organisation's own website (if any) and to a summary of its holdings; it includes a number of overseas libraries that hold British archives.

Out-county Records
It is very rare for record offices not to provide some deeds for any parish in their area, but equally rare for them to hold all that survive. This section considers other places that may supplement local collections. All record offices include what is known as 'out-county' material. Sometimes this has arrived by chance, with no real local connection, but more often it relates to isolated property owned by someone whose main interests are in another locality. Occasionally, such collections have been divided between different record offices when major sections relate to widely separated areas; an example is the estate archive of the Dukes of Bedford, split between the

Bedfordshire and the Devon record offices. More often such collections have been kept as a unit wherever they have arrived. A few record offices do pass on information about their out-county holdings, so it is worthwhile asking about this.

Finding out-county material is not easy, unless a major landowner can be identified and the location of the family archives discovered. It is often useful to visit adjoining counties, which are the most likely to hold relevant documents, and it is of course worthwhile enquiring of record offices believed to contain specific estate collections with local connections. If the archives of an estate that is of interest cannot be located, TNA's Discovery catalogue may provide the answer, through a search by 'Record Creators'. This provides access to material formerly held by the National Register of Archives, including some 30,000 reports describing individual collections, mainly prepared by record offices. The search can cover family name or title, or the name of a business or organisation (and also diaries and manors), but to see the reports themselves you have to visit TNA or the record office holding the collection.

Out-county sections of record office holdings are no doubt incorporated into their online catalogues when the relevant collection is listed, but otherwise the only standard means of access will be through a place index. This can be expected to include out-county documents and normally these are organised by county, so that the related documents and places can be easily located. Frustratingly, a few have only a single sequence of places in- and out-county, making the location of, say, Warwickshire material almost impossible, unless you are looking for one specific place. No doubt they have a significant proportion of mis-identifications as well (always a hazard with unfamiliar material).

National Collections

Two places in London (TNA (see the next section) and the British Library) and one in Wales (the National Library of Wales, Aberystwyth) have collections of deeds on a national scale, and may well hold deeds related to any given place in England or Wales respectively.[2] The Bodleian Library, Oxford and the Cambridge

University Library have superb holdings of manuscripts, but include substantial, rather than enormous, numbers of deeds. These relate principally, though not exclusively, to the Midlands and East Anglia respectively. Both libraries have indexes of places but not people. Most of the Bodleian Library's holdings were acquired by various antiquarians and presented to the Library. They are calendared in W.H. Turner and H.O. Coxe, *Calendar of Charters and Rolls preserved in the Bodleian Library* (Oxford, 1878), continued on microfiche as Bodleian Library, *Calendars of charters and rolls in the manuscript collections of the Bodleian Library* (Chadwyck-Healey, 1992); unfortunately very few libraries hold copies of either of these calendars (although the original calendar is available online as a PDF). Its online catalogue gives information about a number of individual collections (mainly from particular family estates) that include deeds; some are catalogued in fair detail, but others only briefly as, for example, 'Cornish deeds', comprising twenty deeds of unknown provenance, 1588–1773. However, none of the deeds in the calendars are included in the online catalogue.

Because the National Library of Wales was founded many years before any of the Welsh county record offices, its manuscript holdings include much material, estate archives, solicitors' deposits, parish records, etc. that might elsewhere be in county offices. It has a place index and an online catalogue (though some of the entries are only in Welsh). The library is clearly an essential place to look for deeds relating to anywhere in Wales. It also has some English material, mainly derived from Welsh landowners with property in England. Cardiff Central Library also collected material for the whole of Wales, and its archive holdings are now in Glamorgan County Record Office.

The Manuscript Division of the British Library has large holdings of deeds, many of them medieval; they are arranged in various series – Harleian Charters, Additional Charters, etc. depending on when and how they were acquired – but these series are of no significance for the type of deed. Brief descriptions of the Additional Charters (the largest series) are included in the online catalogue and are also covered by two series of people and place indexes (on open shelves in the Manuscript Reading Room), which may be helpful in resolving ambiguities. Some of the smaller deed series are not yet included in the online catalogue, but are being added gradually.

The National Archives
Deed Classes

TNA holds deeds in overwhelming numbers and frankly overwhelming complexity, in more than sixty different classes.[3] The online catalogue, Discovery, covers the major classes (not always completely), and is complemented by paper catalogues.[4] However, some of the smaller classes are unindexed.[5] Table 3.1, A–B, below, lists the major TNA classes that are made up of deeds. It also shows the number of items, their date range and the availability of lists or indexes. Table 3.1, C–D covers deeds in court exhibits and in other TNA classes.

> ### Table 3.1: Deed Classes in The National Archives: Ancient and Modern Deeds
>
> #### A. ANCIENT DEEDS (TO 1603)
> Each group of deeds was originally identified by a letter depending on its provenance (e.g. Ancient Deeds Series A), which is still used for reference; each was divided into a main series together with large deeds (AA, etc.), and deeds with fine seals (AS, etc.). Each section now has a standard class number. Only parts of the main series are listed in Discovery (see below). Much of the remainder are included in the *Descriptive Catalogue of Ancient Deeds* (*CAD*), 6 vols (HMSO, 1890–1915), online at http://www. british-history.ac.uk/ancient-deeds/vol1, etc.), and the rest can be found in unpublished lists on the TNA Map Room shelves. Two series have been omitted from the table, as they are principally financial, E 213 (RS – receipts with fine seals separated from E 210) and E 404 (W – warrants, bundled by date, without a detailed list; E 43, WS, warrants with fine seals are listed individually in Discovery).

Class and Letter	No. of Deeds	Comments
E 40 (A)	15,910	A-series: Treasury of Receipt (part in Discovery, 6,123-10,426 in *CAD*, Vol. 4; 10,427-13,672 in *CAD*, Vol. 5; remainder in unpublished list)
E 41 (AA)	533	All in Discovery
E 42 (AS)	549	All in Discovery
E 43 (WS)	760	Mainly receipts and warrants but includes a few deeds
E 326 (B)	13,676	B-series: Court of Augmentations (property of dissolved monasteries) (part in Discovery, 4,232-4,837; 6,900-7,661; 8,973-9,000; 9,099-13,677 in unpublished list) *For Conventual leases, see Table 3.1D*
E 327 (BX)	783	BX deeds were published in Thomas Madox, *Formulare Anglicanum* (1702); all in Discovery
E 328 (BB)	433	All in Discovery
E 329 (BS)	483	All in Discovery
E 315/29-54	6,756	E315, Vols 29–54 comprise the *Cartae Miscellaneae*, deeds bound into volumes (unpublished list, not covering E315/29-30); not in Discovery
C 146 (C)	11,087	C-series: from Chancery records (part in Discovery; 1287-1780 in *CAD*, Vol. 1; 1781-2915 in *CAD*, Vol. 2; 2916-3674 in *CAD*, Vol. 3; 3765-8060 in *CAD*, Vol. 6; 8,061-11,030 in unpublished list)
C 147 (CC)	1,310	Descriptions for C 147/1-373 only in Discovery
C 148 (CS)	171	(card index to C-series deeds in C 148/172-183)
E 210 (D)	11,325	D-series: Queen's Remembrancer (similar to B); all in Discovery
E 211 (DD)	724	All in Discovery

Where

E 212 (DS)	139	All in Discovery
LR 14 (E)	1,178	E-series: Land Revenue (Crown Estates); dates up to 1730
LR 15 (EE)	322	Larger deeds. Descriptions in Discovery only for LR 15/126-322
WALE 29 (F)	516	F-series: Wales and Cheshire
WALE 30 (FF)	51	Larger deeds. Some now at National Library of Wales
DURH 21 (G)	9 boxes	G-series: Palatinate of Durham; post-1557
PL 29 (H)	63	H-series: Palatinate of Lancaster
DL 25 (L)	3,652	L-series: Duchy of Lancaster. Digital images of seals in DL 25-27 can be downloaded
DL 26 (LL)	105	Larger deeds
DL 27 (LS)	332	Deeds with fine seals
DL 36	268	Bound up, as *Cartae Miscellaneae* Printed list, not in Discovery
E 354 (P)	50	P-series: Pipe office
E 355 (PP)	301	Larger deeds. Unlisted

B. MODERN DEEDS (1603 ON)

Several of the Ancient Deeds classes (Table 3.1A, from LR 14 onwards) also include post-1603 deeds; no DL (L) series of modern deeds was created.

Class and Letter	No. of Deeds	Comments
E 44 (A)	535	All in Discovery
E 330 (B)	50	All in Discovery
C 149 (C)	65 boxes	Unlisted
E 214 (D)	1679	All in Discovery
LR 16 (E)	14 boxes	Unlisted
WALE 31 (F)	11 boxes (c. 700 deeds)	Wales and Cheshire; includes also Shropshire deeds. Part transferred to National Library of Wales

53

C. COURT EXHIBITS CONTAINING DEEDS AT THE NATIONAL ARCHIVES

Several series of court exhibits include deeds. Apart from the specific deed classes (WARD 2 and C115), most contain a great variety of other items and the deed evidence is most likely to be identified during searches for people or places.

Class	Date Range	Comments
WARD 2	twelfth century–Charles I	Court of Wards and Liveries. 65 boxes (each including many items), boxes 1–12, 47–65 being added to Discovery; others uncatalogued. Some deeds in other Ancient Deed classes also seem to derive from the Court of Wards
E 140	post-medieval	Queen's Remembrancer exhibits; 246 bundles
E 219	post-medieval	Clerks' working papers, including some deeds; 720 bundles and single items
C 45	1691–1816	1 bundle (identified as exhibited deeds); listed in Discovery
C 171	fourteenth–nineteenth century	Chancery Six Clerks exhibits; 54 bundles, listed by bundle, with some places named; includes Acle, Norfolk and Alrewas, Staffordshire
C 103-C 114	mostly post-medieval	Chancery Masters Exhibits. Listed by suit, with some places named
C 115	twelfth–nineteenth century	Duchess of Norfolk's Deeds (estates of Scudamore family) About 9,000 deeds, partly listed in Discovery; see also IND 1/23396; some of the catalogued items no longer survive
C 150	medieval	The cartulary of Abbey of St Peter, Gloucester and 11 deeds, formerly in C 115

J 90	sixteenth–nineteenth century	Supreme Court Exhibits; 2,101 files listed by suit with some additional detail
PL 12	1795–1860	Palatinate of Lancaster; 17 bundles, many relating to Hopwood and Hathershaw Moor, Lancashire
(WALE 27		1 bundle, transferred to National Library of Wales)

D. OTHER SERIES

Class	Date Range	Comments
ADM 75	thirteenth century–1931	236 bundles. Greenwich Hospital property. Mainly Kent, and Northern England, including former estates of Earl of Derwentwater (forfeited 1715); brief descriptions in Discovery
C 47	Medieval	Chancery Miscellanea; Bundle 9 (63 items) includes deed transcripts; all in Discovery
(COAL 1)	1548–1850	(33 deeds for coal mines; now in Derbyshire and Staffordshire record offices)
CRES 38	thirteenth century–1964	2,219 items, relating to lands owned by the Crown; all in Discovery
DL 14	Henry VIII–George III	112 bundles, Duchy of Lancaster, draft leases; MS index, not in Discovery
DL 15	Edward VI–1875	110 bundles, Duchy of Lancaster, counterpart leases; MS index, not in Discovery
DL 47	1572–1715	6 bundles, Savoy Hospital estate, counterpart leases; not in Discovery
E 116	1578–1715	110 deeds, relating to Chatham, Kent, and Harwich, Essex; land bought for fortifications, listed in Discovery

E 299	1525–46	19 bundles, Augmentation Office, counterpart leases; dates only in Discovery
E 118 E 303 E 311	1330–1552	Conventual Leases (leases made by religious houses); E 118, 1 bundle; E 303, 29 portfolios; E 311, 51 bundles, copies of leases; MS lists and calendars; not in Discovery
E 304	Commonwealth	8 bundles, Conveyances of Crown lands; listed in Discovery
E 305	c. 1536–53	532 deeds for purchase and exchange of Crown lands; MS list and index; parties and dates in Discovery
E 307	Commonwealth	49 bundles, Conveyances of fee-farm rents; MS calendar in IND 1/16995-6; not in Discovery
E 311	Henry VIII–James I	59 bundles, Counterparts of Crown leases, etc.; MS calendar; not in Discovery
E 312	1509–58	35 bundles, surrendered leases; some details in Discovery
F 15	1781–1894	10 deeds, Forest of Dean; in Discovery
FEC 1	1552–1744	1724 bundles (including non-deed material), estates forfeited in 1715; see *Records of the Forfeited Estates Commission* (HMSO, 1968); in Discovery
IR 10	1513–1816	68 deeds, Board of Customs; in Discovery
LRRO 5	sixteenth-century–1917	69 bundles. Mainly deeds required by statute to be deposited; in Discovery
MAF 6	1720–1863	47 deeds, Manor of Paglesham, Essex; in Discovery

MAF 9	1841–1925	369 boxes, Deeds of enfranchisement of copyhold land; see also MAF 20; registers in MAF 76; names of manors and tenants only in Discovery
MT 21	1639–1939	468 files, Ramsgate Harbour; in Discovery
SC 3	1719–47	147 files, Rolls Estate (Chancery Lane) leases, etc.; in Discovery
SC 4	1670–1720	6 bundles, Grants of Crown fee-farm rents; in Discovery
T 64	1668–1803	Treasury Miscellaneous Records, includes a few deeds for Crown lands; summary listing in Discovery
TS 21	1539–1947	2,034 items, not all deeds, Treasury Solicitor. Listed in Discovery
WORK 7	1700–1915	84 boxes, Office (then Ministry) of Works, Series I, deeds, etc. for ancient monuments and other properties; listed in Discovery
WORK 8	1710–1904	82 boxes, Deeds Series II; continues WORK 7; listed in Discovery
WORK 24	1614–1929	8 boxes, Deeds Series IV (Series III contains building contracts); listed in Discovery

The most important of these groups need further comment. The majority of the medieval deeds were collected at the end of the last century into a series of artificial classes known as Ancient Deeds (containing about 60,000 deeds in all). Evidence of their original source or arrangement was lost in the process, except for the division into four major groups, though the provenance of some deeds is clear from internal evidence. The largest group consists of Ancient Deeds series B and D (which belong together). They derive from the archives of the dissolved monasteries and chantries, and it is usually possible to recognise the particular sources. Series D especially seems to comprise fairly large numbers of deeds from a limited number of archives. For Warwickshire, for example, they relate mainly to the property of Stoneleigh Abbey, Arbury and Monks Kirby priories, and the chantries at Aston, Birmingham and Erdington. One other large series also has a monastic source. This is the *Cartae Miscellaneae*, consisting of monastic deeds without their seals, bound into volumes in the series of Court of Augmentations Miscellaneous Books.[6]

Series C is from Chancery, and its deeds presumably relate to lawsuits, though this is not easy to prove; fewer deeds seem to relate to each individual place or estate than in the other series. In Series A, some deeds derive from confiscated estates, and form very large groups indeed. A particularly notable example is the archive of Robert Catesby, relating to estates in Northamptonshire and Warwickshire, forfeited after the Gunpowder Plot. This has never been precisely enumerated, but appears to represent more than 10 per cent of Series A deeds (1,500+ deeds). Another substantial group relates to Cornish property of the Reskymer family, though the reason for these deeds being in Crown hands is unclear.[7] It is important to realise that the Ancient Deeds are by no means a random collection, and that most derive from fewer individual sources than might be supposed. Thus, the presence or absence of a particular place from the collection has very little to do with its importance in the medieval period. With luck, the Ancient Deeds include a mass of information for a given place, but equally they can be totally unhelpful.

Modern Deeds classes corresponding to the Ancient Deeds were also set up (Table 3.1, B, above), but they are very much smaller, a few thousand documents in all; some but not all are now in Discovery.

Exhibits

The second important source for deeds (especially post-medieval ones) is the Exhibits, documents produced as evidence in lawsuits but never returned (Table 3.1, C, above). These contain an immense variety of fascinating material, frequently including deeds. Various series of exhibits survive, relating to the different courts. The largest group is the Chancery Masters' Exhibits, from the Court of Chancery. For the most part, they are still in bundles by lawsuit, grouped according to the relevant 'Six Clerks' office (the subdivisions of the Court of Chancery). Thus, if a particular case is known to be of interest, it is well worth checking for an exhibit. Locating relevant material directly is more difficult: only for a minority of the groups do the lists include even a summary of the places concerned. One exhibit has been given a specific class number (C 115), The Duchess of Norfolk Deeds. These are a remarkable collection that reached the Chancery in the early nineteenth century, and include the muniments of Llanthony Priory with many early deeds relating to the Welsh borders.[8] The exhibits to the Court of Wards (WARD 2) also contain many deeds, with other fascinating material. They are at the present time in the course of being listed in detail.

Other Deed Classes

Most of the other TNA deed classes (Table 3.1, D, above) are more closely defined, relating to specific places or estates. Some form interesting groups, such as the Greenwich Hospital deeds, and the Crown Estate documents, both of which go back to the medieval period. Many but not all are listed in Discovery.

Enrolled and Registered Deeds

As well as original deeds, TNA holds many *enrolled* deeds, i.e. deeds copied onto the rolls of one or other of the royal courts (Table 3.2

and see below), and also the records of the fictitious lawsuits used for property transfers, Recoveries and Fines, which are described later (p. 118). Many copies of deeds were enrolled when the deeds were originally written, either to validate them (see p. 128) or to give the owners greater security against the original being lost. Such copies do not approach a complete record, but they should not be neglected. Some deeds were also enrolled locally or recorded in the various local deed registries. All these have now been replaced by the Land Registry (p. 67)

Table 3.2: Deeds Enrolled in the Royal Courts

None of these classes have online lists giving details of the individual items enrolled, so the only means of discovering deeds is through the indexes and calendars.

Class and Series		Comments and Indexes
Court of Chancery		
C 53	Charter Rolls	Enrolments until c. 1330. Published calendar
C 54	Close Rolls	See p. 63. Published calendar to 1509. Full indexes to grantees and grantors only; IND 1/9455-9457 (1,2) gives a list of people and places for 1558–66, and a list by county exists for 1680 onwards
J 18	Enrolment Books	Continuation of C 54 for 1903–57
C 66	Patent Rolls	Enrolled copies of Letters Patent, including Licences to Alienate. See p. 125
Court of Common Pleas		
CP 40	Plea Rolls	(Also known as De Banco Rolls) Listed Ed. I–18 Ed. II; IND 1/17174, 17168 for Ed. IV– Hen. VII

CP 43	Recovery Rolls	Continues CP 40, from 1582–1833; Index to deeds for 1555–1629 in CP 73/1; lists of deeds for 1555–1836 in IND 1/16943-16949

Exchequer

E 13	Exchequer of Pleas: Pleas Rolls	Selective list by place and party 1229–1820, including deeds with other local material. The principle of selection and the proportion of deeds covered is unclear
E 159	Queen's Remembrancer Memoranda Rolls	Includes a section of enrolled deeds. Indexed 1-35 Ed. I, otherwise, IND 1 indexes year by year only, without summaries; E 368 is similar but apparently does not include a section for enrolled deeds
E 315	Augmentation Office Miscellaneous Books	Vols 209–47 (mostly) contain enrolments of Crown leases; printed index of names

Court of King's Bench

KB 26	Curia Regis Rolls	In print down to 1249, in Curia Regis Rolls, vols. 1-20 (1923–2006)
KB 27	Coram Rege Rolls	Continuation of KB 26 after 1272. List of deeds enrolled Ed. I–II. IND 1/1385-7 list parties in enrolled deeds 1595–1649; List of parties 1656-1805 (KB 173/1-2)
KB 122	Judgement Rolls	Continuation of KB 27 after 1702; see preceding entry

Miscellaneous

JUST 1	Eyre Rolls	Contains a handful of early enrolments. No list or index, but many early rolls have been printed
E 372	Pipe Rolls	Before 1195, these contain frequent enrolments. Many early rolls have been printed by the Pipe Roll Society
C 52	*Cartae Antiquae*	1106 charters on 46 rolls (Rich. I–Ed. II), mostly royal charters to monasteries, apparently continuing the practice of enrolment on the Pipe Rolls. Calendar, partly published (rolls 1–20) in Pipe Roll Soc. NS17 (1939) and NS33 (1957)
CHES 29–30	Plea Rolls	For Palatinate of Chester; first 4 rolls printed; printed calendar of deeds (Hen. III–Hen. VIII)
CHES 32	Enrolments	For Palatinate of Chester
DURH 13	Judgement Rolls	For Palatinate of Durham; no calendar but some year-by-year lists
PL 2	Close Rolls	For Palatinate of Lancaster; calendared
PL 15	Plea Rolls	For Palatinate of Lancaster
WALE 16–26	*Welsh Plea Rolls*	Now in National Library of Wales

NATIONAL ENROLMENTS

Deeds were being been copied onto the rolls of the royal courts at Westminster from the thirteenth century onwards.[9] The increasing popularity of this form of record probably provided one stimulus for the Statute of Enrolments of 1536, which laid down that all transfers of freehold land had to be enrolled. Although it never achieved its objective, very many enrolled deeds do exist. Several series of enrolments are found, within the 'Courts of Record', listed in Table 3.2, above.

In these series, the most important are the vast numbers of enrolments in the Court of Chancery (Close Rolls), and to a lesser extent those in Common Pleas (Plea Rolls). The latter have lists or indexes of places for the post-medieval period which are relatively easy to search, but the rolls themselves are extremely daunting, piles of parchment sheets bound together at one end, anything up to a foot thick and 3ft long. Some of the indexes (but not all) give the membrane number; on all the rolls, the deeds are in a separate section at the end. Feet of Fines (described on p. 119) are also records of the Court of Common Pleas, though they are not strictly enrolments of originals. The Plea Rolls and the Recovery Rolls also contain the original enrolled court judgements, whose copies are the Exemplifications of Recoveries (see p. 118).

The Close Rolls initially provided a record of letters sent by the King, but this use rapidly declined from the fifteenth century onwards. In the fourteenth century, the texts of deeds began to be copied onto the backs of the rolls (the *dorses*), and this eventually overwhelmed the original purpose, so that only the dorses were written. Enormous numbers of deeds were recorded in the later sixteenth and seventeenth centuries, with, for example, 1,195 rolls (perhaps 75,000 deeds) for the reign of Elizabeth, compared with 206 rolls for the reigns of all the earlier Tudors.[10] The great majority of the enrolments are of deeds, though they also include financial transactions and other matters. By the eighteenth century, enrolments were declining, until in the nineteenth century the rolls were used mainly for a few types of deeds, in particular the grants of property to the trustees of charities; these trust deeds have a special index.[11]

The medieval Close Rolls have been published up to the end of the reign of Henry VII, including the enrolled deeds. After this, unfortunately, the finding aids become very unsatisfactory, just as the number of deeds increases. The only indices are two sets of contemporary year-by-year lists of the grantors and grantees (sellers and purchasers) in the deeds, arranged alphabetically by initial letter, but not sorted for each initial; the indexes give the surnames of both parties, and from 1671 onwards the county is included. The provision of a full index of parties and places for this immense mass of material would be an outstanding aid to historians of all kinds, but seems unlikely to be undertaken in the foreseeable future. With the available indexes, it is possible to follow the acquisitions by a person of fairly high social status as he built up a landed estate, or his declining fortunes as he sold land, but topographical study is virtually impossible.

One systematic group of enrolled deeds from the eighteenth and nineteenth centuries are those by which the assets of a bankrupt were transferred to the trustees who would sell them to repay his creditors; these were required by law to be enrolled in one of the national courts. Occasionally, a private deed, say for the sale of a small part of a larger property, refers to the previous purchase of the whole property having been enrolled in Chancery (i.e. on the Close Rolls), and these references can then be located from the name of the original purchaser. Otherwise, the only possibility of finding deeds relating to a particular place is a speculative and usually unsuccessful search for the name of someone who might have bought or sold land there.

Local Enrolments

One of the reasons for the failure of attempts in the eighteenth century to create deed registries was opposition from various boroughs which claimed already to hold 'Courts of Record' in whose rolls deeds were registered. Although they were successful, these objections were specious as by the eighteenth century this registration was virtually extinct.[12] In the medieval period, enrolling of deeds was carried out energetically in many boroughs, and several important series survive. G.H. Martin has discussed these enrolments, but no list has been made of those that survive, let alone the boroughs which made them but whose records are lost; the making of enrolled copies can be established from the endorsements applied to the deeds on enrolment.[13] However, for anyone studying either the people or the topography of a borough which has surviving rolls, they provide a major source of evidence. The most important series is that for London, starting in 1252 and enrolled in the Court of Hustings. It has some 3,000 entries before the end of the thirteenth century, and 30,000 for the whole medieval period. Wallingford, Oxfordshire has the earliest roll (1231–2) which is particularly interesting, as it seems to record oral rather than written transactions; the next roll (1252–3) recites written charters, but no later rolls survive. Another major series comes from Norwich, starting in 1285, where a study has examined the process of enrolment.[14] It also applies the evidence of the enrolled deeds to the topographical reconstruction of part of the city, and to the analysis of its trades and economic structure.

The other sets of locally enrolled deeds are those created following the Statute of Enrolments in 1536. This allowed feoffments to be valid without seisin (p. 128) if they were enrolled either in the national courts or before the Clerks of the Peace in each county.[15] Locally, the 'Enrolled Deeds of Bargain and Sale' are included among Quarter Sessions records. Their popularity and survival is extremely variable. Thus, for Devon a good series starts in 1536 and includes some 1,300 deeds in the sixteenth century, while the earliest roll for Essex has only 100 deeds in the date range 1536–1624. As another example, the rolls for Warwickshire do not survive before 1612, and thereafter are very sparse; curiously, the latest ones consist almost entirely of the sales of former toll houses by disbanded turnpike trusts.

DEED REGISTRIES

In England, local deed registries were established in the early eighteenth century in Yorkshire (1704–36) and Middlesex (1708), and also in Ireland in 1708, but attempts to extend their activity to the rest of the country were defeated. For these areas, the registers provide comprehensive sources covering more than 2 million deeds in each county; all the registers are now in the appropriate record office. Registration was not compulsory, but the advantages of having deeds registered soon became so obvious that few if any eligible deeds were omitted; however, leases for less than twenty-one years and deeds for copyhold property could not be enrolled. At each registry, when a deed had been signed and sealed, the details were recorded by the registrar in a 'Memorial', and the original deed was endorsed with a note of the date and time it was registered. The registers are not a complete substitute for the originals because the memorials usually only include abstracts: dates, parties, witnesses and property descriptions, omitting the consideration and any conditions or covenants; from the later nineeenth century on, they include copies of any plans in the original deeds.[16]

The indexes to the memorials vary in quality. All the registries have indexes to grantors (usually arranged annually by initial letter but not sorted into precise alphabetical order), but only the East and West Ridings of Yorkshire have indexes to grantees (from 1828 and 1763 respectively). The Middlesex registry has no place index at all, and that for the West Riding covers only 1704–86 and 1885–1923. It would be an exceptionally valuable aid to local and family historians if these indexes could be made more comprehensive – a very worthwhile task for volunteer work.[17] Despite these qualifications, this mass of material provides a historical source for people and places that is the envy of anyone concerned with other counties. The registers also provide complete blocks of deeds without any problems of survival that can be used for wide-ranging surveys, for example, of variations in the land market.

Private Copies of Deeds

Individuals and corporate bodies attempted to safeguard their title deeds by making copies, particularly in the medieval period. The resulting volumes, known as cartularies, are a major source for medieval deeds, and something like 1,300 have survived. Most are no longer to be found with the deeds and other records with which they once belonged, and the best way to locate them is from G.R.C. Davis, *Medieval cartularies of Great Britain: a short catalogue*.[18] The great majority of cartularies were produced by monasteries, and they are listed by Davis according to the monastic house concerned, followed by the few lay cartularies. There is no overall index of places covered, so the easiest way to discover possible cartulary evidence is by identifying former monastic owners. Davis's catalogue stops in 1535, and so omits the occasional later cartularies (for example, the fine 'Grenville evidences' for Wootton Underwood, Buckinghamshire, now in the Henry E. Huntington Library, San Marino, California); however, these later examples are more likely still to be associated with their estate archives.

The Land Registry

Only recently has registration at the English Land Registry become compulsory (gradually extended since the beginning of the twentieth century and finally applied everywhere in England and Wales in 1999), but this only takes effect when property is transferred, so even now the Registry does not have complete information on land ownership. This is in contrast to Scotland (see p. 2) or the US where title deeds have been recorded comprehensively in local courthouses from the seventeenth century onwards. However, for property that is registered, the Land Registry provides a great deal of information (though not usually the deeds themselves). Its information is publicly accessible as of right (irrespective of the ownership), though charges are made.

TRACING DEEDS AND OWNERSHIP THROUGH THE LAND REGISTRY[19]

Many people will want to start by tracing the history of their own house (or perhaps of a house or houses whose history they are researching), and this should be easy, assuming the title is registered.[20] The first step is to download the Title Register and the Title Plan. You can find the relevant property either using the post code, address, etc., or by searching on a map.[21] The Plan is useful to check precisely what is covered by the title, and the Register will show the ownership and also the date of first registration. The Land

Registry do not retain the main body of deeds for the property, but they should hold copies of any deeds 'referred to' in the Register, i.e. for which the date and information (e.g. about covenants) is given in the Register. Apply for copies using the form from the Land Registry website (Form OC2). You may also find that the property concerned is part of a larger registered property, in which case, of course, you will need to follow that one back.

It is far from certain that the deeds survive for a particular property before its ownership was registered at the Land Registry (*the pre-registration deeds*), but using the following procedure you should be able to find information about them.

> 1. If title registration took place at the time you bought the property, your solicitor should have received the pre-registration deeds, or he should be able to obtain them from the seller's solicitor.
> 2. If the property was already registered, ask the previous owners and their solicitor and, if possible, also the owners before them.
> 3. Before undertaking further searches, it is obviously worthwhile asking the local record office, to see if the deeds have been passed on to them, or if earlier deeds for the property have landed up there.
> If these enquiries have been unsuccessful, some information can always be obtained through the Land Registry. In particular, although they do not advertise its existence, the Registry should always hold the form submitted when the property was registered, which lists the deeds being provided to register the property.
> 4. Request a copy of the form submitted on first registration (ask for: 'either DL or A13' under 'documents not referred to in the register'). These forms list the documents submitted, with brief descriptions and dates.[22] The name of the solicitor applying for registration should be on the form but is sometimes omitted, in which case you will need to ask for the name. It will be on file, even if it's not given on the form. The

deeds will have been returned to this solicitor by the Land Registry, so you can then ask them what has happened to the deeds. If the firm is no longer in existence, the Law Society can tell you who was their successor.

PLACES IN MIDDLESEX AND YORKSHIRE
In principle, you don't need to attempt to find the pre-registration deeds for these places, because all the early deeds should be recorded in the Deed Registers. However, finding them may not be easy, and the list of pre-registration deeds obtained from the Land Registry is particularly useful, because it pinpoints precisely which names and dates need to be searched in the Deed Registers' indexes to find the memorials relating to the property concerned.

Deeds in Private Hands
UNREGISTERED PROPERTY AND MAJOR LANDOWNERS
All the deeds so far described have become detached from the properties to which they relate, but of course deeds also exist in the 'right' place. Legally, it is only necessary for title deeds to prove ownership for twelve years, while most property ownership relies on Land Registry certificates. Despite this, many deed bundles include old deeds, usually extending into the nineteenth century, and quite often to the eighteenth or sometimes the seventeenth centuries. On one astounding occasion, I was shown the deeds of a west Devon farm which included a mid-fourteenth-century charter, though it was not clear if it related to the farm itself, or to other property which had once belonged to the same family.

Private deeds can obviously be very useful, but tracking them down and obtaining permission to inspect them may be an onerous task. It is probably not advisable to undertake this systematically until the publicly accessible sources have been checked. The procedure begins naturally with a tactful request to the owner; they may well need to provide written authorisation if the deeds are held by a third party. Commercial property may pose particular problems, starting with that of identifying the owner, as opposed to the occupier. However, by polite enquiry coupled with formal application by letter (emphasising that it is only the historical evidence of the old deeds that is of interest), I have been given access to deeds by a considerable number of organisations and firms (and I should here express my gratitude to them all).

Naturally, if the local record office contains a long run of deeds identifiable as referring to a particular house or farm, then its later deeds may well not add much (though from the mid-nineteenth century onwards, they may include plans). When part of a big estate was sold, it was very rare for any earlier deeds to be passed on. Any that survive are almost certainly among the estate records, which may or may not be in a record office.

Some corporate bodies own very large amounts of property. Almost all the Oxford and Cambridge colleges have their own muniment rooms, with their deeds reasonably well organised, including many relating to property they have sold. Breweries hold vast numbers of deeds for public houses, generally in regional offices. Some have made extensive deposits in local record offices (for example Watney-Mann in Norwich, Trowbridge, the Greater London Record Office and elsewhere). It is to be hoped that this commendable practice will be adopted by other businesses. The major banks have their own archive offices in London, and their archivists generally have the deeds for the banks' own premises in their care, together with the occasional ownerless deed bundle that has come to light in their vaults. City, district and county councils own remarkable quantities of property, acquired especially through urban redevelopment and housing. Sometimes some of the early deeds have been passed on to local record offices, but in my experience they still hold much important historical material. They generally have large-scale maps showing what they own. The government in the form of its various ministries has also acquired property for motorways, airfields and other defence installations, hospitals, etc. Some of the related deeds have reached TNA (and more may do so in the future), while some are held locally, but most are in the keeping of the Treasury Solicitor; in principle it is possible to obtain permission to inspect the deeds for particular properties for historical purposes.

Where

Network Rail own much property, almost all acquired more than a century ago, whose deeds should be of great interest. This applies particularly to urban areas where they were likely to buy complete properties. For their rural land, large deed bundles are much less likely, because they normally bought strips of land forming parts of larger properties, and received only abstracts of the earlier deeds. Occasionally their deeds have reached local record offices by accident (e.g. those for the Leamington–Rugby branch of the London and North-Western Railway in WCRO). Apart from these, their deeds are held by their National Records Centre in York. The only ones I have inspected (for a small part of the former London and Birmingham Railway) were rather disappointing in that they had been weeded of almost everything except the purchase deeds themselves, but in other regions the bundles are apparently much more complete, occasionally including deeds dating back to the sixteenth century. Any request for information should be sent to their Freedom of Information Section, emphasising that the information is wanted for historical research purposes (see Further Resources, below). Before enquiring, as much research as possible should be done using the deposited plans, to help identify the particular property of relevance.

Similarly, the various canal companies acquired large amounts of property – again, most often strips of land rather than complete properties. Like the railways, some canal deeds have reached local record offices, but the remainder should be held by the Canal and River Trust. Also, before seeking information from them you should examine the deposited plans.

One point should be re-emphasised. Especially when examining any private deeds, it is essential to make one's notes as detailed as possible, even noting material that does not seem directly relevant, such as other property included in the deeds. It is clearly unreasonable to expect owners to permit access to the same documents time after time.

Dispersed Deeds
All the deeds described so far have come to rest in safe keeping and

are accessible (apart perhaps from those in private hands), even if indexes to them are not as complete as one would wish. Sad to say, some deeds are suffering much worse fates, being sold as collections, or as single documents, or even being destroyed. It seems that most of the dispersed material originates in solicitors' offices. Despite attempts by the Law Society and the British Records Association to educate them, some solicitors are still throwing away the unwanted contents of their strongrooms or giving dealers the chance to 'sort' through them. The result is that deed bundles are broken up, the unsaleable but historically vital abstracts of title and other papers destroyed, and the deeds taken off for sale. All this is clearly a breach of their professional responsibility, because the deeds do not belong to solicitors, but are in their possession for safe keeping. Furthermore, every archivist in the country can be expected to collect the unwanted material and keep it safely, while it remains formally the property of the depositor.

A particular danger time for deeds comes when ownership is first recorded at the Land Registry (see p. 68). At that moment, the old deeds are legally of no value. Even so, conservative solicitors tend to retain them in the deed bundle. Happily, others arrange for the deeds to reach the local record office, but sometimes they are thrown away or sold.

Building societies (and also banks) in their capacity as granters of mortgages hold immense numbers of deed bundles, almost always for properties which are recorded at the Land Registry. The majority of these bundles no doubt include only modern deeds, but a substantial minority certainly contain early ones as well. The problem posed for the societies by the bulk of their deed bundles is understandable. As the deeds are technically under the building societies' control, it is to be hoped that they would combine their refusal with a strong recommendation, or even a requirement, that the old deeds are depositied at the local record office.[23]

Some deeds come on to the market as individual items or in substantial collections through the major sale rooms and antiquarian booksellers.[24] The latter will probably eventually reach libraries (though not always accessible ones). Others are sold as single documents for a few pounds each through small booksellers, antique markets or even, as I have seen, in a shop at Disneyland in California. Thankfully, the fashion for parchment lampshades has passed, but despite this, with the deeds scattered among innumerable owners, they are lost as far as historical study is concerned. We can only hope that eventually they may be passed on to record offices or libraries. The absence of an individual deed may be regarded as unimportant, because of the overlap of information between one deed and another, though most deeds do provide some unique facts. Unfortunately, the dispersed material does not originate as isolated deeds, but as collections and deed bundles, whose sale from a stall in the Portobello Road does serious damage to the historical evidence available for the particular place concerned. There seems little chance of completely halting the trade in old deeds, though perhaps public-spirited individuals might be able to rescue some for record offices. The best hope may be to stop the trade at source, by persuading solicitors and owners to treat the material in their possession more responsibly.

DEEDS OVERSEAS

As well as the scattered deeds that eventually reach collections in this country, a considerable number are now in North America, and a few in Australasia.[25] Finding any of these that relate to particular places of interest is even more difficult than locating out-county material in British collections. Three or four US libraries have acquired major estate archives more or less intact. The most important is the Henry E. Huntington Library, San Marino, California, whose biggest collection is the archive of the Dukes of Buckingham (Stowe, Buckinghamshire and many other places); they also have the Ellesmere (Cheshire) records, and medieval documents from Battle Abbey, Sussex, as well as a number of smaller collections. All these are described in the *Guide to British Historical Manuscripts in the Huntington Library* (Huntington Library, 1982), which includes an index of the places most frequently mentioned.[26] The Joseph Regenstein Library, University of Chicago, holds the Bacon family archive (with a good unpublished catalogue). The archives of the North family of Kirtling, Cambridgeshire, have been acquired by the Kenneth Spencer Library, University of Kansas, Lawrence, Kansas (a detailed list exists but is not accessible online).[27] Finally, the Folger Shakespeare Library, Washington, DC, has the estate collections of Paget of Blithfield and Ferrers of Tamworth (both from Staffordshire);[28] its smaller groups and numerous individual deeds are included in the published catalogue, but the major collections have separate lists (unpublished). These collections should show up in Discovery in an Advanced Search under 'Record Creators'. Clearly, if the place you are studying formed part of one of these estates – or the people of interest lived there – then, for thorough research, you will need to find out what might be relevant in the archives and perhaps arrange a visit.

Unfortunately, as well as these reasonably well-known archives, very many other American university and public libraries own deeds, in numbers ranging from thousands down to handfuls; I know of more than thirty such collections. Without exception they are unloved, poorly catalogued if at all and in particular not listed by the National Register of Archives. Those that I have examined are rather mixed in character, and are clearly artificial collections, but they tend to emphasise a few places, for which they may be of great significance. Thus, Harvard Law Library includes what are recognisably the medieval deeds for Worth in Washfield Parish, Devon, whose later deeds are in the Devon Record Office.[29] Happily, what was the largest group, the Wakefield collection at the Library of Congress, Washington DC (including about 1,000 deeds relating to Rothersfield, Hampshire and the estates of the Tylney family) has now been returned to the UK and the documents distributed to the relevant record offices (although not necessarily catalogued in detail by the recipients); the Library does still retain a small number of miscellaneous deeds obtained from other sources.[30]

DEED CATALOGUES

An indication that the dispersal and sale of deeds is not exclusively a modern problem comes from a substantial number of catalogues of deeds for sale that were printed in the early years of the twentieth century. Three main groups are known to me: the Coleman, Marcham and Moulton catalogues.[31] Even though the information they provide about each document is very sparse, they can be useful; the Marcham catalogue gives the only clue to the builder in 1671 of an unusual Buckinghamshire farmhouse.[32] Copies of these catalogues can be found in various libraries, and the Society of Genealogists has all of them, and also holds a slip index of personal names (but not places) in the Coleman catalogues. Some of the deeds listed in these catalogues may now be in libraries or record offices (for example, most of the Warwickshire deeds from Moulton's catalogue are in the Library of Birmingham), but, for the majority, the catalogue remains the only evidence.

ON THE TRAIL

With good luck, private deed bundles will give good runs, perhaps back into the eighteenth century, but if not, the situation may not be hopeless. One of the principal reasons for the absence of early deeds is that they were not passed on to a purchaser because they were relevant to other property belonging to the seller. If so, the sale deed is likely to include an agreement ('covenant') to produce the previous deeds. A covenant of a date much earlier than 1900 is probably not worth pursuing; one must hope that the old deeds come to light in one of the places already discussed. With a twentieth-century sale, the chance of successfully following up such a lead is very much better. It should be noted that, although the covenant to produce previous deeds is in principle legally enforceable, strictly speaking this only applies to the original seller and purchaser. In any case, the most interesting deeds will be the earliest, probably preceding any included in the covenant. However, the main problem is not getting permission to look at the deeds, but locating them. If the property belonged to an estate which is still a going concern, then the deeds can reasonably be expected to be either in a local record office, or still with the estate. Often though, the seller or his descendants cannot be identified. Usually the existing deed bundle contains an Abstract of Title (very important documents, discussed in detail on p. 93), and this is invaluable for making further progress, as well as giving a summary of the previous ownership. The abstract generally carries on the cover the name of the solicitor who prepared it, and he is likely either to have the deeds, or to be able to locate them. If the name is not on the cover, then it can almost certainly be found in the handwritten notes made on the abstract by the purchaser's solicitor, when checking the correctness of the abstract. These take the form 'Examined with the original at the offices of . . . (solicitor's name and address) . . . (date)'.

A success story about a small farmhouse in the Breconshire hills illustrates what can be achieved. The first original title deed was no earlier than 1967, when the house was sold off from the farmland. The abstract of title only went back to a sale in 1945 following the death of the then owner, and attempts to follow up his relatives achieved nothing. Progress came through the help of the owner of the farm's land. His deeds went no further back, but did include one vital document, the abstract of title for the 1945 sale. This started with a will of 1875, which set up an elaborate family trust, eventually wound up in 1935. It also gave the name of the Brecon solicitors who had produced the deeds for inspection. Enquiry from them revealed that they held a bundle of documents which included not only the deeds from 1875 to 1935 but also those back to 1786, with a recital of one of 1759. So, with several people's assistance, a solid 200 years of the farm's history were documented.

NEW WAYS TO FIND DEEDS
It will be clear from the previous sections that one of the biggest problems with using deeds for any sort of historical research is that of finding relevant documents, which may be in any of hundreds of record offices (even apart from those in other collections). Many record offices do now have electronic catalogues which can be searched online, although for only a few does the catalogue cover all their holdings. But, to use these successfully one first has to decide

which record office is likely to hold material of interest. The first steps to change this were taken through a project called Access to Archives (A2A), completed in 2008. This undertook the 'retro-conversion' from paper catalogues to an electronic database of about 10 million descriptions of archive items held by 437 record offices. Initially, the descriptions could be searched on a stand-alone website, but this has now been integrated with Discovery, TNA's own catalogue. Thus, we do have for the first time a database that provides detailed access to more than one repository. What has not yet become possible, although it has been promised for several years, is for new electronic catalogues to be added to Discovery, and for corrections and updates to be made to the A2A descriptions. When this is put in place, those looking for deeds (and also, of course, for other archives) will begin to be able to find them, even without knowing where to look.

Two more limited overarching databases should also be mentioned. The Archives Hub includes catalogues from some 300 repositories, principally universities and specialist collections. The descriptions tend to be relatively general and, from their nature these repositories do not hold large deed collections. Thus, the description of a collection at the University of Nottingham, 'A Collection of Miscellaneous Deeds, 13th century-1896 (701 items)' gives no further information, though the university's own catalogue shows that it includes deeds for Nottinghamshire (principally), Derbyshire, Leicestershire, Lincolnshire and eight other counties.

The AIM25 database covers collections from London (within the M25). They are held by higher education institutions, learned societies, cultural organisations and livery companies within the region. It includes records held by London Metropolitan Archives, but not generally those of the London borough archives (the largest group). More importantly, the database only contains *collection level* descriptions and not details of individual items, though a number of places, particularly in London are named.

Tracing History Through Title Deeds

Notes

1. Only some of their collections are included in the online catalogue or on Discovery (A2A, see p. 77). It is essential to scan both their old and more recent place indexes (the former in red binders by county) to be sure of finding deeds for any particular place, and they have no person index. Worse, several thousand of their deeds are not covered in these indexes, and the only way to access them is to scan the two enormous accession registers which give a scanty list of places. Recataloguing of the earlier accessions is now under way, though it will take considerable time before this is complete.

2. Using these national collections may not be as easy as visiting a county record office. Reader's tickets are required for them all, and may need to be obtained in advance, so it is advisable to check their websites; some major libraries (but not the national ones) may charge some applicants for tickets. Unfortunately, it often difficult to identify the precise references to the documents of interest without visiting the collections, although the online catalogues may help, so a preliminary visit mainly to obtain references may be needed.

3. I am most grateful to Sean Cunningham of TNA for updating the information about progress with cataloguing the deed series.

4. Partly in the *Descriptive Catalogue of Ancient Deeds*, partly in typescript lists on open shelves in the Map and Large Document Reading Room. Because of the omissions from Discovery at the time of writing if some useful references are located there, it is important to follow them up by searching the corresponding section of the *Descriptive Catalogue* and the typescript lists. For searching, note that the catalogue entries generally include the county name, but in abbreviated form, e.g. *Suff* for Suffolk. The descriptions also often use eccentric spelling, so several alternative spellings (or wild cards) may need to be tried.

5. Because it often does not take long to abstract a deed, it is useful to know that if one is working with deed classes in which every deed has to be requested separately (the majority), it is possible to place an advance 'bulk order' for thirty to fifty documents in the same class.

6. Two volumes in the same series, E 315/29-30, known as *Cartae Antiquae Diversorum Regum* (Ancient Charters of Various Kings) also contain bound-up deeds without seals but apparently are derived from other sources (uncatalogued).

7. TNA, E40/14702 is a 1564 Reskymer family settlement including a vast list of their properties. TNA also holds family correspondence (SP 46/58, 1535–1612), presumably for the same reason as the deeds.

8. The introduction to the class explains that a number of the deeds relating to the Holme Lacy estate were returned to the Earl of Chesterfield in 1899 and are now lost, but their descriptions are still included in the catalogue and in a schedule (the only available information about them).

9. See S.J. Bailey, 'Thirteenth-Century Conveyancing from the Charter Rolls', *Cambridge Law Journal*, 19 (2) (1961), 200–22.

10. A study of the evidence of the sixteenth-century enrolments is Madeleine Gray, 'The Close Rolls as a source for sixteenth-century history', *Archives*, 17 (1966), 131–7.
11. See R.W. Ambler, 'Enrolled trust deeds – a source for the history of nineteenth-century nonconformity', *Archives*, 20 (1993), 177–86.
12. Apart from the copyhold transactions recorded in manor court rolls (see p. 151).
13. G.H. Martin, 'The Registration of Deeds of Title in the Medieval Borough', in D.A. Bullough and R.L. Storey, *The Study of Medieval Records* (Oxford, 1971), pp. 151–73.
14. S. Kelly, E. Rutledge, M. Tillyard, *Men of Property: an Analysis of the Norwich Enrolled Deeds, 1285–1311* (Centre of East Anglian Studies, University of East Anglia, 1983).
15. The East Riding Deed Registry (but not apparently the other Yorkshire registries) also enrolled deeds as well as registering memorials; these enrolments include more than 170 enclosure awards dating between 1735 and 1847, which would elsewhere be among Quarter Sessions records.
16. For an excellent description, see F. Sheppard and V. Belcher, 'The Deeds Registers of Yorkshire and Middlesex', *J. Soc. Archivists*, 6 (1979–81), 274–86. Registries also exist for the Isle of Man and Jersey and (as already noted) in Scotland, where the land law was very different from England. Surprisingly, the earliest English registry to be established (in 1663) was that covering a 75,000-acre tract in the Fens, which was granted to the Adventurers as recompense for providing the funds for drainage (registers in Cambridgeshire Record Office). See also Peter Roebuck, 'The Irish Registry of Deeds: a comparative study', *Irish Historical Studies*, 18 (1972), 61–73. The Irish memorials are considerably more detailed than in England, including much more of the information in the original deed.
17. The person and place indexes for the North Riding Registry for two five-year periods have been entered on a searchable database. We must hope that the success of this project will lead to its extension to other periods. A crowd-sourcing project is under way to index the memorials at the Irish Registry of Deeds (http://irishdeedsindex.net/), which has so far indexed some 25,000 memorials (from about 2,000,000) up to 1900, covering about 200,000 person and place names.
18. A revised edition by Claire Breay, Julian Harrison, and David M. Smith was published by the British Library in 2010.
19. This section is based on guidelines prepared by the author for the British Records Association (http://www.britishrecordsassociation.org.uk). Any future modifications or updates will be included in these guidelines.
20. If your own property is unregistered, then your solicitor may hold your deeds, though often, of course, a bank or building society has them, but they should allow them to be examined on request.
21. Avoid commercial sites which offer Land Registry services, as they charge much more than the Land Registry itself.
22. If the Registry say they don't have this form, ask them to search the file – inexperienced assistants may not know about it.

23. Regrettably, I have been told by solicitors on several occasions that building societies have suggested that the old deeds be thrown away. See also a note in the magazine *Traditional Homes*, April 1986, p. 4.

24. The National Archives scans sale catalogues from many of these sources and alerts county record offices to items of interest. Unfortunately, they do not also index the listed items by place or person, so that any items which are not acquired by record offices vanish again.

25. Such as the Bright family archives at the University of Melbourne.

26. However, the deeds are mostly not catalogued in detail, and cannot be searched online.

27. They also hold deeds and other archives from the Kaye family of Woodsome, West Yorkshire, and a considerable number of deeds for other places.

28. See N.W. Alcock, 'The Ferrers of Tamworth Collection: Sorting and Listing', *Archives*, Vol. 19 (1991), 358–63.

29. This collection can be searched online though rather cumbersomely using the Harvard Library HOLLIS catalogue, with keyword 'deeds' and type 'archives/manuscripts'. Their website includes the text of an exhibition of 150 of their deeds, with informative descriptions, though images of the deeds are not included (http://hls.harvard.edu/library/historical-special-collections/exhibits/history-in-deed-medieval-society-the-law-in-england-1100-1600).

30. For a brief description with a summary of the most important places represented, see N.W. Alcock, 'English Archives at the Library of Congress, Washington D.C.', *Archives*, Vol. 16 (1984), 273.

31. J. Coleman, *Sale Catalogues of Deeds, etc.* (265 catalogues, 1860–1913); F. Marcham, *The Antiquaries List of Deeds for Berkshire*; same for *Buckinghamshire, Middlesex* and *Surrey* (4 vols, c. 1909); H.R. Moulton, *Palaeography, Genealogy and Topography* (1930).

32. Cowcroft, Latimer, Bucks; see N.W. Alcock, 'From Palladio to Potters Bar', in N. Burton (ed.), *Georgian Vernacular* (Georgian Group, 1995).

Chapter 4

HOW

This chapter explains how to recognise the important types of deed, and how to extract their historical significance from the legal jargon. The links between the various types are examined, but the purely legal aspects of how conveyancing was undertaken and how it has changed through the centuries are not over-emphasised, as this is relatively unimportant for the historical application of deed evidence. Instead of quoting a series of complete deeds as examples, the key sections of individual deeds are examined separately. This is intended to make it easier for the reader to match the content of the deeds they are studying with the examples described. Typical complete texts are included in Appendix 4 to illustrate these sections in context.

 Understanding deeds becomes much easier at the very end of the medieval period (around 1550). At this time, deeds change from being written mainly in Latin to being mainly in English, the handwriting becomes easier to read and new types of deeds appear. The chapter is therefore split between post-medieval deeds (in English with minor exceptions) and medieval deeds (in Latin). A third section deals briefly with various documents which are not title deeds proper but are often found in deed bundles or are related to deeds, and a fourth examines property transactions in manor courts. A detailed discussion of palaeography is not included, but some aids are listed under Further Resources (p. 190). Most deeds are fairly easy to read from about 1700 onwards and, before then, they tend to be very much better written than, say, letters or informal accounts. However, even eighteenth- and early nineteenth-century deeds may have occasional words that can only be deciphered with great difficulty, by much comparison between an individual letter and the same (or perhaps different) letters in words that can be recognised; this arises because of the very stylised letter forms used by the lawyers' clerks. It can be rather easy to misread names, unless particular care is taken, and even nineteenth-century abstractors made mistakes on occasion. As a help for this period, a page of letter forms is given in Appendix 2.

TENURE

An important idea for understanding the meaning of deeds (especially medieval ones) is that of *tenure*, that one person holds property from someone else. In legal principle, all land in England belonged to the king (by right of the conquest by William I) and everyone except him held their land from someone else. The king granted it to his nobles to hold of him as his tenants. They in turn granted manors to their retainers to hold by knight service (sending knights to fight when required). Finally, the various inhabitants of the manor held of its lord, paying a money rent and/or doing work on his land.

By the post-medieval period, we can recognise three main types of tenure: *freehold*, property held freely and for ever (effectively ownership as we know it now), *leasehold*, property held by a lease for a given period from a freeholder, and *copyhold*, property held as part of a manor, whose ownership was recognised by a copy of an entry on the manor court roll. Other forms of tenure/ownership, e.g. burgage tenure, tenure in free socage, ceased to have any substantial legal significance in the post-medieval period.

POST-MEDIEVAL DEEDS
Introduction
STUDYING A DEED BUNDLE

When you have identified a bundle of deeds relating to a place or family of interest, you will probably want to make an abstract of each, listing the significant information – but the time taken to make a word-for-word transcript will almost always be wasted, and will bury what you need to know in a mound of legal jargon. Occasionally, of course, you will be lucky and the record office itself will have prepared an abstract. Even so, you will probably want to look at the original – you might, for example, see your ancestor's signature (or his or her mark).

It is generally best to work in chronological order, as later deeds often repeat the information of earlier ones (sometimes with less detail); thus, if an earlier deed has been covered, a later one can be dealt with quickly. Exceptionally, if the latest deeds give a clear modern description of the property (e.g. with its street number), it may be useful to start with them. The first step will probably be to skim through the bundle and check the endorsements and dates, only opening those deeds without dates on the outside. Even though most deed bundles are out of order, the actual order of the documents should never be altered without permission from the record office staff, because this order may convey 'invisible' information which, once lost, can never be regained (see Illus. 1.4). It is also worth remembering that the precise chronological order may not be the most informative. For example, if a bundle contains deeds for two properties which were later combined, the earlier deeds belong in two distinct sequences.

Endorsements

Even before a deed is unfolded, the writing on the outside (the endorsement) may explain what it is, and this is particularly useful when starting work on a bundle of deeds. In the nineteenth century it was standard practice to write an identifying

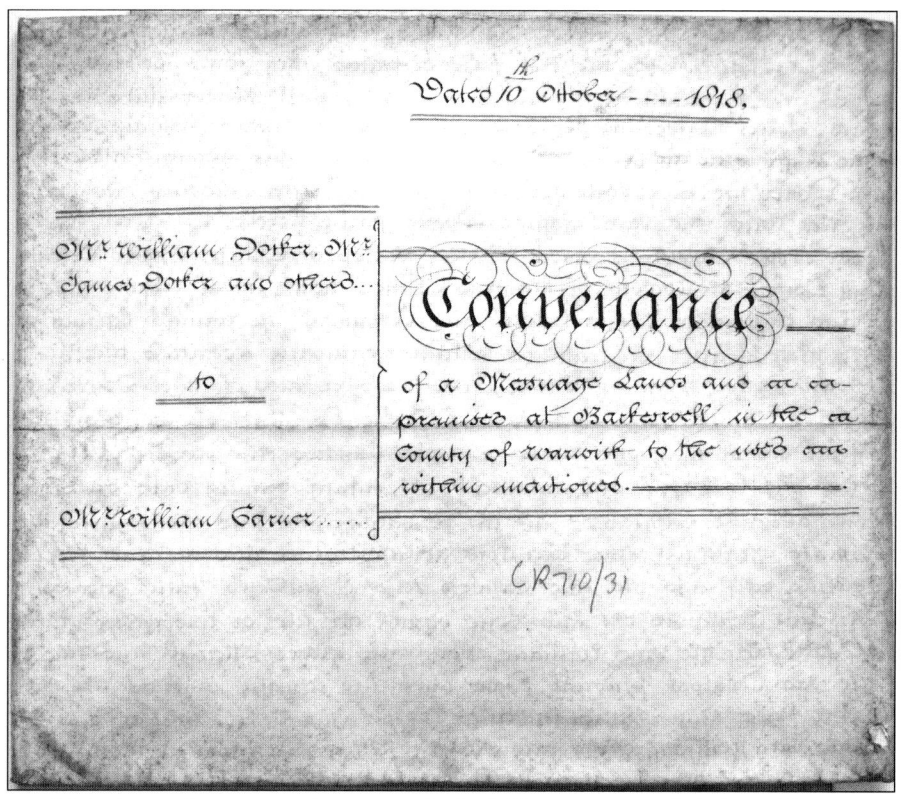

4.1 A nineteenth-century endorsement of a deed. These are a great help in working out the significance of the deed. (WCRO, CR710/31)

endorsement when the deed was drawn up (Illus. 4.1). This gives the date, the type of deed, the two principal people involved (sometimes saving much effort identifying them among half-a-dozen or more in the deed itself), and the property involved. However, the deed itself should always be looked at as well, because it gives much more information on all these aspects.

Original endorsements of this sort were not a normal seventeenth- or eighteenth-century practice (with a few exceptions, such as leases granted by major estates). However, the majority of deeds of this period have been endorsed, usually somewhat later than they were written. Series of numbers are common, indicating the order of deeds in the bundle, which are helpful in showing whether any have been lost. They are often accompanied by a brief note of the date and subject (Illus. 4.2,

How

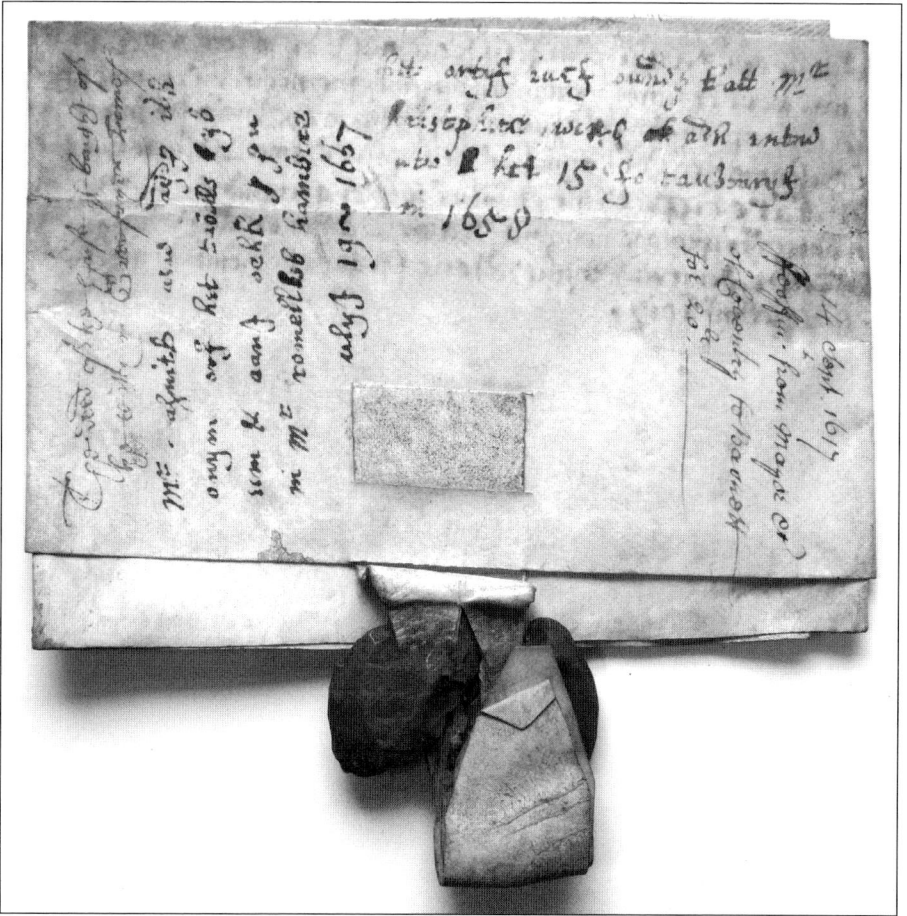

4.2 Endorsements on a seventeenth-century Coventry deed. The main endorsement (a – left side) 'The deed of the house I bought of the Citty in Greefryer Lane' is typical of the period, as is the eighteenth-century note (b – right side), '14 Sept 1617. Feoffment from Mayor, etc. of Coventry to Basnett for £20'. However, the two 'secret' endorsements are unique. The initial impression is of 'Double Dutch', though the code is not difficult to break, merely involving writing the initial letter of each word at the end. The combination of the code and some eccentric spelling makes the text unusually difficult to transcribe, but my best reading is: (c – top) het ortyf oundp hatt Mr ristpherC wenO adh intw uto het 15 fo eauboaryF ni 1658; (d – left side) Mr AsnitB asw aydp ish onym het tabells yb eem & aanJ ocr pu ni Mr romellsb hamberc ulyJ 19 1667. (WCRO, CR607/Coventry)

items a–b). More exotic endorsements are sometimes found, though rarely as bizarre as the secret writing on the example illustrated (Illus. 4.2, items c–d). An endorsement reading 'Examined and produced in the case of A v. B' is particularly significant; it indicates that the deed was used as evidence in a lawsuit. From the date and the names of the participants, it should be possible to find further records of the case.[1]

When the deed is unfolded, the dorse (back) often carries other text, not connected with the endorsements which identify it. Most of this is formal, and virtually repeats information more easily found in the deed itself. The dorse also has the signatures of the witnesses to the deed. In contrast to the medieval period (see p. 143), these were usually lawyer's clerks, and the names are of little importance (but for an exception, see p. 128). Receipts for purchase money or mortgage repayments may also be recorded. Occasionally, this text is significant, and it can include such things as schedules of furniture, lists of debts or of strips in open fields. More often, such details are on extra sheets of parchment attached to the bottom of the deed. These schedules are sometimes extremely interesting as, for example, in two deeds for the manor of Faccombe, Hampshire; the first of these (1583) attaches 'a pedigree . . . from whome the landes . . . did descende', chattily reciting the complicated ownership of the manor; the second (1634) lists room by room the goods that were to be removed by the owner when he passed the manor on to his son (University of Kansas, Kenneth Spencer Library, MS 239/326, 356).

Finally, especially in the nineteenth century, one may find a complete second deed, or a reference to one, written on the back of the original. These are likely to be either the reconveyance of a mortgage (its cancellation after repayment); or a note that part of the property has been sold, possibly with a record of the agreement to produce the deed on request to some other interested party (usually the purchaser).

How

Dating
The only major problem with dating post-medieval deeds comes from the practice of starting the year on 25 March, which was in use until 1752 ('Old Style', as opposed to 'New Style'). Without overwhelming evidence to the contrary, any date from 1 January to 24 March before 1752 can be assumed to belong to the next calendar year, e.g. 17 February 1724 is really 1725. This should be recorded as 1724[/5], using square brackets because this is your inference; sometimes original documents follow this style, and then your abstract can show 1724/5 without brackets. If there is any doubt, the date can be checked from the alternative method used in deeds, dating by *regnal year*. For example, consider the case of '10 February in the second year of King George the First'. George I came to the throne in 1714, but this date is 1716, because the day of his accession was 1 August. It is not difficult to work out the year from a list of the accession dates of the sovereigns, but much the easiest way is to consult the excellent tables in C.R. Cheney's *A Handbook of Dates For Students of British History* (Royal Historical Society Guides and Handbooks, Cambridge University Press, 2000).[2] Indeed, this book is so useful that anyone working with deeds should probably buy their own copy, so that precious record office time can be saved for looking at documents.

Both year and regnal date are given in deeds from the Restoration until about 1840, but before 1650 the year is less common (though it is sometimes included at the very end of the deed). The convenience of including the year probably became clear during the Commonwealth, when deeds were dated 'In the year of our Lord God, according to the computation of the Church of England'.[3] Curiously, the only omission from *A Handbook of Dates* is a table covering the Commonwealth period, and showing the dates of Easter, the Calendar Table, etc. This is provided in Table 4.1, below.

Table 4.1: Calendar Table for the Commonwealth Period

Year	Regnal year of Charles II*	Easter Day	Calendar Table in Handbook of Dates
1650	1, 2	14 April	24
1651	2, 3	30 March	9
1652	3, 4	18 April	28
1653	4, 5	10 April	20
1654	5, 6	26 March	5
1655	6, 7	15 April	25
1656	7, 8	6 April	16
1657	8, 9	29 March	8
1658	9, 10	11 April	21
1659	10, 11	3 April	13

* Charles II counted his reign as starting from the day his father was beheaded (30 January 1649), though I have never encountered deeds dated by his regnal years before his Restoration in 1660.

SHAPES AND PATTERNS

Most post-medieval deeds share a common physical shape, with an indented (wavy) top, and are therefore generally called 'indentures' and start 'This indenture'. In theory this implies that, as in the medieval period, two copies were made, one for each party, that could be fitted together (see p. 138), but in practice most deeds had only one copy and when more were made (e.g. for a lease and counterpart), they probably did not fit together; there are also often many more than two parties, but not all would receive copies of the deed. It is also helpful to know that when a multi-page deed is unfolded, the first (indented) sheet is at the bottom and the last sheet with the signatures is on top. By the nineteenth century, indentures were usually of a standard size with sheets of parchment measuring 33 by 25in (85 by 65cm), folded up to 11 by 9in (28 by 23cm).

How

Some other forms of deed are found, which can be recognised from their appearance and their initial phrases. Most of these are not indented, because ostensibly they were declarations by one person rather than agreements between two. The different types of post-medieval deed are summarised in Table 4.2, below, and Appendix 1 (Sections B–C) provides a flow-chart to help identify them.

Indentures follow a standard pattern in their text as well as their shape. Each consists of one monstrous sentence, followed by a second short sentence witnessing the first. This first sentence is always made up of a number of sections or clauses dealing with

Table 4.2: Types and Shapes of Post-medieval Deeds

Form	Initial phrase (English or Latin)	Shape	Illustr./page	Comment
Indenture	This Indenture	Rectangle with top edge indented, as it involves two parties. Can have many sheets	4.4 p. 99	The most important form
Feoffment	*Sciant presentes* Know all men	Rectangle. In principle not indented, as it is a declaration by one party, but generally written as an indenture		Survival of medieval deed form
Quitclaim	To all Christian people	As feoffment		As feoffment (commoner)
Fine	*Hec est finalis concordia* (until 1733) This is the final concord	Long rectangle, two edges indented	4.7 p. 120	Specialised handwriting
Bond	*Noverint Universi per presentes me* Know all men by these presents	Upright rectangle, two sections, first Latin later English (often printed) Second section usually English, starting 'The condition of this obligation . . .'	4.6 p. 113	
Recovery	George by the Grace of God . . .	Rectangle with suspended seal (often in tin box)	4.8 p. 123	Specialised and difficult handwriting
Letters Patent	Elizabeth by the Grace of God . . .	Rectangle, ornamented with royal portrait, suspended Great Seal	4.9 p. 126	
Copy of Court Roll	Name of Place View of Frankpledge, or Court Baron	Rectangle, two paragraphs, sometimes in Latin	4.13 p. 153	
Will	In the name of God . . .	One or more rectangular sheets; sometimes with attached grant of probate		

different aspects, arranged in broadly the same order. It is essential to be able to recognise these clauses in order to identify the various types of indenture and to extract their historical evidence.

The different clauses are described in Table 4.3, below. Not all occur in every deed, while some may be repeated. Each clause

Table 4.3: Clauses of Post-medieval Indentures

The phrases are usually more repetitive than shown here, e.g. the action clause of a Release might read 'hath, granted, bargained, sold, released, and confirmed, and doth grant, bargain, sell, release and confirm'.

Clause	Text	Comments and Significance
Introduction	This Indenture tripartite	Bipartite (2), quadripartite (4), etc., depending on the number of parties
Date	dated the	See p. 87 for how to convert dates in regnal years
Parties	Between ... of the first part and ... of the second part, etc. Witnesseth that	The people concerned. One party may consist of several people
Recitals	Whereas ... Now the said ...	Describes previous transactions – sometimes very numerous 'Now' ends the recitals
Consideration	for and in consideration of ...	Often the actual sum of money; sometimes a cautious 'for good and sufficient consideration', or 'for natural love and affection'; 5s. for minor parties. The end of the recital may explain how the consideration was to be paid
Action	doth demise (lease) *or* grant *or* release *or* assign ... unto ...	These are the main alternatives though each is wrapped up in many more words
Property	All that messuage ... together with all ways watercourses, ... (and also ...) together with all title deeds ...	The property involved. The inclusive clause 'together with' at the end does not mean that the property included any watercourses, etc., but guards against any omissions Another property, or something like a right of way Alternatively 'such deeds as relate solely' to the property
Tenure	To have and to hold the said messuage ... to the said ... his heirs and assigns ...	
Period	For the term of ... *or* For ever	An important distinction between a permanent grant and one for a limited period, long or short
Lordship	To be holden of the chief lord ...	Not always included. A medieval survival that can be ignored
Rent	Yielding and paying ...	The rent, if any
Uses	to the use of the said ...	Who benefits – this clause can be very complex
Conditions and Covenants	Subject to ... and the said ... further covenanteth ...	By far the most variable clause with both formal and significant covenants
Warranty	And the said ... warranteth that he hath not done any action ...	A re-statement of the right of the seller to the property. Sometimes this section includes useful information, e.g. the name of the seller's wife or even parents or grandparents
Witness	In witness whereof the said ... hath hereunto set his name and seal the day and year above written	
Seals and Signatures		Applied to the folded base of the parchment. Post-medieval seals normally have little significance
Dorse		Carries the witnesses to the signing, sometimes with receipts and additional memoranda

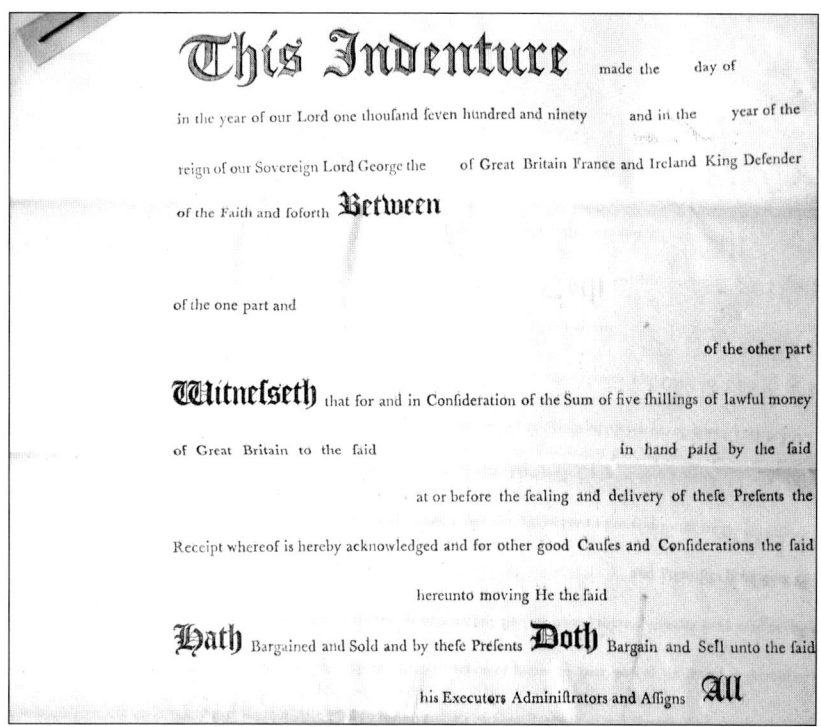

4.3 Printed blank deed form, dating from the 1790s, one of a variety of examples from an old-established solicitor's files. The image shows the start of a mortgage by lease and release (original size 28 × 38cm). (WCRO, CR1596/box 91/2/1)

usually starts with a characteristic phrase, that is sometimes written in capitals or otherwise emphasised. These phrases are so standard, that it was even possible for them to be printed, leaving blanks for the significant text to be written in (Illus. 4.3).[4]

The differences between the various clauses in different types of deeds are the main concern of the following sections. A little practice, coupled with a knowledge of the standard pattern, makes the study of deeds very much more rapid than might seem possible at first. For example, you come to a pair of deeds (a lease and release) in the middle of a sequence of deeds, identified on the outside as a conveyance by A and mortgagees to B. First, the small lease is passed over, and probably need not even be opened (its function is explained later). In the release, the parties are examined, and consist of A, who has been seen before, though now his abode has changed from the local town to a nearby village; his mortgagees, as named in an earlier mortgage deed (already examined); and B and his dower trustee (see p. 101), who are new and must be recorded in full. 'Whereas' introduces a long recital of the mortgage which is skipped through as it repeats the earlier deed. On the last page, 'Now' is immediately followed by the consideration, which is new information, and the property, which is the same as before, except that B is named as the occupier. A glance over the covenants and conditions shows only formal clauses, except that a lease to B made two years earlier is excepted from the conveyance, because still current; even though B is apparently the beneficiary, he might have assigned it to a third person. This lease is not in the bundle and so a final note is made. In a total time of less than 5 minutes, all the unique information has been gleaned. Of course, if this is the earliest deed in the bundle, and it does not contain an abstract of earlier ones, a careful summary would need to be made of the deeds recited and the property because these are new and not repeated.

It is often convenient to record the evidence of a deed on a standard form, and a possible layout is included in Appendix 2. This can be particularly useful if the type of deed is not immediately clear, as much of the form can be filled in before the deed is completely understood. Also, if the logical order of the deeds is uncertain, the forms can be shuffled. It is possible to use file cards for individual deeds, but unfortunately a standard 5 by 3in card is really too small for most deeds. With experience, and with a well-ordered deed bundle, an alternative to either forms or cards is to record the deeds in the same way as on an abstract of title (next section). This involves listing for each deed the date on the left, and the details on the right, following on one after another.

The primary analysis of a deed bundle should not depend on whether it is for local or family history. The local historian needs all the information on property and its changes, but must also keep a watch on the people involved. The family historian's concern with people should not cause him to ignore the property. In due course he may want all the details available to help him locate it and understand its significance for his ancestors' social standing and financial dealings.

Abstracts of Title
In principle, every bundle of title deeds should contain one or more abstracts of title, covering all the deeds and possibly running back before the first original. In practice, lawyers' clerks seem to have thrown out old abstracts, so that it is common to find deeds without abstracts even in coherent bundles, while when the deeds have been scattered, the abstracts have almost always vanished. Naturally, when an abstract describes deeds that are not in the bundle, notes should be taken with the utmost care, because it contains evidence that may now exist nowhere else at all. A good example is that for Chapel Street, Warwick, described above (p. 37), which includes details back to 1723 although the earliest deed is of 1819. As here, the abstract often covers about 100 years, which was considered a sufficient period to establish a secure title. When the deeds in the bundle are being examined, the abstract can save a lot of effort, but the aims of the abstractor should be borne in mind. His vital concern was to ensure that the seller (whose title to the property was described) was clearly the owner. Thus he paid great attention to the legal details of each deed to make sure it had the right form and included the right people. He was rather less concerned with the descriptions of property, particularly when the property of interest was only part of that in the deed, and he might omit the irrelevant sections with the comment *inter alia* (among other (property)). He might also simplify some of the personal details. Thus for historical purposes, an abstract of title makes an excellent route-map through a deed bundle and saves a lot of work, but if the deeds exist it is important to check their details against the abstract.

Types of Post-Medieval Deeds

How the general pattern of clauses in deeds (Table 4.3, above) appear in different types of deed will now be described. If there is no convenient endorsement, it may not be at all clear at first what sort of deed is being looked at (and this applies just as much to 'experts' as to 'beginners'). Even if the deed does not follow a standard pattern, working through clause by clause will eventually locate the key phrases. These phrases for the major types of deeds are summarised in Table 4.4, below. The most common deed types that do not follow the pattern are instantly recognisable, being the bond, fine, recovery and copy of court roll (see Illus 4.6–8 and 4.13). Others are sufficiently straightforward that they can be easily identified, and their analysis should not need extra help (e.g. articles of agreement or building contracts). There remain a few more types of deeds or deed-like documents

Table 4.4: Post-medieval Indentures: Summary of Principal Clauses

Type	Page	Clause	Nature
Lease	95	Action	Demise, set and to farm let
		Period	Various, e.g. twenty-one years; life; three lives
		Rent	Full market rent or small reserved rent
Lease and Release	99		*Sale of property (sometimes used for mortgages)*
(i) Lease for a year		Consideration	5s.
		Action	Bargain and sell (usually)
		Period	Year (sometimes six months)
		Rent	Peppercorn
(ii) Release		Consideration	The sale price
		Action	Hath granted, bargained and sold . . . being in his actual possession
		Period	For ever
Mortgage (by demise *or* in fee)	109	Action	Grant, bargain and sell and demise
		Period	500 or 1,000 years (usually)
		Rent	Peppercorn
Assignment of Mortgage	110	Action	Assign and set over
Assignment to attend inheritance	112	Uses	To B in trust for A, to wait upon and attend the inheritance
Feoffment *and* Bargain and Sale	127	Action	Given, granted, alienated, bargained and sold and enfeoffed
		Endorsement	Feoffment: Livery of seisin
			Bargain and Sale: Enrolment in court
Quitclaim	130	Action	Remise, release and for ever quitclaim

that are extremely rare. If you encounter one of these, then it is very reasonable to seek help from an archivist.

LEASE AND COUNTERPART LEASE; ASSIGNMENT OF LEASE

The lease makes a convenient point to start. It is a common and relatively straightforward deed that usually means what it says, while its derivatives are involved in several other types (especially the lease and release and the 'perpetual lease', pp. 99 and 130). Properties such as small cottages were often held 'at will', without any written lease, but for anything more substantial, two copies of the lease were prepared. One was signed by the owner and given to the tenant. This is the *Lease* itself. The other was signed by the tenant and kept by the owner. This is the *Counterpart lease* or *Counterpart*. The distinction between the two can be useful in deciding where a particular document comes from, though if a lease was given up before it expired (was *surrendered*), the surrendered lease (sometimes endorsed to this effect) would be returned to the owner. Alternatively, the tenant might assign his rights to someone else by an *Assignment of lease*. He might also sub-let (under-lease) the property or part of it, though both assignments and sub-leasing were often controlled by conditions in the original lease (usually requiring the owner's permission). The main difference between the two is that with an assigned lease, the owner would receive his rent from the new tenant, but a sub-tenant paid the original tenant who then paid the owner. In eighteenth- and nineteenth-century building development in towns such as Bath and London, whole nests of leases are found, with the property owner granting a ninety-nine-year lease of a block of land to a developer, the latter laying out plots and under-leasing to a builder, and the house when built being under-leased again to the tenant.

A *Reversionary lease* or *Lease in reversion* starts after some specified future event has taken place, e.g. the death of a life tenant or the expiry of a current lease, and the property has 'reverted' to the landlord.

The special features of a lease are as follows:

Parties: These are (1) the true owners or perhaps the trustees of a marriage or family settlement (which will be mentioned in a recital), and (2) the tenant who is usually, but not necessarily, the occupier.

Consideration: A sum of money, an *entry fine*, was often paid for a lease, especially if the rent was a token one. The surrender of a previous lease may also be recorded here.

Action: The key words are 'demise, set and to farm let'.

Property: See below (p. 104).

Period: This is either a term of years (fourteen and twenty-one being common, as is ninety-nine years for building leases), or sometimes one year, to continue year by year until notice is given by either party (a yearly lease), or until some event takes place, e.g. during the life of the tenant (a life lease). A form of the latter particularly popular in south-west England, but not uncommon elsewhere, was the 'three-life lease', for ninety-nine years or until the death of the last of three named people (all living when the lease was granted). For example, a lease of 1613 for Sowton, Devon, was for the lives of Thomas Pyne, his wife Agnes and their son, Leonard.[5] This made a very secure tenure for the farmer and his immediate family which could later be extended. We are told that for some farms this went on for centuries, so that only the owner and the farmer himself were aware that it was not a freehold.[6] In the eighteenth century, such leases were calculated by estate administrators as equivalent to sixty-year terms; during this century they were gradually replaced by twenty-one-year leases.[7] Three-life leases were also used in Ireland, where they caused considerable trouble in the nineteenth century, as the 'lives' emigrated and no one knew whether they were alive or dead.

With three-life leases, reversions were often granted 'to add one life to two'. This lease started on the death of the first of the lives, and so brought the number of people on whom the tenancy depended back to three. Alternatively, the surrender of the original lease might be part of the consideration for a new lease for three lives. This had exactly the same effect, unless the reversionary lease was granted to a different tenant, possibly even one who had outbid the original tenant for the renewal. The starting date of a lease is always stated, and Lady Day (25 March) and Michaelmas (29 September) were usual.

Rent: This is a real sum, not a token (peppercorn) as in a lease for a year or mortgage. It was usually paid in two parts, on Lady Day and Michaelmas. Some leases, especially those for 'three lives', had rather small rents, e.g. 6s. 8d., coupled with large entry fines. The fines might then vary from renewal to renewal of the lease, while the rent was constant. A 'rack rent' is occasionally referred to in a deed (though more often in rentals and estate documents). It has two very different meanings. Originally, it described a rent comprising a very high proportion of the holding's profit, the term being derived from the instrument of torture. Such a rent might be extorted if the landlord wanted the maximum immediate income, irrespective of the future decay of the property; thus, nineteenth-century Irish landlords frequently demanded them. However, generally speaking, in estate practice of the late nineteenth century the term had lost its pejorative flavour, and the rack rent merely represented the full market rental. This was often calculated by a rule of thumb allowing one-third of the holding's profit to the owner (as rent), one-third to the tenant (his living expenses) and one-third for the land (the return on the tenant's capital, used for purchase of stock, etc.).

Other payments and services are listed with the rent. These might include 'suit of court' (attendance at the manor court, usually twice a year) and 'heriot' (in three-life leases, a payment on the death of one of the intermediate lives). A rent of a cock or a hen at Christmas or Easter is not uncommon, and other rents in kind sometimes occur, e.g. '500 couples of conies [rabbits]' from the tenant of a warren or the 'two firkins of barrel butter all good, swete, merchantable and of the best, every firkin to waye threescore and foure poundes' to be delivered every year at Michaelmas (1611 lease of a farm in Hoo, Suffolk; University of Kansas, Kenneth Spencer Library, MS 239:3038).

Covenants and conditions: Conditions were frequently attached to leases. Some are formal, almost always present, rather obvious and not very important. However, the end of a lease should always be checked for unusual conditions, and a few samples are given in Table 4.5, below.[8]

Type	Comments
1. Formal	
Quiet enjoyment	The landlord will not prevent the tenant using the property
Maintenance	To maintain the buildings in good condition
Distraint or re-entry	Usually, if the rent was unpaid, the landlord could distrain after, say twenty-one days, i.e. collect goods to the value of the rent. After a year's arrears, the lease was void, and the landlord could re-enter. As most leases ran to completion without trouble, these clauses were rarely invoked
2. Significant	
Building	Tenant or landlord to build or rebuild a house or barn, etc. within a specified time. Usually with a detailed description of the new building
Carriage	E.g. to carry two cartloads of coal per year from Nuneaton to Stoneleigh Abbey, Warwickshire (1683; SCLA, DR18/1/992); may be part of the rent clause
Husbandry	E.g. a financial penalty on ploughing more than a specified part of the land within the last five years of the lease, or to apply specified amounts of manure or other fertilizer
Social	'to attende and bee ready with a nagge, horse or mare to ride with ... Henry Raynsford [*lord of the manor of Clifford Chambers, Warwickshire*] when he shall bee thereunto requested, the said Henry Hobbins [*the tenant's son*] having his livery cloake or coate allowed unto him by the said Henry Raynsford' (1623; SCLA, DR33/10)

Table 4.5: Conditions in Post-medieval Leases

The structure of an *Assignment of lease* is not very close to that of a lease, but as they are closely related in their function, the assignment is described here. Its significant clauses are:

Parties: The usual parties will be (1) the original tenant, (2) the new tenant, possibly with (3) the owner, if his permission was needed for the assignment.

Recital: The grant of the original lease is always recited.

Consideration: Something can be expected here.

Action: The key phrase is 'assign and set over'.

The remaining clauses will either be repeated from the original lease, or will be covered by phrases like 'as in the hereinbefore recited indenture . . .'.

LEASE AND RELEASE

Unlike most other indentures, the two linked deeds which make up the lease and release do not perform a single function, but rather provide a form which was employed for many tasks. However, the form originated as a conveyance to transfer property from one person to another, and this function is described here. The lease and release was invented in about 1600 to provide a secret but legally valid conveyance. The first part of the lease and release is a lease of the property by the vendor to the purchaser for one year at a nominal rent (Illus. 4.4). This puts the purchaser in possession as tenant. Then, on the following day, the vendor and anyone with an interest in the property release their rights to the purchaser, leaving him in full ownership. Because the release only transferred an *interest* in the property (the reversion after the expiry of the lease) rather than the freehold itself, it did not have

4.4 The Lease of a *Lease and Release* of 1692 for a house in Derby. Although smaller than most post-medieval indentures, this shows their typical form. Its archival place is folded up inside the Release, and in the nineteenth century it was sometimes physically attached to the bottom of the Release. For the text, see p. 175. (TNA, E 330/31)

to be made public by enrolment or livery of seisin (unlike the bargain and sale or feoffment, p. 127). The earliest example I have encountered is of 1657, apart from one of 1636, which differs in several respects from the standard later ones.[9]

The lease and release gained popularity steadily during the seventeenth century until in the eighteenth and early nineeenth centuries it was virtually the only form of conveyance. The lease part of the lease and release was no longer needed after 1841 with the passage of 'A Statute for rendering a Release as effectual for the conveyance of a freehold estate as a Lease and Release' (as it is sometimes referred to in deeds of the period). The Real Property Act of 1845 finally allowed freehold property to be conveyed by a single private deed.

The details by which the two parts of a lease and release can be recognised are as follows:

1. *Lease for a year* (also called 'bargain and sale for a year') (Illus. 4.4):

Parties: These are usually the actual owner and the actual purchaser.

Consideration: Normally 5s. (useful for identification).

Action: Either 'demise' as for an ordinary lease or 'bargain and sale' (or both).

Property: Full details of the property are always given.

Period: One year (occasionally six months in the seventeenth century).

Rent: Usually 'a peppercorn if legally demanded'.

Uses: 'To the end and intent that . . . the said B [purchaser] may be in actual possession'.

2. *Release*. Although releases may be fairly simple if the conveyance has no complications (as in the text of the example on p. 185), they can be very lengthy, particularly in the recital section. The extent to which this can be skipped depends on whether the deeds referred to have already been seen, or are described in an abstract of title. Because the release is the single

most important type of title deed, this is the best point to examine the parties and the property (p. 104).

Parties: The simplest possibility is (1) the seller, (2) the purchaser, and this is common until the mid-eighteenth century. Quite often the description of the seller includes his connection to a previous owner, e.g. 'John Clarke, son of Jeremiah Clarke, late of Ettington, deceased'. Joint owners were usually the result of a joint inheritance, but occasionally two people made a purchase as partners; such joint owners were generally 'tenants in common', implying that they owned a half share each, and their shares could be sold, left by will, etc. The alternative of 'joint tenants' or 'tenants in survivorship' meant that, if one purchaser died, the other automatically succeeded to both shares.

A very important distinction has to be made between straightforward ownership as just described, and the more complex situation in which the owners in the eyes of the law purchased or sold property on behalf of someone else. The latter was the 'beneficial' owner, who received the benefit of the property. Trustees make up the main group of these legal owners, and executors of a will are another example; they were frequently instructed to sell the deceased's property, and they would then be the first party in the deed. Among trustees, apart from dower trustees (see below), those of marriage or family settlements (p. 114) are most common, but trustees in bankruptcy are also found. For all of these, the recital should explain their position, but it does not always make quite clear who was the previous owner.

For the purchaser, an important change took place in the later eighteenth century. Before this he acted straightforwardly as an individual, but thereafter he was usually associated with his own trustee, a dower trustee. The legal title to the property was held by the trustee, so that, on the purchaser's death, his widow would not be entitled to one-third of the property for life (her common-law dower rights). The dower trustee is rarely so-called explicitly, but can be recognised either from the uses (see p. 103), or from his description among the parties, for example, 'William Townsend of Coventry, glazier, and Edward Lea of the same city, tailor, a person nominated by and in trust for the said William Townsend' (CHC, TC/1/L/325). He may be listed after the purchaser, or may be combined with him as a single party. It is also worth noting that dower trustees, unlike the trustees of settlements, do not usually enter into succeeding transactions, because the 'uses' include the ability for the real owner to dispose of the property. The dower trustee was no longer necessary after 1833, when dower could be 'barred' by a declaration in the deed itself. Later deeds often include the phrase 'who was a bachelor (or "unmarried") on 1 January 1834', to make clear the position in regard to dower. Another party frequently present in a release is the mortgagee — invariably so if the owner has mortgaged the property. In order to extinguish the mortgage satisfactorily, the purchaser may also have another trustee in whom the mortgage will be vested 'to attend the inheritance' (see p. 112).

Recital: One main concern is to justify the seller's title. Details of wills are often given, including the date of writing and of probate (and where it was proved). These should be recorded, because it is often informative to examine the complete will. It is noticeable how often deed bundles start with a will; it gave a particularly unassailable title, and no doubt lawyers were glad to lose sight of whatever had gone before. As already mentioned, the appointment of trustees is also recorded. This recital is particularly long and tedious for bankruptcy trustees, though, if the original deed appointing the trustees is found, it may give interesting lists of the debts involved and be signed by numerous creditors.

The second main concern of the recital is the mortgage (if any), usually including its establishment and some or all of its assignments. These repeat the mortgage deeds, and so can be ignored if the latter exist.

Finally, the agreement to purchase is often recited, perhaps with the date and place that the property was auctioned (to demonstrate that the sale was at full market rate). Sometimes the buyer at the auction had resold it to the final purchaser and this is explained; the original buyer may then be a party to the deed. The division of the purchase money between any co-owners, mortgagees and other recipients is also described.

Consideration: This clause tends to be short, with any more interesting details in the recital. People with minor interests in the property – trustees, widows resigning dower rights, etc. – generally received a nominal sum of 5s. each, which is noted in this clause.

Action: 'Hath granted, bargained, sold, alienated, released and confirmed, and by these presents doth grant, bargain, . . .'.

Property: See p. 104.

Period: A conveyance of freehold by release is always 'for ever'. If the conveyance includes the assignment of a paid-off mortgage, then this will be assigned for the residue of the original term (often 1,000 years). A perpetual leasehold (see p. 130) is often conveyed by lease and release. It will have the same 1,000-year period (usually), but can be distinguished from a mortgage because it is assigned to the purchaser, rather than to a trustee to 'attend the inheritance'; it can also be recognised in the recital.

Rent and tenure: If any rent has to be paid, it is usually included in the covenants. The tenure clause depends on the legal status of the property, but can be ignored for practical purposes.

Uses: Normally to the use of the purchaser, his heirs and assigns, i.e. with freedom to sell, mortgage or transfer the property, etc.; later, the dower trustee holds to the same uses. If, say, the money of a marriage settlement was used for the purchase, then the uses will be the same as in the settlement.

Covenants and conditions: These are generally formal, mostly intended to give the purchaser as strong a title as possible and normally do not need to be studied in detail. They can include an agreement to levy a *fine* – '*sur cognisance de droit com ceo*' (see p. 119) – or to execute any extra deed requested by the purchaser (sometimes within time or distance limits, e.g. without travelling 'more than ten miles' (1700), or 'outside the counties of Warwickshire or Staffordshire' (1692)). A warranty to defend the title may mention relatives of the vendor who do not appear elsewhere, and so need to be noted. Sometimes there are exclusions, either of a rent that has to be paid, or of a lease that has been granted and is still current.

One of the few important covenants arises when the seller is not handing over the previous title deeds. He then covenants first to produce copies if requested, and secondly to take reasonable care of, and produce on demand, the earlier deeds (often listed in a schedule at the bottom of the deed). These will have been described in an abstract of title, but, if that has disappeared, the schedule may give the only clue to the earlier history of the property. Schedules are rather difficult to interpret, as they usually only list the dates and parties, leaving one to guess if they are describing conveyances, mortgages, settlements or whatever. Alternatively, this type of covenant might be made the subject of a separate deed.

Property: Property clauses can cover anything from an entire ducal estate to a strip of land 6in by 12ft for the footings of a wall. Like the other clauses, part represents real information, part is formal. Four property clauses will be quoted in detail, to illustrate their character and this distinction.

The first is a fairly simple example for rural property:

> All that quarterne or fourth parte of one yardland of arable, meadow, and pasture ground with the appurtenances, lying and being in the fields, precincts and territories of Napton upon the Hill in the said county of Warwickshire, and now or late in the tenure or occupation of the said Robert Crofts, his assignee or assignes, and heretofore purchased by the said Robert Crofts, deceased, uncle of the said Robert Crofts, party to these presents of and from one Elizabeth

Greenoway and John Greenoway, Together with all and singular lands, leyes, hades, balkes, meadowes; pastures, lott grasse, parting grasse, feedings, comons and comon of pasture, profitts, commodityes, advantages, emoluments, and hereditaments whatsoever to the said quarterne . . . belonging (1681; WCRO, D19/591).

Only the first part of this contains much useful information, though the second part suggests that common grazing rights were involved. It did not include a house, which would have been stated explicitly, as in the next example. The description of the number of yardlands or their fractions is typical of open-field land in dispersed strips.

Terriers (detailed lists of strips) are occasionally included with deeds, especially if an open-field holding is being subdivided, and give very valuable topographical information (Illus. 4.5, p. 106).

The next example shows how enclosed fields might be described. The term 'messuage or tenement' is standard for a house, though occasionally 'tenement or cottage' is found for a small dwelling. As in the last example, the end of the property clause can be ignored.

One messuage and tenement with the appurtenances situate, lyinge and being within the parishe of Stoke Gabriell in the countie aforesaide [Devon], sometymes being but a bakehouse, barne, courtlage, garden, and orchard, and also certen parcells of land, meadow, and pasture with the appurtenances called the South Downes, the Millake, the Waleteane, and Waleteane meadow, conteyninge in the whole by estimacion five and twentie acres or thereabouts, be the same more or less, together with common in Myllake Green, all which premises are scytuate, lyinge and beinge in Stoke Gabriell aforesaid, now or heretofore parte and parcell or reputed to be parte and

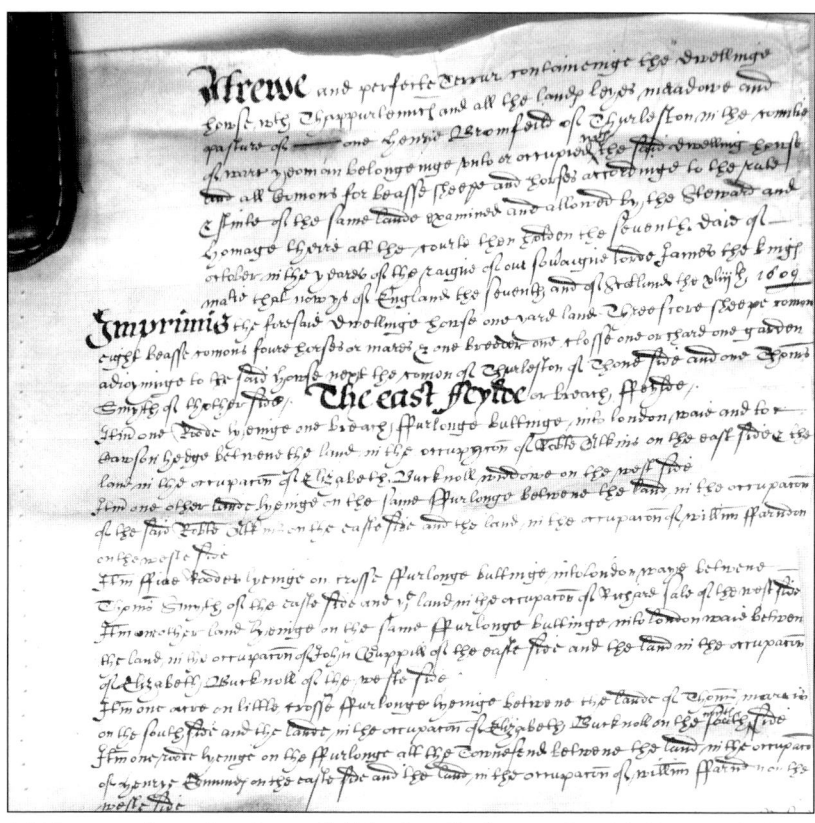

4.5 The start of a terrier of open-field land at Thurlaston, Warwickshire, attached to a deed of 1616. For text, see p. 177. (WCRO, CR2015/Box2/50)

parcell of the Lordshippe or mannor of Paignton in the said countie of Devon, and now in the tenure, manurance [= *tenure*], or occupation of Gilbert Tully the elder, Gilbert Tully, son of Odes Tully, and Gilbert Kinge or one of them, their or one of their assignee or assignees, for and during their natural lives according to the custome of the said mannor of Paignton, And all houses, edifices, buildings, barnes, stables, shippens, courts, courtlages [courtyards], gardens, orchards, lands, meadows, lesowes, pastures, feedings, wasts, commons, common of pasture, wayes, pathes, waters, watercourses, easements, profits, commodities, annuities, and hereditaments whatsoever ... [*etc. for several more lines*] (1637; WCRO, L3/4).

Next comes a simple example for urban property, just recording the street in which the house lies and the occupier.

> All that messuage, cottage, or tenement, garden, backside, hereditaments, and premises, situate, standing and being near a certain place called Saint James's Hill in the parish of Saint Mary in the Borough of Warwick, in the County of Warwick, formerly in the occupation of John Hill, and now of Edward Baron, And also ... [*another house*], Together with all ... (1784; WCRO, CR1886/BB213).

The main description here occupies just one-and-a-quarter lines of text in the original, but the 'Together with' clause, covering every conceivable appurtenance possibly associated with the property, extends to no less than seven-and-a-half long lines.

The final example shows how complex an urban property description could become, even without details about the building. It was probably made so precise to define clearly what part of the original larger plot was involved. The names of people owning adjoining houses (the abuttals) are often included in urban descriptions and are particularly helpful in locating property on the ground. The example also illustrates the concentration of a particular occupation in one part of a city. (For the full text of this deed, see p. 185.)

> All that messuage or tenement with the appurtenances called or knowne by the name of the Tolbooth, and heretofore in the several tenures or occupations of Thomas Hope, father of the said Samuel Hope, party to these presents, and John Holloway, clothworker, and heretofore part of a messuage or tenement sometime in the tenure of Elizabeth Sharratt, widdowe, which said messuage or tenement hereby granted is situate, lyinge and beinge in the City of Coventry aforesaid, in or neere a certaine streete there called or knowne by the

name of Muche Parke Streete, between a messuage and yard there of one Samuel Clarke of Coundon in the said county of Warwickshire, gentleman, now or late in the tenure of Anthony Edwards, clothworker, on the north and west parts, and a messuage and garden there being the land of one Mary Coles, now in the occupation of Thomas Webb, clothworker, on the south part, and Much Parke Street aforesaid, on the East part, and conteyninge in breadth by the said streete side twenty three foote, and in breadth on the west side towards Anthony Edwards said yarte [sic] nineteene foote, and in length on the north side towards the said Anthony Edwards house thirty seaven foote, and in length on the south side towards the said messuage in the occupation of the said Thomas Webb fourty two foote With all houses, . . . (1678; deed in private ownership).

Other information that may be included in the property clause has been discussed in Chapter Two. In the nineteenth century, especially in the case of urban property, plans of the site and buildings may be found, with the phrase 'which said premises are more particularly delineated in the map or plan drawn in the margin of these presents'. In general, property descriptions were often unchanged from one deed to another, apart perhaps from amending the list of occupiers from, say, 'in the occupation of John Anstye', to 'formerly in the occupation of John Anstye, and now of Richard Porter'. It is not safe to deduce from such phrases that the former occupant had been there shortly before. Similarly, a phrase like 'newly rebuilt' can be repeated for a century!

A somewhat curious description occasionally found is 'the site of the ground where a messuage stood', which may not indicate that the house is no longer there – sometimes the description continues with 'together with the messuage there standing'.

Mortgage

Fundamentally, the mortgage is a lease for a long period at nominal rent, but it has three particular features: first, it is granted in consideration of a specified sum of money. Secondly, the deed will be cancelled if the money is repaid with interest by a certain date, but, if not, the mortgage becomes 'absolute'. At that moment, in theory the *mortgagee* (who lends the money) becomes owner of the property; in practice this very rarely happened. Thirdly, the property is still used by the *mortgagor* (the original owner); this is not stated in the deed. However, the last two points only became established during the seventeenth century, and before that mortgages had a very different character (p. 30).

Various forms of deed are used for mortgages. The lease is the simplest (a *Mortgage by demise*), and has the following characteristics:

Parties: (1) The owner, i.e. the mortgagor, (2) the lender of the money, i.e. the mortgagee(s), who may be an individual or a group of trustees, executors of a will, etc. holding money in trust to invest.

Recital: Occasionally describes the owner's purchase. Usually states that he needs money, and that the mortgagee will lend it.

Consideration: The money being lent (the principal).

Action: 'Grant, bargain and sell and demise, set and to farm let', i.e. a mixture of a grant and a lease, of which the lease is the effective part.

Period: Usually 500 or 1,000 years 'without impeachment of waste', i.e. without the mortgagee being liable for any reduction in the value of the property. Terms of ninety-nine years are found in the seventeenth century.

Rent: A peppercorn.

Conditions: The key clause in a mortgage, 'provided upon this express condition that if the said A (mortgagor) shall pay . . . [the principal and interest, at stated times], this present indenture of mortgage shall be *absolutely void*'. It continues, 'and if default shall be made [in repayment], it may be lawful for B (*mortgagee*) to enter on, have, hold, possess, and enjoy the same'. The form of repayment is also laid down. A sum of, say, £50 is typically either to be paid as £51 5s. in six months, or as £1 5s. in six months and £51 5s. after a year. Both correspond to repayment with 5 per cent interest; the rate at any time in the eighteenth and nineteenth centuries hardly varied outside the range of 4 to 5 per cent, though it was as high as 8 per cent in the mid-seventeenth century.

In reality, both as a loan for the mortgagor and as an investment for the mortgagee, the mortgage was intended to continue indefinitely, with interest paid regularly. Indeed, during the course of the seventeenth century, the courts gradually established that mortgages could not be *foreclosed* (terminated) at the whim of the mortgagee, even if the date set for repayment had passed.[10] Thus they became a secure way for a property owner to obtain a loan without the danger of losing his land; he retained his *equity of redemption*, his right to repay the mortgage. The only way the mortgagee could foreclose was to apply to the Court of Chancery. A court order for the sale of the property would only be granted if the money due was not paid on the day set by the court.

In the nineteenth century, second mortgages appear, taken out on property already subject to one mortgage. These avoid the problem of default by including a 'power of sale' among the conditions, which meant that if the interest had been unpaid for a given time, say, six months, the mortgagee could (and often did) put the property up for auction, without needing a court order.

Other Mortgage Deeds; Assignment of Mortgage
The previous example of a mortgage has the simple form of a lease for 1,000 years as a single indenture. Mortgages were also granted by lease and release, and even by fine. In the *Mortgage in Fee*, the property was granted to the mortgagee by a lease and release, so that he actually owned it, although the mortgagor still occupied the property and collected the rents. The release or the

'deed to lead the uses of the fine' (p. 119) then contains the conditions for redemption and repayment, and the key clause 'provided that' if the money was repaid, the release would be null and void.

As we have seen, even if the mortgagee wanted his money back, he could not easily foreclose. Instead, someone else was found to take over the mortgage, and a deed of *Assignment of mortgage* was executed. To judge by the number of assignments that exist, there was no great difficulty in finding mortgage money, but the deeds themselves do not explain how this was done. The assignment is very like the assignment of a lease (p. 98), with the following key clauses:

Parties: (1) The owner, (2) the original mortgagee (or perhaps his executors), (3) the new mortgagee; the parties may, however, be in a different order.

Recital: Date and details of the original mortgage and any earlier assignments.[11] The original mortgage had usually become absolute (i.e. had passed its set redemption time), and this is often stated, as is the wish of the mortgagee to be repaid.

Consideration: The original principal, repaid to the old mortgagee. Sometimes the size of the mortgage was also increased as part of the assignment.

Action: 'At the request and by the direction of A (the owner), B (the old mortgagee) hath bargained and sold, assigned and set over to C (the new mortgagee) . . . all the estate, right, title: . . . and number of years yet to come in . . .'.

Property: Usually as in the original mortgage, but occasionally with the occupiers, etc. brought up to date; if new houses have been built, this may be noted to justify an increase in the value of the mortgage. Sometimes the property description is only given in full in the recital and this clause only notes 'the said messuage . . .'.

Conditions: The assigned mortgage is subject to the same conditions as the original one, and they are usually repeated.

The End of a Mortgage: Assignment to Attend the Inheritance
The simplest way of terminating a mortgage was for the money to be repaid and a receipt endorsed on the back of the original deed. However, this was felt to be unsatisfactory. The 1,000-year lease had been granted and not properly terminated. Thus what was adopted was an *Assignment* of the mortgage (as just described) to a trustee for the owner *in trust to attend the inheritance*, with the following key phrase in the uses: 'to have and to hold to B (the trustee) ... in trust for A (the owner), to wait upon and attend the inheritance'. This assignment may be incorporated in a release if the mortgage is being paid off at the same time as the property is sold, or may be a separate deed. In either case, the only new historical information is the name of the trustee, likely to be a friend of the owner. The deed also recites the original mortgage and the details of the property, which are valuable if the earlier deeds have not survived. In the later nineteenth century, with changes in the law, mortgages were paid off more simply; by reconveyance of the rights originally granted, and this was usually written on the back of the original deed.

If the mortgage could not be paid off, then the mortgagee might with difficulty enforce a sale (as noted above), or more usually the property would be put up for sale with the agreement of the owner. Occasionally, the mortgagee himself might buy it, in which case the owner would convey it to him by lease and release, releasing what was known as the *equity of redemption* (the right to repay the mortgage).

BOND

The bond does not have the form of an indenture, and it had many uses other than in relation to title deeds. However, it is often associated with a mortgage and so is conveniently described here. The bond has a characteristic appearance (Illus. 4.6). The formal first section was in Latin until 1733, and was often a printed form with gaps for the names, amount and date to be inserted. It simply states that one party is *bound* ('firmly bound and obliged') to pay a certain sum to the other party. The second part states that 'The condition of this obligation' is that, if a specified action is performed, then the first part will be void. This

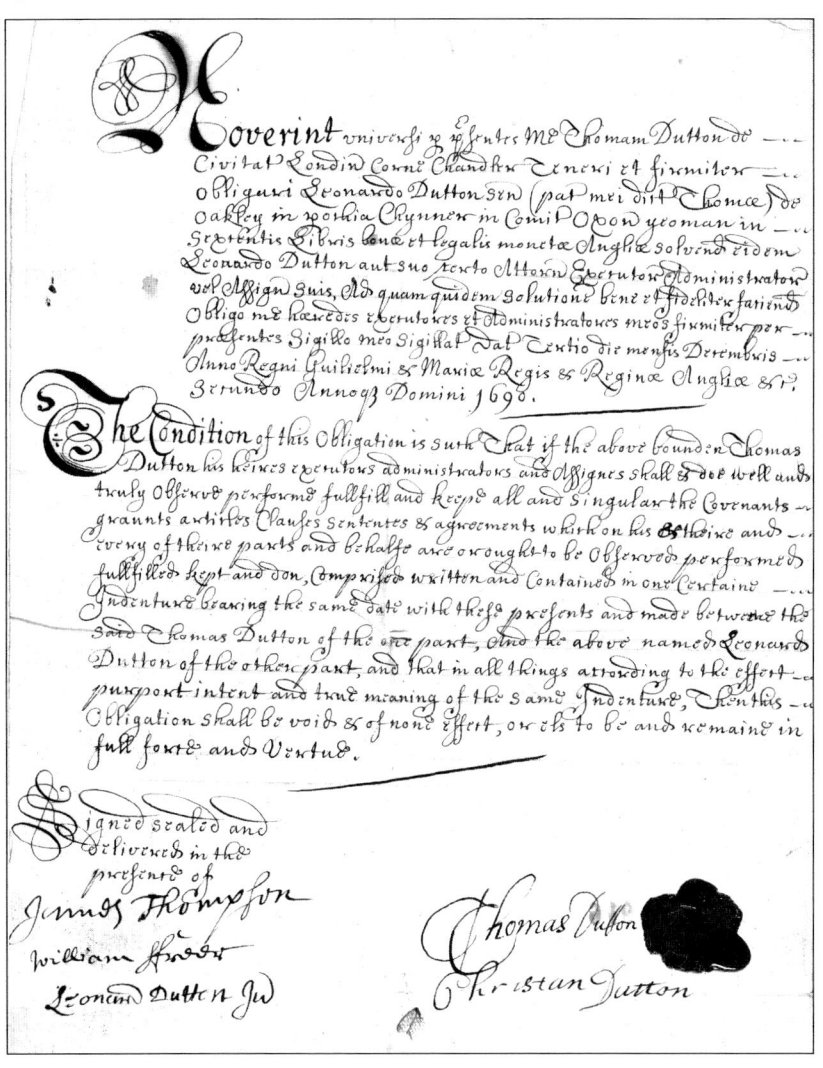

4.6 A bond of 1690, for keeping the covenants in a deed-selling property in Crowell, Oxfordshire. For text, see p. 178. (TNA, E 214/946; the corresponding deed is /945)

could be simply the payment of a stated sum of money at a stated time, as in the case of a straightforward debt, but bonds were also regularly used to strengthen a mortgage. The bond had the advantage that it could if necessary be enforced in a court of law, as an alternative to applying to foreclose the mortgage. By convention, the bond was for a *penal* sum, twice the amount actually due.

Bonds were also made to accompany conveyances as in Illus. 4.6. With these, the penal sum would be twice the purchase cost, and the seller would be bound either to give the purchaser 'quiet enjoyment' of the property, or to observe the 'covenants in a certain pair of indentures of even date' (i.e. a release executed on the same day as the bond). In the seventeenth century bonds often included a description of the property, but by the eighteenth century their only useful information is likely to be the names of the parties.

Settlements

Two types of settlement are common among title deeds: the *family settlement* in which family property was entailed, i.e. assigned to trustees so that it would descend in the family's ownership; and the *marriage settlement* in which property was held for the joint benefit of husband and wife and their children. Both take the form of conveyances to trustees, usually by lease and release in the eighteenth century, and by bargain and sale before then (see p. 127).

The *marriage settlement* is generally the simpler type, with the following sections:

Parties: These include the husband and wife and a pair of trustees (one associated with the husband's family and one with the wife's). If either husband or wife is not the property owner in his/her own right (or is not of age), then their parents or trustees also appear (e.g. the father whose son is being married). Sometimes, the settlement deed involves the purchase of a property, when its owner will be among the parties (confusingly, as he generally has nothing to do with the other persons concerned).

Recital: Usually commences 'Whereas a marriage has been agreed and with God's grace will shortly be performed . . .' (a post-nuptial settlement, when the marriage had already taken place, was less common). The payment of money either as a marriage portion for the bride or by the husband's family is sometimes noted, but its omission does not necessarily mean that no dowry was involved. Sometimes more unusual items are mentioned, such as a *Bride Cart*. In the marriage settlement of John Spyer of Burton Hastings, Warwickshire and Sarah Hitch of Dunton Bassett, Leicestershire, the groom's father settled the family farm on the trustees, including about 30 acres of land (one yardland), while the bride's dowry was £65 and 'a Bride Cart to the value of at least £15' (WCRO, CR1391/2/2); this was a cart that was loaded with 'bedding, linens, furniture, pewter, brass and other household stuff', which the bride brought with her.[12]

Property: It can be important to remember that the property in the settlement often did not include everything owned by the husband. In general, a balance was sought so that the land settled by the husband's family was about equal in value to the wife's dowry.

Uses: The uses to which the trustees are bound in a marriage settlement are normally fairly standard, and have four stages:

1. Before the marriage, for whichever family originally owned the property.
2. Jointly for husband and wife, and for the survivor after the death of his or her partner.
3. After the deaths of both parents, for the children of the marriage (sometimes in separate portions for elder and younger sons and daughters).
4. In the absence of children, to the heirs of the original owner (sometimes named).

Occasionally, a much simpler form is found in which the husband or wife after the other's death can assign the property as each chooses. This was probably used particularly for the marriage of an elderly woman when children were not expected.

Family settlements were often made for families of wealth and status, generation after generation, on such an occasion as the eldest son reaching the age of 21, or marrying.[13] Whenever a new settlement was made, the previous settlement would be annulled by a recovery (p. 118). Their aim was to preserve the family estate intact for future generations, and they therefore arranged that the head of the family had the use (and profits) from the estate *during his life only*, and so could not sell it without the consent of both his heir and his trustees. Such a settlement is usually instantly recognisable because of its size (Illus. 1.6)! Its principal sections are:

Parties: These include the father and eldest son, together with old and new trustees.

Recital: Of a previous settlement.

Property: Generally, most but not all of the family estate was covered, leaving a part that could easily be mortgaged or even sold if necessary. It was also possible for the trustees to mortgage the settled estate which presumably provided good security, though foreclosing would have been even more difficult than for an ordinary mortgage. Private Acts of Parliament were sometimes passed to allow the sale of settled estates to pay the owner's debts.

Uses: Although the property description in a family settlement can be lengthy, its bulk generally comes from the uses. The first concern has already been noted, to make the head of the family 'tenant for life', with his eldest son to succeed him (the 'tenant in tail'). The sequence after that had to be laid down, with 'remainders' to the eldest son's children in order; to his brothers and their children successively; to his sisters and their children – to the limit of the lawyer's patience and his client's purse. The settlement also provided an income for the owner's wife and lump sums for younger children. The details of these arrangements are usually of minor historical interest, although they indicate the financial strain placed on an estate by the children's portions. However, in the process of laying them down the settlement gives a clear view of the family, including for example the children's order of precedence.

Married Women's Property
One important aspect of marriage and family settlements is the ownership of property by wives. In principle, until the later nineteenth century, the law held that everything belonging to a woman passed to her husband on their marriage, and was his to dispose of – to sell, give or gamble away – legally known as her coverture (or couverture). The position only changed with the passing of the Married Women's Property Acts in 1870, 1882 and 1893; the first allowed a wife the right to her own earnings, and the second and third Acts finally gave wives the same legal control as unmarried women. However, the reality was not always so draconian. In the eighteenth century, wills making bequests to married women quite often specified that the bequest was to be for her own use, not withstanding her coverture, and that her husband was not to 'intermeddle' with it; such bequests were generally made to trustees to hold on the wife's behalf.[14]

A more systematic way to circumvent coverture involved the marriage settlement itself, as seen for Mary Harris of Stoneleigh, Warwickshire in 1615. She was the wife of Richard Harris and left a will (Lichfield Joint Record Office). This is very unusual indeed for a wife, but in her case before their marriage it was 'agreed by consent and before witnesses' (but perhaps not in writing) that she could 'give away and dispose of at myne owne pleasure and liking' her 'household stuffe'. A more substantial example is that of Susannah Hubert of Wolston, Warwickshire, the wealthy widow of Michael Hubert (d. 1737).[15] Before she remarried in

1751, she executed a settlement, transferring to trustees both her lands (the manor of Wolston) and her personal property, jewels and household goods (itemised in an attached schedule and valued at £2,845). These were to be held to her use, 'notwithstanding her coverture' and not to be liable to the control of her husband to be. Such precautions were perhaps more common than is realised and, indeed, this real life settlement corresponds almost precisely to the situation described in William Congreve's *The Way of the World* (1700), in which widow Languish, before her re-marriage to the scheming Fainall, secretly executed *A deed of Conveyance of the whole Estate Real of Arabella Languish*, that was produced to confound him in the last act!

In relation to the transfer of property, it was a common-law principle that if husband and wife were jointly selling or mortgaging property (e.g. that included in the marriage settlement), she had to be a party to the deed. A clause in the Fines and Recoveries Act of 1833 required that she had to be interviewed separately, to confirm that she was of age, and that she was not being forced to consent to the transaction, despite her coverture. This examination was recorded in a Certificate of Acknowledgment of a Deed by a Married Woman, which may be attached to the main deed, or included inside it.[16] Surprisingly, in transfers of copyhold property even in the medieval period and regularly from at least the seventeenth century wives were 'solely and secretly examined' by the steward of the manor, to confirm their agreement to the transaction – a much earlier date than for freehold conveyances (see p. 155).

FINES AND RECOVERIES

Of all the variety of deeds that are encountered, the fine and the recovery are the most extraordinary – and also the least useful.[17] They are the official records of entirely formal legal cases, undertaken to confirm a change of ownership, or to cancel a previous deed. The clerks who wrote them had their own archaic styles of handwriting unlike those encountered in any other documents, and often this is extremely hard to read. Worse, probably because the official record was open to anyone to inspect, the property descriptions are formal and impossible to identify (e.g. 'two messuages, two gardens, one orchard, ten acres of land and two acres of meadow in Kenilworth'). Because of their formality, post-medieval fines and recoveries were always accompanied by private deeds giving full details of the transactions involved. Complete sets of fines and recoveries exist at TNA, and are fully listed though they are exhausting to search except for short periods. Thus the individual documents themselves have little independent historical value, though the complete sets can give information about land transactions in particular places. Isolated fines where the associated deeds have not been preserved are more significant as they record transactions which could otherwise only be found by an extensive search of the TNA copies. Both fines and recoveries were abolished in 1833. Medieval fines are of considerably more historical importance than the post-medieval ones and are discussed below (p. 148).

1. Fine; Deed to Lead the Uses of a Fine
The *fine* or *Final Concord* (so-called from its opening phrase: *Hec est finalis concordia* ..., or after 1732, 'This is the final agreement') was the record of a case in the Court of Common Pleas. It was prepared in triplicate (see Illus. 4.7), and the 'Feet of Fines' were kept by the court (TNA, CP 25).[18] Left and right 'indentures of fine' were for the plaintiff and defendant (called *querent* and *deforciant*), i.e. the purchaser and the seller. Because the seller had no use for his part, the purchaser often kept both copies. Occasionally deeds contain an *Exemplification of a fine*, i.e. a copy prepared by the court of its record (the Foot of Fine); this looks like a recovery (see below), except that the text in the document is that of a fine.

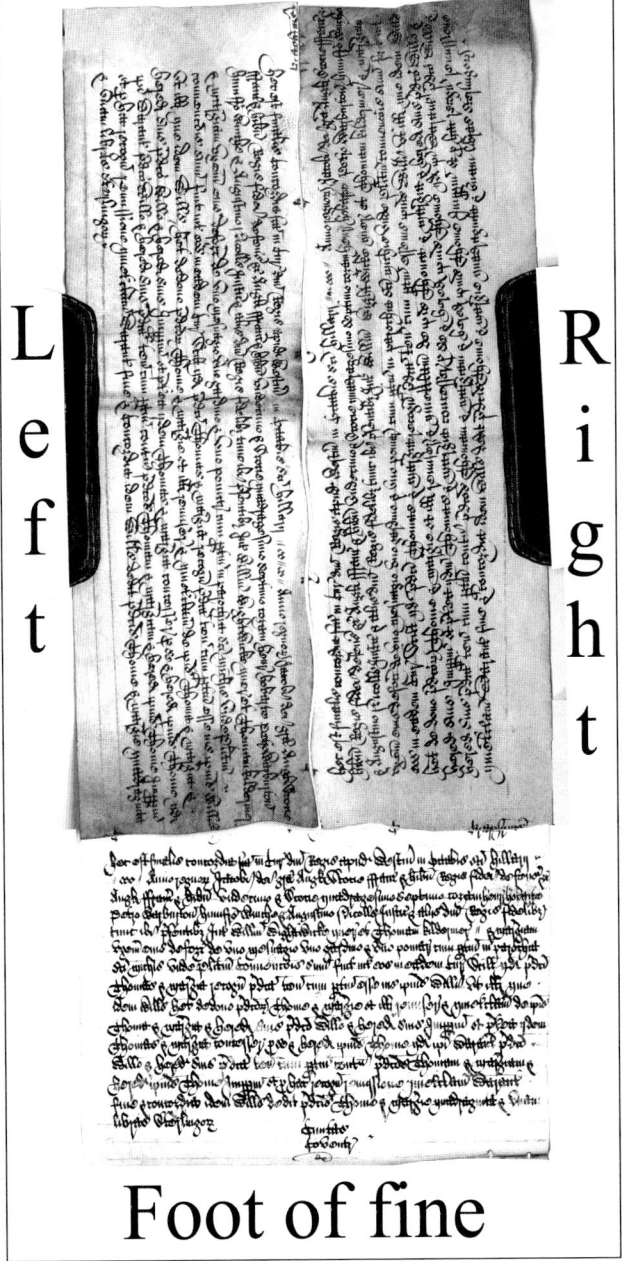

4.7 Left- and right-hand Indentures of Fine (Final Concord) of 1623 for Coventry, combined photographically with the Foot of Fine, from the Court of Common Pleas. For the text, see p. 179. (WCRO CR607/Coventry; TNA, CP 25/2/389/11JASIHIL)

How

After its opening phrase, the fine gives the date by regnal year and law term (Michaelmas (autumn), Hilary (spring), Trinity (summer)), then the names of the justices (which can be ignored). The main part runs '*Inter A, querent et B, deforciator de* . . . [the land]', or after 1732 'Between A, plaintiff and B, deforciant of . . . [*Querent* and *deforciant* are alternative terms for *plaintiff* and *defendant*]'. At the end, a fictitious sum is recorded, and B warrants to defend A's title. With a joint defendant, e.g. husband and wife, if only one of them is named in the warranty, it may indicate which of them was the original owner of the property.

The fine often accompanies either a conveyance or a mortgage: in either case, the main deed for the transaction would then include the agreement to levy a fine. Otherwise, a special deed was drawn up, called a *Deed to lead the uses of a fine* (or, if the fine has already been levied, to *declare the uses*). This takes the form of an indenture with the following sections:

Parties: The seller and purchaser (for a sale). The plaintiff in the fine may well be a nominee or a trustee, and will then be included as a party.

Action: The deed 'witnesseth that in pursuance of covenants . . . it is covenanted, granted, and agreed' that A (the seller) will 'before the end of the next law term acknowledge and levy one Fine *sur cognisance de droit com ceo etc.* of (the property) . . . by the name or names of one messuage [as in the fine]'.

Uses: 'And it is agreed and declared that the cognizee (the plaintiff) shall be seized' to the uses listed.

A form of 'Deed to lead the Uses of a Fine' that is particularly intriguing is found in the later seventeenth century. It covers a whole collection of properties with their individual sellers and purchasers. Each transaction would have its own conveyance but all the parties joined together to levy a single fine, no doubt to reduce the expense, and they drew up a single *Portmanteau Deed* (my name) to lead its uses. This lists all the properties and their new owners, and the appropriate number of copies was prepared.

121

Each therefore includes information about the whole set of unconnected people and property, for some of which other evidence may not have survived. With such a deed, it is therefore useful to record the different parties and property descriptions in detail.

2. Recovery; Deed to make a tenant to the Precipe
Fines were levied as a form of title insurance in relatively straightforward transactions, when the seller had a full legal right to dispose of the property. If it was entailed, i.e. required by earlier deeds to descend in the family (see above, under 'Settlements') before any sale or new family settlement could be effective, it was necessary to destroy or *bar* the entail. This was achieved by a *Common Recovery* (Illus. 4.8). The court action in which the final owner 'recovered' the property was entirely formal, and the rolls of the court's records (see p. 61) merely state the stages by which his title was established. The impressive document finally produced is the *Exemplification of a Recovery*. This has the form of a royal declaration in which the king states that the rolls of the Court of Common Pleas for a particular year contain the recovery. Following this, comes the text from the roll itself, followed finally by the date that the exemplification was made. The Latin version of the preamble to the main text is given here, to help in finding the only useful part.

> Georgius Secundus Rex . . . omnibus ad quos presentes perveniunt salutem [to all to whom these presents shall come, greetings] Sciatis quod inter placitis terre irrotulatis apud Westminster coram . . . [Know that among the pleas of land enrolled at Westminster before (judges' names)] in rotulis de banco de terminis Sancto Hillarii anno regno . . . rotulo xxxi continetur sic [in the rolls of the [King's] Bench of Hilary term (year), in roll 21 is contained] Warr' [i.e., Warwickshire, but could be any county] A [the plaintiff in

the case, called the *demandant*] in propria persona petit versus [in his own person demands against] B [the defendant, called the *tenant*] decem messuagia . . . [the property].

The description of the property is formal, but truthful as far as it goes. A, the demandant, may be the final recipient of the property; B is often the family lawyer. The exemplification continues with a description of the court case. The recovery is sealed with the seal of the Court of Common Pleas, usually enclosed in a tin box (a 'skippet').

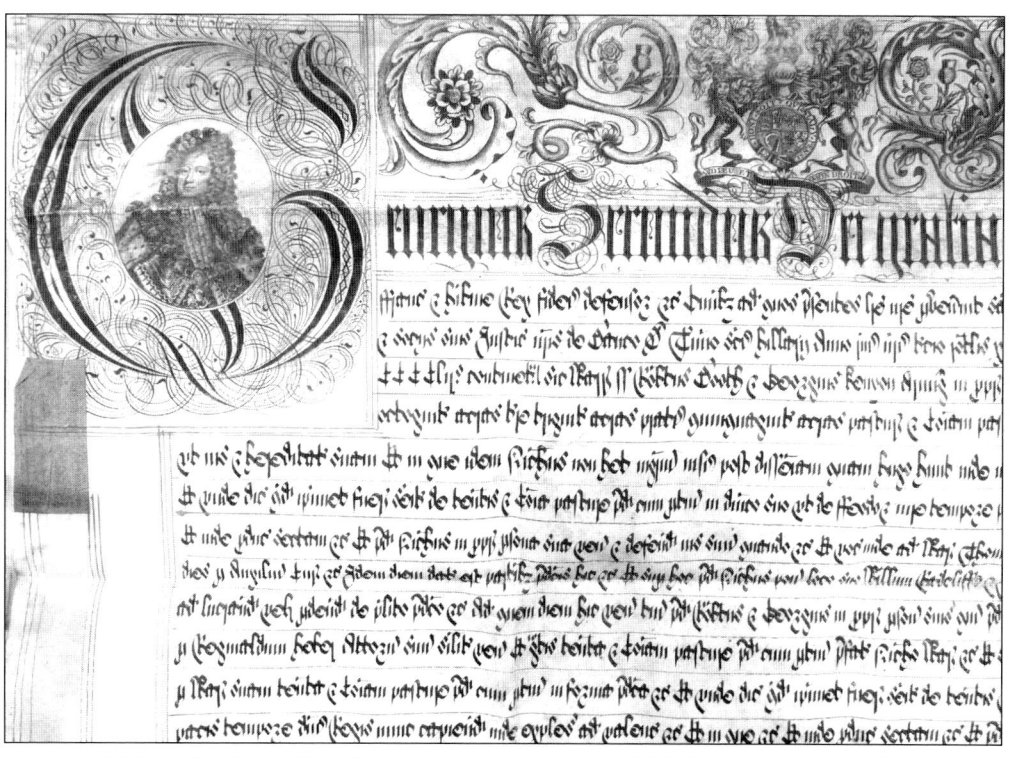

4.8 Part of the Exemplification of a Common Recovery of 1730 for property in the parish of St Nicholas, Warwick. It shows the characteristic script used for these deeds. (WCRO, CR1886/BL/8449)

As with a fine, a private deed was drawn up to explain the purpose of the recovery. This could simply declare the uses of the recovery, but more often involved a conveyance by lease and release. It was known as a 'Conveyance to make a tenant to the Precipe for the purpose of suffering a Common Recovery'. The property (fully described) was conveyed by the owner himself (who probably held it for life only) and his heir to B, a trustworthy third party, the 'tenant' (the *precipe* being the writ by which he would be summoned to court). Another party is the person who will carry out the recovery (the 'recoverer'), who is the family lawyer, or the purchaser or his lawyer if a sale is involved, rather than just the freeing of the property from an entail.[19] The deed also includes:

Recital: the right of the owner and his heir to the property, and any agreement to purchase.

Consideration: The purchase money (if any), and nominal sums to the other parties, with the phrase 'for the docking, barring, defeating, and destroying all estates tail'.

Uses: The 'tenant' will hold the property 'as a good and perfect tenant', and a recovery will be carried out. The 'recoverer' will hold the property to whatever use is finally intended. As the uses come at the very end of the deed, they can be fairly easily located.

After 1833, if an entail was to be barred, it could be done by means of a straightforward disentailing deed, though this had to be enrolled in the Court of Chancery.

The complete text of a recovery is not included here because of my strong view that wading through it will give no information worth the effort. However, for those who wish to marvel at the contortions the legal mind could dream up, the sequence of events in a recovery is described below (adapted from a real example cited by A.A. Dibben (ed. Clive H. Knowles), *Title Deeds, 13th–19th Centuries* (Historical Association, 1990)). (See also Illus. 4.15.)

1. A messuage and land held by John Shed as 'tenant for life'

and his son Thomas as 'tenant in tail' is to be disentailed and sold to Robert Denny. They jointly convey the property to a lawyer, Robert Baxter who becomes the 'tenant to the precipe'; this conveyance is not actually valid because the property is entailed. The same deed has another party, Stafford Squire, the recoverer, who will eventually hold it to the use of Robert Denny.

2. Stafford Squire starts a case against Robert Baxter in the Court of Common Pleas (asking for a writ of *precipe* to be served), claiming that the property was his, but that he, Stafford, had been illegally ejected (disseized) by one Hugh Hunt (a fictitious person), after which Robert Baxter had obtained possession.

3. In defending his title, Baxter calls on Thomas Shed to confirm his ownership (to *vouch to warranty*). Thomas, however, calls on a third party to vouch for the title, Francis Martin (who is the court crier); he is known as the *common vouchee*.

4. Stafford Squire and Francis Martin beg leave to *imparle* (confer privately) before the case is heard. Stafford returns, but Francis does not come back into court when solemnly summoned.

5. Thus, Thomas Shed's and Francis Martin's support of Robert Baxter's title fails and judgement is awarded to Stafford Squire.

6. He therefore owns the property, held to the use of Robert Denny – the intended outcome. The exemplification of the court record is prepared and all retire to pay the lawyers' fees.

Letters Patent

Royal grants were made by *letters patent* sealed with the Great Seal (Illus. 4.9). They look like recoveries but have more legible writing, with a handsome royal portrait starting the first line. The majority of letters patent found with title deeds are of the sixteenth century, because this was the great period for the disposal of property obtained by the Crown at the dissolution of the monasteries. Small pieces of land were granted 'to be held in

4.9 (a) Part of Letters Patent of 1604, granting Warwick Castle to Fulke Greville; (b) its ornamental leather case. (WCRO, CR1886/BB404)

free socage, as of the manor of East Greenwich', and these could be bought and sold freely. However, complete manors were usually held of the Crown *in chief* (i.e. by feudal tenure), paying a modest annual rent. Permission was needed before they could be sold, and this was also granted by letters patent, giving a 'Licence to Alienate' the land.

Apart from the somewhat different appearance, the distinction between letters patent and a recovery is also clear from its start, e.g.:

> [Charles the Second . . .] to all to whom these present letters shall come, greeting, Know ye that we for divers good causes . . . have given, and granted, and by these presents

for us, our heirs and successors do give and grant unto our beloved Laurence Hide, esquire . . .

All letters patent are enrolled on the Patent Rolls (TNA, C66), and a long series of calendars is in print, extending to the end of James I's reign; these are always worth checking for any place of interest.[20] The property descriptions are often detailed, including the names of occupiers (though rarely abuttals for urban property), and where monastic or guild property is concerned, the original owner is almost always stated. Some of the details may be omitted in the published calendars (though this is always noted), which may make it necessary to check the enrolled copies. It can also be useful to know that the details were usually based on the *Particulars for Grant*, valuations for prospective purchasers (TNA, E 318 and LR 10). These in turn were taken from surveys of monastic property (see PRO, 'List of Rentals and Surveys', *Lists and Indexes*, Vol. 25, for the religious house concerned). It is not uncommon for errors to occur when the property description was copied from one document to another. Of these descriptions, those in the surveys are often the most useful because they show all the property of the original owner, which may not all have been granted to the same purchaser; they can also have valuable marginal notes indicating the purchasers of different parts of the property.

Bargain-and-Sale; Feoffment

These are forms of conveyance used especially in the sixteenth and seventeenth centuries before the lease and release became standard. They represent the development of medieval deeds following the Statute of Uses (1535); this is of great legal importance, but of less significance for the interpretation of straightforward deeds. The distinction between the bargain-and-sale and the feoffment lies not in their wording, but in the method used to render them valid.

1. *Feoffment*: The feoffment continues the medieval tradition in which the actual transfer of property only took place through the ceremony of livery of seisin, in which a token part of the property, e.g. a key or a piece of turf, was handed over to the new owner in the presence of witnesses. The written deed merely confirmed the seisin.

The post-medieval feoffment was written and signed first, but was only made effective by the seisin. Its form is straightforward, with *parties*; the *consideration* (often not stated in money terms); the *property*; and the *covenants* (usually concerned with providing a good title). The *action* clause is distinctive and reads 'given, granted, alienated, bargained and sold, and enfeoffed'. The seisin is recorded in an endorsement. The names of the witnesses are important historically, as they are the worthy neighbours who were present at the ceremony of seisin. This clause sometimes includes the witnessing of the deed, but a typical wording is as follows:

> Memorandum that on the tenth day of August in the yeare of our Lord God first within written, quiet and peaceable possession, together with livery and seisin of all and singular the said premises was given and delivered to the within-named John Kemsey in his proper person to hold to him and his heirs and assignes forever, according to the tenor and effect of these presents, in the presence of Thomas Wyse, The marke of John Hill the younger, Alexander Dougan, John Courte. (1657; WRO, CR1886/5687, slightly edited).

2. The *enrolled bargain-and-sale* was created by the Statute of Enrolments (1536), as an alternative to the feoffment; the bargain-and-sale itself had existed previously but transferred only the use of the property, not its ownership. The text differs from the feoffment only in its action clause, 'granted, alienated,

bargained and sold'. The main distinction is that it was valid without seisin, but had to be enrolled within six months either at the royal courts at Westminster (usually on the Close Rolls), or by the Clerk of the Peace for the county, on rolls forming part of the Quarter Sessions records (see p. 65). The enrolment of the deed is always recorded in an endorsement giving the date when this was done, e.g. '*Irrotulatur in dorso clausarum Cancellarie . . .*' ('enrolled on the dorse of the Close Roll of Chancery') (Illus. 4.10).

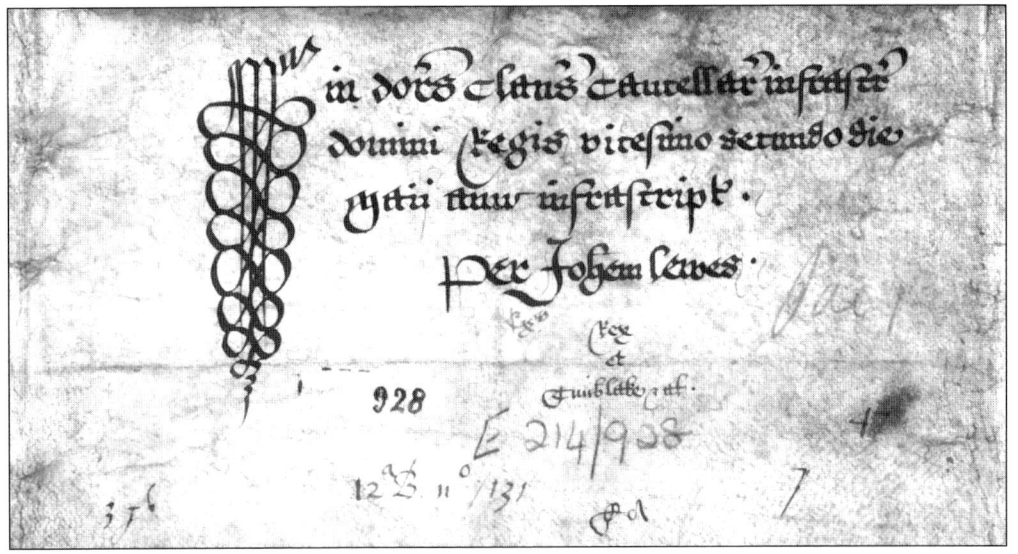

4.10 Endorsement, recording enrolment in Chancery, on a lease of 1609 by the Crown, for property near the Tower of London. For text, see p.181. (TNA, E 214/928)

Landowners disliked both the bargain-and-sale and the feoffment because of their publicity. Either the seisin ceremony, or the enrolled and publicly available copy left no secrecy about their actions. This was the reason that the lease and release became the principal form of conveyance, because it provided a deed that was secure and at the same time secret. Occasionally, deeds of bargain-and-sale are seen without either seisin or an endorsement of their enrolment. Some of these concern such small pieces of property (e.g. half a well), that presumably nothing more formal was thought necessary. Others seem at first to be legally invalid but on a careful look they turn out to be counterparts. Rather than the conveyance by A to B, signed by A, they are duplicates signed by B, and kept by A to confirm that B would observe any covenants involved; such counterparts were also retained as a record that A had sold the property. In other cases, the non-enrolled bargain-and-sale was accompanied by a separate deed, a feoffment or *quitclaim* with seisin.

QUITCLAIM

Quitclaims are occasionally found among sixteenth- and seventeenth-century deeds, and like feoffments are medieval in origin. They are not difficult to understand in themselves, but it is not always obvious why they were used. Their actual function was to *release* or *quitclaim* the rights of the first party to the second party, and some concern the possible rights of someone who was not actually the property owner. Others are endorsed with livery of seisin and were used as feoffments. Quitclaims are not indented, and are rather more often in Latin than other post-medieval deeds, starting '*Omnibus Christi fidelibus* . . .'. In English their opening phrase becomes:

> To all Christian people to whom this present writing shall come I, [A], send greeting in the Lord everlasting, Know ye that I for divers good cause have remised, released and for ever quitclaimed unto [B] all estate, right, title . . . of me the said A, in . . . [the property].
>
> An alternative wording is 'Know all men by these presents . . .', continuing broadly as before.

PERPETUAL LEASE

This seventeenth-century type of deed is relatively uncommon, but worth describing, particularly as examples are easily confused with mortgages (sometimes even in record office lists). Although technically leases, they have the effect of conveyances, because they last for a very long time, often 500 or 1,000 years (and thus can conveniently, though loosely, be called 'perpetual'). As with quitclaims, the reason for their use is unclear, but they probably represent another way to avoid the problems of the bargain-and-sale, because only the leasehold interest is being transferred. They also have some similarity to medieval grants in fee farm (see p. 146), which are sometimes found in the post-medieval period; these are conveyances *for ever*, but with a significant 'fee farm' rent reserved, to be paid to the seller. The distinctive features of a perpetual lease are:

Action: 'Demise, set and to farm let', as for other leases.
Period: Usually 500, 1,000 or more years.
Rent: Some small sum, e.g. 5s., but not simply a peppercorn.
Covenants: In contrast to a mortgage, the perpetual lease does not have a provision for redemption.

COPIES OF COURT ROLL

All the deeds so far described were used for freehold land, perhaps covering three-quarters of all property in England by the seventeenth century. However, in a considerable number of places, land was held by *copyhold*, for which the title deed was the *copy* of an entry on the manor court roll. Many such copies survive in bundles of title deeds but the primary record of the copyholder's title was in the manor court rolls. For this reason, although the appearance of copies of court roll has been described above so that they can be recognised, they are discussed in detail in a separate section (p. 151); a post-medieval and a medieval copy of court roll are shown in Illus. 4.13 and 4.16.

MISCELLANEOUS POST-MEDIEVAL DEEDS

A variety of other deeds may occasionally be encountered, and a few should be mentioned. *Deeds of Partition* and *Deeds of Exchange* are rather similar. Each uses the lease and release form, with two copies of an identical release (one for each party) describing two separate transfers of property, one from A to B, the other from B to A. Each party also executes a lease for a year to the other, but these are different, each concerning one of the two pieces of property which are either being partitioned or exchanged; sometimes a trustee is the recipient, holding both parts of the property for the benefit of the two owners.

A *Deed of Enfranchisement* was used to convert a copyhold into a freehold. It has the normal indenture form. The lord of the manor, in return for a substantial consideration 'for the freeing and extinguishing of the copyhold tenure from all copyhold services, fines and heriots', granted the specified property, to be held 'for ever', subject only to the payment of the rent and to attendance at the manor court (see p. 97).

A *Covenant to Produce Deeds* was executed when a seller retained some or all of the title deeds, usually because they also related to other property. The covenant has an action clause, 'doth covenant and agree', to produce the deeds, and in addition it recites the sale of the property, including a full description. At the end, a schedule of the deeds to be produced is given, similar to those occasionally included in a release (see p. 104).

Articles of Agreement usually have a heading identifying them, followed by a series of numbered clauses. They are fairly easy to follow as they describe what was actually intended before it was converted into the legal language of the deed itself. Agreements for a marriage settlement are perhaps the most common, followed by those for the purchase of a property.

Contracts are occasionally found in deed bundles, concerning building work in particular, and they can be extremely interesting. They have the form of indentures between A, the landowner, and

B, a carpenter or mason, in which B agrees to erect a building to a stated specification and timetable and A will pay him agreed sums of money at stated times. They also normally include agreements for arbitration in the event of dispute.

Two documents are not considered in detail here, because they are financial rather than directly concerned with property. The *Recognisance in the nature of a Statute Staple* was a strong form of bond, more readily enforced if necessary. It was usually cancelled by a separate document, the *Defeasance of a Recognisance*.

The Contents of Deed Bundles

This section describes documents which are not themselves deeds, but which are relevant to their evidence and are often found in deed bundles in addition to deeds themselves. The main alternative to transfer of property by sale is transfer by inheritance. Wills are therefore frequently included with title deeds. They may be the 'probate copies', on parchment with a copy of the grant of probate attached.[21] However, if the will deals with more than one piece of property, then each deed bundle may contain a paper copy.

Abstracts of title also refer to wills, but they only give details about the actual bequests of property. Naturally, anyone searching for wills for family or social history will look first in diocesan or county record offices rather than deed bundles, but the latter can also be helpful. It is very rare for the wills in deed bundles to have survived better than those in record offices, but wills with deeds can still be of value.[22] First, the associated deeds usually clarify the relationships between the people named in the will and those in other records. Secondly, the description of property in a will is often rather vague, e.g. 'the house wherein I dwell' or 'my messuage and land in the parish of X', and the only way to locate it precisely may be through the related title deeds. Achieving this can be particularly valuable in relation to *probate inventories*. These are lists of the deceased person's possessions (excluding property), which frequently accompany the wills in the diocesan records. They are immensely valuable for social history, particularly if they can be related to specific houses or farms. Unfortunately, the vagueness of wills generally leaves the identity of the house unclear, but deeds help to overcome the problem.[23] Finally, wills were sometimes not proved in the church court (perhaps when the executor was the only person inheriting and was also the legal heir), in which case the copy in the deed bundle may well be the only one that exists.

Other documents in deed bundles are also concerned with descent. Frequently, certified copies of *baptism, marriage* and *burial certificates* are included to give proof of relationships, and sometimes drawn-out *pedigrees* are found, when the family links are particularly complicated. *Statutory declarations* (statements made under oath following statutory requirements) may also explain family connections, though they also cover other matters. They were most commonly used if no deeds could be found, to declare that the owner had been in undisturbed possession for many years. Between 1833 and 1882, *Married Women's Certificates of Acknowledgement of Deeds* are also common (see p. 118).

Deed bundles may also contain miscellanea relating to the property itself. These can include *sale particulars* and *auction announcements*, which often give details about the property, numbers of rooms, tenants' names, etc. that are not in the deeds. *Insurance policies* were often kept with deeds, and the early ones have brief descriptions, particularly covering the construction and materials of houses. *Building contracts* are more informative still, though very rare.

A final group is of legal papers. These may include *counsel's opinions*, for example on the validity of a title deed. Most frequent are *solicitor's bills* for carrying out purchases. They are not generally very significant for the history either of the property or the people concerned, though contemplation of the level of costs is salutary.

MEDIEVAL DEEDS
Introduction
Before medieval deeds can be understood, two barriers have to be overcome, the writing and the language. As compensation, their text and structure are much simpler than for most post-medieval deeds, so that extracting their historical evidence is generally less difficult. Record offices have also tended to calendar and index their medieval deeds in preference to later ones, often providing an outline to start from. For the handwriting, various guides exist (see Further Resources, below) of which K.C. Newton's *Medieval Local Records: A Reading Aid* (Historical Association, 1971) is by far the best for medieval deeds (though unfortunately out of print); those by Grieve and Hector are also to be recommended, but cover a wider range, with less specifically medieval material. One particular problem is that abbreviations were used on every possible occasion. C.T. Martin, *The Record Interpreter* (repr. Phillimore & Co., 1982) is useful as an aid to deciphering them, and also as a Latin vocabulary, while E.A. Gooder, *Latin for Local History* (Longmans, 1978) and Denis Stuart, *Latin for Local and Family Historians* (Phillimore & Co., 1995) are helpful for Latin translation. They both include deed texts which can be matched with examples being studied. Sometimes deeds are written in English, and these are always intriguing though not necessarily easier to understand. For the rare documents in Norman French, it is reasonable to ask for expert help, particularly as most are unusual in content as well as language. A highly detailed study of the structure and variety of medieval deeds can be found in J.M. Kaye, *Medieval English Conveyances* (Cambridge University Press, 2009). This would be useful to anyone wishing to follow up particular aspects of these deeds.

The earliest surviving deeds are Anglo-Saxon charters, which are almost exclusively royal grants. Charters issued by the nobility appear in the twelfth century, though their texts generally do not follow standard later forms. Most of them have been preserved because they granted substantial property or rights to important beneficiaries (especially monasteries), and their study is bedevilled because these recipients were not above 'improving' their charters, or even producing completely spurious deeds; their forgeries were not necessarily designed to obtain property that did not belong to them, but rather to recover what had been lost in troubled times, and to reinforce their ownership (perhaps when their charters had been destroyed). Detection of forgeries is not made easier because many are only preserved in cartularies or as enrolled deeds (see pp. 66 and 75ff.). Kaye's *Medieval English Conveyances* may help in evaluating whether a particular early deed has been 'improved' and in interpreting it. An informative and less technical discussion of the development of written charters and of the problem of forgeries is also given by M.T. Clanchy in *From Memory to Written Record* (2nd edn Blackwell, 1993).

Deeds in standard medieval form appear at the beginning of the thirteenth century.[24] Some were issued by people of modest status, including burgesses in towns and freeholders in the country. We rarely know exactly when they were written, as the inclusion of dates in deeds only became standard practice in about 1300, and much later undated deeds are occasionally found. The earliest deeds that regularly include dates are leases for specific periods of time (e.g. seven years), when it was obviously important to state when the lease started. A good example is in Illus. 1.2 (p. 5); as here, such early deeds are usually not dated themselves, but can be assumed to have been written just before the lease was due to start.

Dating

With undated deeds, a very approximate date can be obtained from the handwriting (e.g. by matching it with examples in palaeography texts). The only way to achieve greater accuracy is

How

from the people named as parties and witnesses in the deed. If prominent men are involved, the dates of their death may be known, giving limiting dates. Otherwise, to make progress a moderately large number of deeds needs to be studied. The earliest dated ones will include names also found in undated deeds, which therefore cannot be very much earlier. These deeds in turn will contain other names which cannot be directly dated, but must somewhat precede the last group. In this way, with the help of a few fixed points, a framework can be built up to provide dates with an accuracy of about a generation (see also p. 42 for the application of computers to this problem).[25]

When the text of a deed contains a date, this is hardly ever in modern style, and it needs to be interpreted. The year is normally given as the 'regnal year' (p. 87), while until the mid-fifteenth century, the day is hardly ever specified by the day of the month. Instead, it is related to a church festival, e.g. 'Wednesday before the Feast of Saint Martin, in the year of the reign of King Edward, the third after the conquest, the twenty fourth'. In working out such problems, C.R. Cheney's *A Handbook of Dates For Students of British History* is indispensable. First, the table of regnal years gives 24 Edward III as 25 January 1350 to 24 January 1351, and refers to calendar tables 7 (for 1350) and 27 (for 1351). Then, the list of saints' days (which includes all the likely day and festival names as well) gives St Martin's Day as 11 November.[26] Calendar table 7 shows that, in 1350, 11 November was a Thursday, so the deed was executed on 10 November 1350. The procedure is the same for dates relating to the moveable church feasts (Easter, Whitsun, Trinity, etc.), except that their dates have to be found from the calendar tables themselves. Two special terms are *in vigilia* and *in crastina*, respectively the day before and day after the feast.

SHAPES AND PATTERNS

Medieval deeds are much shorter than post-medieval ones, hardly ever larger than a smallish piece of parchment. In physical shape they have one of the forms listed in Table 4.6, below, and a flowchart for identifying them is in Appendix 1 (Section A).

Table 4.6: Shapes of Medieval Deeds			
Edges	Seal	Type of Deed	Illus.
Straight	Suspended on tag	Gift or quitclaim	4.11
Indented top	Suspended on tag	Lease or counterpart; Agreement	1.2
Indented side and top		Fine	(as 4.7)
Straight	On sideways tongue	Bond*; Letter (of Attorney, generally)	1.1 4.12

* A medieval bond has its condition on the dorse.

Medieval leases and other indented documents (agreements, etc.) were always produced by cutting up a single sheet of parchment (unlike post-medieval ones). Occasionally both parts survive and can be fitted together; the word '*cirographum*' is often written across the join, and these indented documents are therefore sometimes called 'chirographs'. A bond or a letter of attorney has its seal attached to a strip cut from the bottom of the sheet of parchment, and it should have another thin strip at the very bottom, though this has often been torn off. These deeds were formally private rather than public, and so were designed to be folded and tied up with this strip (see Illus 1.1 and 4.12).

As well as their shape, the first words of medieval deeds are useful in suggesting at a glance the sort of medieval deed being examined (see Table 4.7, below). The full identification comes from the *action* clause but this can be difficult to spot, as it is not picked out with capital letters.

CLAUSES
Like post-medieval deeds, the texts of medieval deeds are arranged systematically in clauses. The most common arrangement can best be illustrated by an actual example, a Deed of Gift (Illus. 4.11) with its translation, divided up to show the

Table 4.7: Initial Words and 'Action' Clauses of Medieval Deeds

Type of Deed	Normal Start	Action
Gift (conveyance)	*Sciant presentes et futuri quod ego presenta carta confirmavi* Know (all men) present and future that I	*Dedi, concessi et hac* have given, granted, and by this present charter confirmed
Quitclaim (three alternatives)	*Omnibus Christi fidelibus* To all the faithful in Christ *Pateat Universis per Presentes* Be it known by these presents *Noverint Universi* Know all men	*Remisisse, relaxasse, et quietclamasse* Remise, relax and quitclaim The initial phrases often continue *ad quod hoc presens scriptum pervenit* (to whom this present writing comes)
Lease	*Hec indentura facta inter* This indenture made between (occasionally starts as quitclaim)	*Concessuit et dimisuit* have conceded and leased
Fine	*Hec est Finalis Concordia* This is the final agreement	Identified by this first phrase
Letter of Attorney	Generally as second or third quitclaim forms	*Attornasse et in loco meo possuisse . . . dilectos in Christo* Attorn and in my stead place . . . beloved in Christ
Bond	As last	*Firmiter teneri et obligari* Am firmly bound and obliged
Agreement	*Hec conventio facta inter* This agreement made (or sometimes *Hec indentura*)	Indicated by this first phrase or by *conventio* in the text

4.11 A medieval gift (conveyance) of 1422, transferring land in Weston Underwood, Buckinghamshire. For text, see below. (WCRO, CR1998/J1/553C)

various clauses in the deed. After this the special features of the individual types of deed will be considered.

Example of a Deed of Gift

Introduction: *Sciant presentes et futuri* (Know all men present and to come).

First party: *quod ego Willelmus Tebowde de Westun Undyrwode* (that I William Tebowde of Weston Underwood [Buckinghamshire]).

Action: *Dedi, concessi et hac presenti carta mea confirmavi* (have given, granted and by this my present charter confirmed).

Second party: *Johanni Batell, clerico de Olney, Willelmo Bulbek, clerico de Ravenestun, Johanni Bolter de Westun Undyrwode, Thome Hobyndone et Thome Hento de eadem* (to John Batell, clerk of Olney, William Bulbek, clerk of Ravenstun, John Bolter of Weston Underwood, Thomas Habyndone and Thomas Hent of the same). The presence of several grantees, including chaplains, makes it likely that they were trustees (feoffees) for the real owner; in medieval deeds, unlike later ones, the reason for a gift being made to a group of feoffees is hardly ever stated. The surname of the last party was probably Hent, with the form Hento representing the dative case.

Property: *Omnia terras et tenementa, prata, pascua et pasturas cum sepibus, fossis et fossatis et cum omnibus aliis proficuis et suis pertinentiis quod habeo in villa et in campis de Westun Undyrwode predicto, excepto uno mesuagio vocato Tebowdys Place situato in Alkenwelllane inter toftum Willelmi Fortho ex parte boriali et toftum Magistri Hospitalis Sancti Johannis Norhamtone ex parte australi, et duodecim acris terre et quinque rodis prati, predicto mesuagio pertinentibus in villa predicta* (all lands and tenements, meadows, grazing land and pasture, with their hedges, banks and ditches, and with all profits and their appurtenances which I have in the village and fields of Weston Underwode aforesaid, except one house called Tebowdys Place, situated in Alkenwell Lane, between the toft [house plot] of William Forth [Fortho probably being the ablative form] on the north side, and the toft of the Master of the Hospital of Saint John [in] Northampton on the south side, and 12 acres [arable] land and five rods of meadow, belonging to the said messuage in the said village).

Tenure: *Habendum et tenendum omnia predicta terras, tenementis, prata, pascua, et pasturas cum sepibus, fossis et fossatis et cum omnibus aliis proficuis et suis pertinentiis exceptis pre-exceptis prefatis Johanni, Willelmo Bulbek, Johanni, Thome et Thome heredibus et assignatis suis, de capitalibus dominis feodi illius* (to have and to hold all the said lands . . ., except as before excepted, to the said John, William Bulbek, John, Thomas and Thomas, their heirs and assigns, from the chief lords of that fee).

Rent and service: *Per servicia inde debita et de iure consueta* (by the service thence due [from the property], and of right accustomed).

[**Term**: either before or after the rent, but absent in this example. When a limited period is not involved *in perpetuum* (forever) is normal.]

[**Conditions**: Conditions may be imposed, particularly concerning the future ownership of the property.]

Warranty: *Et ego vero predictus Willelmus Tebowde et heredes mei omnia predicta terras, tenementis, prata, pascua, et pasturas cum* *sepibus, fossis et fossatis et cum omnibus aliis proficuis et suis pertinentiis ut predictus est prefatis Johanni, Willelmo Bulbek, Johanni, Thome et Thome, heredibus et assignatis suis, contra omnes gentes Warantizabimus in perpetuum* (and I truly the said William Tebowde and my heirs, all the said lands . . ., as aforesaid, to the said John, William Bulbek, John, Thomas and Thomas their heirs and assigns, will warrant for ever).

[**Consideration**: Occasionally included, especially in early deeds, usually near the end of the deed.]

Attestation and witnesses: *In cuius rei testimonium huic presenti carte sigillum meum apposui, Hiis testibus Johanne Bagge, Thoma Hawten, Willelmo Bolter, Thoma Goolde, Johanne Candeler et aliis* (in witness of which thing I have affixed my seal to this my present charter, these being witnesses, John Bagge, . . . and others).

Date: *Data apud Westun Undyrwode predicto in die Jovis post octavas Ephiphanie Domini, anno regni regis Henrici quinti post conquestum nono* (Dated at Weston Underwood, Thursday after the octave [period of eight days including and after the feast] of Epiphany [6 January], the ninth year of the reign of King Henry the fifth after the Conquest [15 January 1422].

Seal: [The deed carries the seal of William Tebowde, with a rose design, and an illegible inscription.]

Deeds were authenticated by the seal or seals of the first party. These were much studied in the nineteenth century, but have been neglected since then. Interest in them has recently revived, in such aspects as their artistic style, the social status of people owning seals, and the relationship between this and the character of the seal. It is notable that women usually had their own seals, so a grant by husband and wife together had two seals. Occasionally seals were borrowed, and people living far from the property being sold sometimes used their local town seal, declaring in the deed that their own seal would not be known to the purchaser. Thus, a study of the seal in context can throw considerable light on the parties involved in the transaction.[27]

Types of Medieval Deeds
GIFTS AND GRANTS
The main medieval deed is the *gift*, the permanent transfer of property from one person to another. Although the price paid is not often stated, the name does not imply a free gift, but is the technical term, contrasted to a *grant* of anything other than property, e.g. goods or the right to tithes ('incorporeal property'); otherwise, *gifts* and *grants* are identical. Gifts to monasteries or churches are often distinguished as being *in pura elimosina* (in pure alms), and these were made without any recompense to the giver.

The normal pattern of a gift is illustrated in the example just given. The key points for recognition are the initial phrase and the *action*, signalled by the words '*dedi, concessi . . .*'. This is always in the past tense (in contrast to post-medieval deeds), showing that the deed is a formal record of an action that has already been completed. The actual transfer of ownership took place by giving and taking *seisin* (p. 128). Unlike later feoffments, medieval gifts rarely record the ceremony and the witnesses to it on the back of the deed.

Parties: These are usually straightforward. If the grantor is a woman, she is described as making her grant '*in pura viduetate*' (in pure widowhood), or '*in pura virginitate*', as only widows or spinsters could dispose of their own property. Almost always the former husband or the father of the grantor is named as well. More complicated family connections are also often recorded (p. 128).

Property: The descriptions in medieval deeds tend to be less detailed than later. They often list the features of the property, house, croft, arable land, pasture, etc. without more detail, as in the example. Occasionally open field land is fully described, with each strip listed, furlong by furlong, with the owners of the strips on each side;[28] this is very valuable for the study of agrarian history, and for the information it gives on minor names. To counterbalance this, other deeds say no more than 'all my land in X'. Descriptions giving the number of acres or subdivisions (1 acre = 4 rods = 40 perches) need particular care in their interpretation. Not only were acres of different sizes in different places (e.g. the Cornish acre was five-sixths of a statute acre), but individual open field strips were sometimes described as 'acres'.

The second part of the example describes the house that was not to be conveyed by its *abuttals* – the names of the owners or occupiers of the adjoining properties. Abuttals are very common in medieval deeds for urban houses, but the inclusion of the name of the tenant of the property being transferred is rare (the reverse of post-medieval practice). The abuttals are not always consistent, which can cause difficulty in matching descriptions. For example, deeds for a Coventry house which could be firmly identified from other evidence had the abuttals listed in Table 4.8, below, on one side. Out-of-date names were often used as here, probably to strengthen the identification with earlier documents.

Tenure: The most important distinction depends on whether the deed dates from before or after 1290, when the statute '*Quia Emptores*' (meaning 'Because purchasers', the first words of the statute) was passed. Before this, in a grant from A to B the property was usually held 'of me [A] and my heirs' by some particular rent or service. Thus this grant introduced a new link in the chain of feudal tenure (*sub-infeudation*): B held of A, who was a 'mesne' or intermediate tenant, who held of X, the 'chief' or superior lord, who held from the king (perhaps via other mesne tenants). If A did not pay his rent to X, X would find it difficult to collect because A was no longer in possession of the property. After 1290, any grant had to be made to B, to hold 'of the chief lord', i.e. B would hold directly from X (in *substitution* for A), who would then be able to collect the services due.

> ### Table 4.8: Abuttals of a Coventry House
>
> From an unpublished study by the author. The deeds used are mainly in Coventry Archives and Research Centre, refs BA/H/8: 48/11, 13, 14 & 51/1 and BA/B/16/76, 1, 3, 6.
>
> | Date | Abuttal |
> |---|---|
> | 1257–9 | Land of Robert de London |
> | c. 1300 | Land of Robert de Kenilworth (and in a deed of 1317 for the adjoining property itself Robert le Keu of Kenilworth and Alice his wife) |
> | 1314 | Land of Robert le Keu and Alice his wife |
> | 1331 | Tenement sometimes of Master Robert Cokus (given in the genitive as Coki) (These four are believed to be identical; le Keu means cook, i.e. Cokus) |
> | 1359 | Tenement John Luke holds (as tenant) |
> | 1361 | Tenement sometime of Master Robert Cokus |
> | 1365 | Tenement John Luke holds |
> | 1377 | Tenement that was of Richard Tole (owner of the adjoining property in the 1340s) |
> | 1393 | Tenement John de Wedon holds (life tenant of the adjoining property from 1377) |

Rent and service: The standard late medieval phrase was 'by the service due and of right accustomed'. In thirteenth-century deeds, these chief rents are occasionally specified, sometimes including two or three separate rents to different people (each created by a former grant). Most of the payments were of money, rents of a few pence or shillings which may at one time have represented the value of the property. Others were rents in kind, e.g. a pound of pepper or of cumin (both valuable spices), while some were formal acknowledgements, such as 'a red rose at Midsummer' or 'a clove of gillyflower [a carnation or clove pink flower bud] at Easter'.

In theory, after 1290 no further chief rents were created, but occasional deeds dating from a little later still include them. At the end of the medieval period and later, grants were made that reserved a *fee-farm rent* (a perpetual rent charge); these grants include a condition allowing the grantor to *distrain* (seize goods) if the rent is unpaid. These rents were in effect the same as the old chief rents, but were not so called.

Conditions: The only common conditions in gifts are those reserving the succession of the property to the heirs of the grantee, usually also with *remainder* to the heirs of the grantor (if the grantee has no heirs).

Warranty: The warranty clause, starting '*Et ego*' or '*Et nos*' is standard in medieval deeds. However, it is occasionally absent from very early deeds (early thirteenth-century and before), and this can be a help in dating.

Consideration: This is occasionally included in thirteenth-century deeds (rarely thereafter), with a phrase like '*Et pro hac donacione* (B) *dedit* (A) *decem marcas*' (And for this gift B gives A ten marks [one mark was worth 13s. 4d.]).

Witnesses: The witnesses in medieval deeds deserve careful study. In a village, they will be the most respected inhabitants, while in a town they generally start with the mayor or a leading burgess. The lesser witnesses include people living near or next to the property involved, who could vouch directly for the transaction. The witness lists therefore help locate both the property and the inhabitants in the town. Early deeds often identify witnesses genealogically, e.g. 'A the brother (or the son) of B', while the dates at which witnesses appear and disappear are evidence for their life span. The final witness in early deeds, before the universal 'and many others' is often a priest, e.g. 'Roger *clericus*'. He was probably the actual scribe of the deed, though this needs to be confirmed by comparing the writing styles in deeds witnessed by the same man.[29]

Quitclaims

These are perhaps even commoner than gifts, because medieval purchasers were very concerned to make their ownership proof against any attack. In particular there was a general feeling that property should only pass by inheritance, even if it was not formally held *in tail*. Thus a purchaser might be sued for wrongful occupation by a relative of the grantor. The new owner would therefore obtain a quitclaim which was a disclaimer of interest in the property from anyone who might be expected to make a claim in the future, such as the grantor's father or mother, brother or son. The grantor himself often executed a quitclaim as well as his gift.

The initial phrases of quitclaims (p. 139) take various forms, but with little difference in meaning. The key section is the *action* indicated by the words '*remisisse, relaxasse, et omnio pro me et heredibus meis quietclamasse*' (I [A] remise, relax, and quitclaim everything for me and my heirs) yielding to B '*totum ius et clameu quod habui vel habere potui*' (all right and claim I had or might have). The property is described in the same words as in the corresponding grant. The remainder of the quitclaim merely repeats the action clause in other words. The witnesses are sometimes preceded by a statement of the consideration given by B to A.

Leases

Leases are the most frequent type of medieval indented deed, and correspondingly they usually start '*Hec indentura* . . .', though other phrases are found. Indentures were also used for other deeds, particularly agreements (see p. 148). The full standard opening clause is '*Hec indentura facta inter* [A] *ex parte una et* [B] *ex parte altera testatur quod* . . .' (This indenture made between A of the one part and B of the other part witnesses that . . .). The next phrase describes the action. A '*concessuit et dimisuit*' (has conceded and leased) the property to B. Leases continue with clauses for tenure, rent and period. Medieval leases were normally made either for terms of years, or for the life of the recipient. Some life leases, however, were effectively for a period of years. They might allow the heirs of the tenant to continue the lease if he should die within, say, ten years. Others increased the rent to a penal value after a number of years. Although the tenant could retain possession, it was not worthwhile to do so. Leases for the life of the grantor imply that he himself had only a life interest.

The last section of a lease before the witnesses generally contains several *conditions*. Most are standard, providing for distraint or re-possession if the rent is not paid, and for the tenant to keep the property in good repair (see text of Illus. 1.2, p. 5). The owners usually give a *warranty* to the tenants for the term of the lease. More interesting and unusual conditions are occasionally found, and are worth particular attention. They include building agreements, which can give important evidence about the types of buildings at the period.[30] Sometimes part of the property is reserved for the grantor (e.g. a chamber and use of the fire in the hall for cooking), or special payments in kind are made for his maintenance. These throw light on both social conditions and household structure.

FINES

Medieval fines or final concords are exactly the same in form and function as later ones (described fully on p. 119), with one crucial difference. Post-medieval fines were always produced as part of a transaction which is explained in more detail in an accompanying deed, while medieval fines mostly stand on their own as the only record of a property transfer. Thus they are more important as evidence and should not be ignored, even though the property is described in general terms (as in post-medieval examples); the financial considerations are apparently fictitious, except perhaps in the earliest examples. Feet of Fines exist at TNA from 1195, though fines were made before this, and a few earlier originals or copies survive. For a fair number of counties, some or all of the medieval fines have been published.³¹

Original medieval fines should be looked at closely, even apart from their greater significance as evidence. In many boroughs, the town court had or claimed the right to conduct the fictitious actions which produced fines. The resulting documents start '*Hec est finalis concordia facta in curia libertatis ville de* . . .' (This is the final concord made in the court of the liberty of the town of . . .). They generally continue with the statement that they were transferred there from the court at Westminster. This will have left traces in the records of the Court of Common Pleas, but buried among mountains of unindexed material, and the fines themselves are naturally not among the Feet of Fines. In principle the feet of these fines should be among the borough records, but they may well not have survived. Therefore, if an original fine was not levied at Westminster, it should be fully recorded.

OTHER MEDIEVAL DEEDS

Various other types of deeds are occasionally found, and some should be mentioned. Perhaps the most common is the **Letter of Attorney** (Illus. 4.12). The ceremony of seisin played a vital part in the transfer of property, but on occasion the vendor or the purchaser could not take part in person. He would therefore appoint a substitute, either to give or to receive seisin on his behalf. The appointment was made by a formal letter, which was kept with the title deeds. The following initial clause identifies them: '*Pateat universi per presentes me* [or an equivalent] [A] *attornasse et in loco meo posuisse dilectos in Christo* [B] . . .' (Know all by these presents that I A do attorn and in my stead place the beloved in Christ B . . .). The next clause depends on whether the person appointed was to give or receive seisin. The first typically reads '*meos veros et legitimos attornatos ad deliberand* [C] *plenam et pacificam possessionem de et in* [the property]' (for me truly and legitimately attorn to deliver to C full and peaceable possession

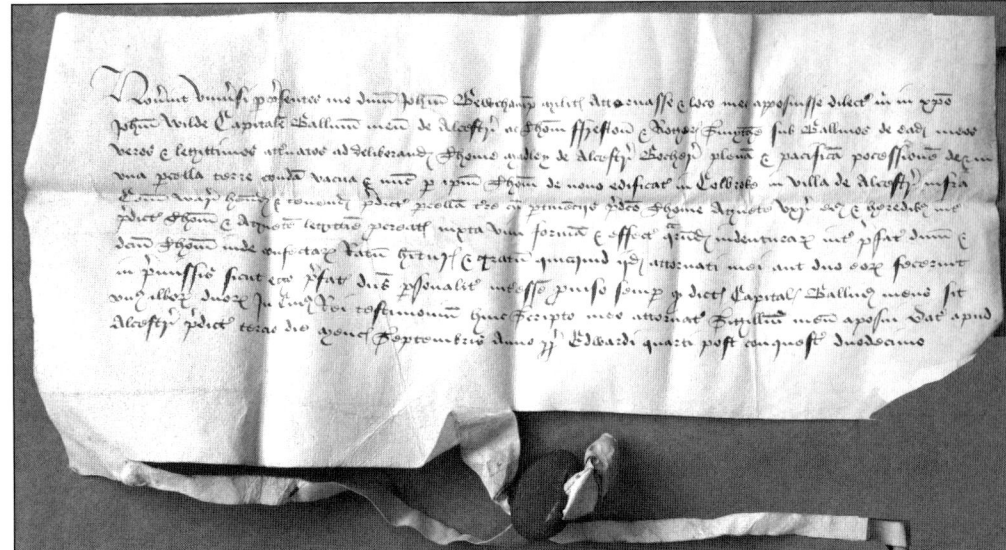

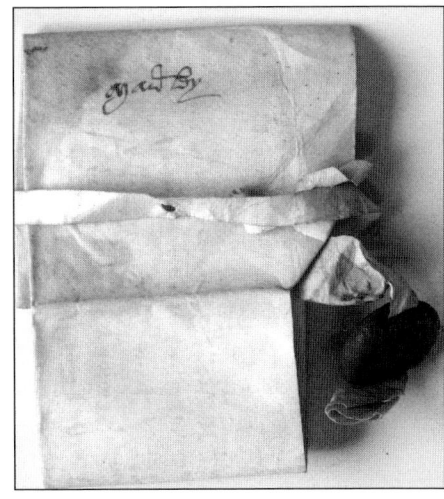

4.12 Medieval letter of attorney of 1472, relating to the transfer of property in Alcester, Warwickshire: (top) open; (bottom) closed, showing how the second strip of parchment (often torn off) was wrapped around the folded letter, leaving the seal showing for authentication. For text, see p. 181. (WCRO, CR1886/113)

of and in . . .). An example of the alternative is '*ad recipiend in nomine meo plenam et pacificam sezinam in . . .*' (to receive in my name full and peaceful seisin in …). The final important section is the property description, which is usually in the same words as the main deed for the transaction. Thus, the letter of attorney can serve as a substitute for this.

Particularly in towns, *Agreements* were needed between neighbours. They generally start either as an indenture, or with the words '*Hec conventio facta inter* [A] *et* [B]' (This agreement made between A and B), and continue with the details of the agreement. They concern such matters as permission to install and repair a gutter, or to overhang the adjoining property. Some agreements mention a payment from one party to the other, or a yearly rent, but often they were of benefit to both sides, and no money was involved.

MANORIAL COURT ROLLS AND COPIES OF COURT ROLL

Like the enrolled deeds described earlier (pp. 128–9), the court rolls or court books give the same information as the individual deeds, the *copies*, but their status reverses that of the enrolled copies.[32] The court roll itself is the original authentic record, and the individual document is the copy, though it was accepted by the manor court as good evidence of title. Importantly, the court rolls or books have generally survived much better than the copies of court roll, and are much easier to locate (see below).

In the medieval period, changes of tenant on most of the 15,000 manors in England were recorded on the court rolls, unless the tenant held 'at will'. This developed into the tenure known as copyhold, because the tenant received a copy of the entry on the roll to prove his tenancy; if the manor was surveyed, he was expected to produce this copy at the special manorial court of survey. Copyhold was governed by the 'custom of the manor', which varied considerably from one manor to another. In some places, copyhold land could be inherited or bought and sold without the permission of the lord of the manor, by paying a standard fee. However, its 'owner' was still technically a tenant of the manor, and the court rolls or books therefore record changes in ownership. He also had to pay a fixed rent, other manorial dues (e.g. heriot, a fine paid on the death of the tenant, consisting of either a sum of money, or the best beast or best possession) and he had to attend the manor court. On these manors, copyhold land was effectively equivalent to freehold.

In other places by the manor custom, holdings could not be inherited, but when a tenant died, the lord could regrant it to whoever he wished for life or for the lives of two or three named people; it was a short step from this to granting it on a three-life lease (and this development frequently took place). Elsewhere, copyholdings were *enfranchised* (converted from copyhold to freehold tenure), with the tenant paying a lump sum to extinguish the fixed rent (see p. 132); after 1852, either the landowner or the copyholder could enfranchise copyhold land without the agreement of the other. Copyhold was finally abolished by the 1922 Law of Property Act, which enfranchised all copyholdings after 1 January 1926.[33]

On manors without copyhold tenure, the keeping of manor courts generally came to an end in the seventeenth or eighteenth centuries, and it is all too common for most or all of the rolls to have been lost. When copyhold persisted, the court rolls were of legal importance as the main record of land 'ownership' (as it was in effect). They were therefore generally both well kept and well preserved, and many copyhold manors have continuous runs from the sixteenth or seventeenth centuries until 1922. The court records are generally actual rolls until about 1700, but court books were very often adopted after that. These frequently have indexes of people, making them very convenient to search. They are an invaluable source of information about both the land and topography of the manor, and the people and families living there.

Most sets of manor court rolls are now in county record offices, but strays are frequent. The Manorial Documents Register is maintained by TNA (in succession to the National Register of Archives) to give the location of all known manorial records. It is online for almost all English and Welsh counties, and requests for information about manors in other counties can be sent to TNA.[34] It is always worth checking for manorial records for any place in which one is interested, especially since the manorial records may be accompanied by other documents. The Register includes all known manorial documents, but of course others do come to light from time to time.[35]

Copies of Court Roll
Court rolls and copies may be in Latin or English, or a mixture of the two. In post-medieval copies, the name of the manor is always at the top left, with a section giving details of the court on the right (Illus. 4.13).

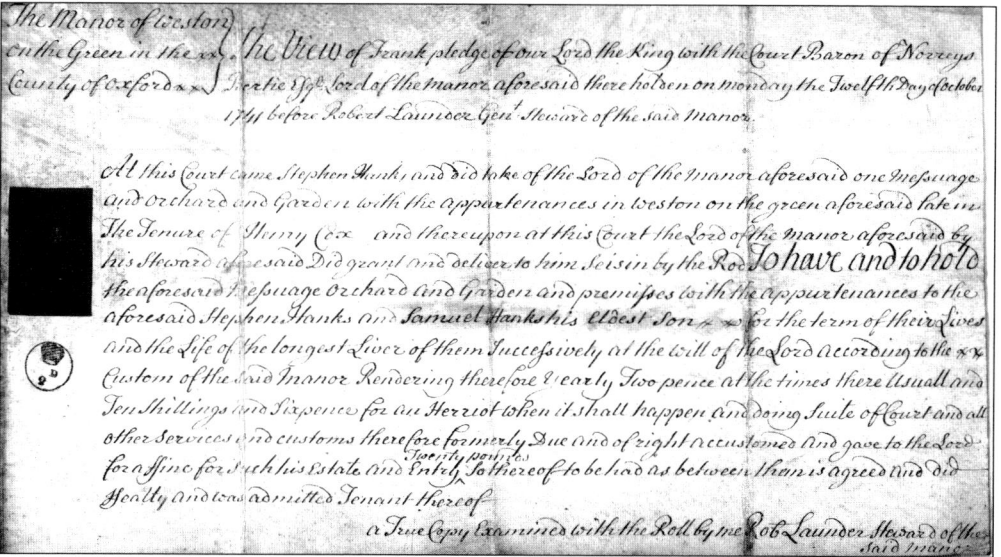

4.13 A copy of court roll of 1741, from the manor of Weston on the Green, Oxfordshire. For text, see p. 182. (TNA, C 103/156)

The heading of a typical Warwickshire example (WCRO, CR1300/6/1) reads:

> Manor of Berkswell. A Court Baron of John Knightley otherwise Wightwick, esquire, Lord of the said manor, held there the second day of July in the thirty-fourth year of the

reign of our sovereign Lord George the second [1760], by the grace of God . . ., Before Joseph Cater, gentleman, steward there.

The second part of the copy gives the details of the property and the change of ownership, as recorded on the roll. Copies of court roll tend to be much less wordy than ordinary deeds, and are easier to follow. The simplest form records the death of the previous owner and the admission of his heir. This was not necessarily the eldest son, as many manors had the custom of Borough English, by which the youngest son inherited. To take over the property, the heir would appear in the court and be admitted and given seisin by the steward, as in the following example. It is notable here that the fine is substantial, indicating that the custom on this manor was not that of inheritance for a fixed fine (usually set by custom at one or two year's rent).

[Allesley, Warwickshire] At this court it is presented by the homage that Mary Beck the Free Bench [holding by widow's right] widow of William Beck late a copyhold tenant of this manor is dead since the last court and that his nephew George Beck an infant of the age of sixteen years and upwards, the only son of John Beck deceased who was the elder brother of the said William Beck, is the next heir to the said William Beck, Whereupon at this court came the said George Beck in his proper person and prayed to be admitted tenant to the copyhold lands and tenements of which the said William Beck died seized (that is to say) to All that messuage . . . [description of property totalling about one acre, including the names of former tenants] To whom the lord of the said manor by me his steward hath granted seisin and he hath seisin thereof by the rod [a ceremony in the court] according to the custom of the said manor to have and to hold the same with the appurtenances to him the said George and his heirs for ever according to the custom of the said manor by the yearly rent of 8 shillings, suit of court, heriott when it shall happen and all other rents, services and customs therefore due and of right accustomed, and he gave the lord for a fine six pounds and is admitted tenant thereto accordingly, but his fealty is respited by reason of nonage [being under age], In witness whereof I the steward have hereunto put my hand and seal.[36] (1755; WCRO, CR623/box 2)

If another change of ownership was involved, then the original owner surrendered the property to the lord of the manor, but could specify the 'use' for the property. This was the feature of copyhold tenure that made it equivalent to freehold. The most straightforward case is that of the sale of the property, when the property was surrendered to the use of the purchaser, as in the following example. The surrender did not have to take place in the manor court, but could be made to two of the manorial tenants at any convenient place (e.g. the bedroom of a dying tenant).

[Borough of Lewes, Sussex] At this court comes William Cooper, gentleman, and Elizabeth, his wife, (the said Elizabeth being first solely and secretly examined by the said Steward and consenting) [to demonstrate that she was not being coerced into relinquishing her rights] and surrenders into the hands of the Lords of the said borough [the borough had joint lords], all that small parcel of land . . ., paying to the lords yearly 6d, To the use and behoof of John Jones of the Parish of All Saints, dyer, his heirs and assigns for ever, And the said John Jones being present in Court desires to be admitted to the said premises, to whom the Lords by the steward aforesaid grant seisin thereof by the rod to have and to hold the same unto the said John Jones, his heirs and assigns for ever by copy of court roll at the will of the Lords, according to the custom of the said borough, by the rents, customs, and services therefore first due and of right accustomed, and he is admitted tenant thereof paying to the Lords for a fine therefore 6d of certain [i.e. a fine fixed by custom and not at the lord's choice]. (1733; private ownership)

Property to be left by will was surrendered while the owner was alive: to the use and behoof of his last will and testament in writing to be declared and when the heir came to be admitted, he would produce the will and the admission would refer to the previous surrender.

This was important if the tenant had several children. If he made no will, his freehold land would pass to his eldest son, but following Borough English, the copyhold land would pass to the youngest son; such a division might well not be intended. It was also possible to create a family settlement, e.g. in a surrender in 1676 by Thomas Abbey in the Allesley manor court:

To the use and behoof of the said Thomas Abbey and the said Joyce his wife for and dureing their naturall lives and the life of the longer liver of them, And ymediatly from and after the decease of the survivor of them the said Thomas Abbey and Joyce his wife, then to the use and behoof of . . . Abbey (onely sonne of Henry Abbey, deceased and grandsonne of the said Thomas Abbey) and of his heirs. (WCRO, CR623/box2)

Copyhold land could also be mortgaged (Illus. 4.14); it was surrendered to the use of the mortgagee conditional on the repayment of the money due:

[South Malling, Sussex] To the . . . use of . . . Walter Brett and John Savage . . . [on the condition that] if the said

Thomas Wynchester, his heires, executors, administrators or assigns or any of them doe at or in the nowe dwelling house of the said Walter Brett situat in Lewes in the county of Sussex well and truly cause to be paid to the said Walter and John, their heirs, [etc.] . . ., being both present in person, the some [sic] of two hundred and six pounds of lawful money in and upon the 3 and 20th day of October next, this surrender to be void or else to remain in force [1654] [Margin] Memorandum that the moneys in the condicion mentioned was payd according to the tenor of the condicion. (British Library, Add. Mss. 33183).

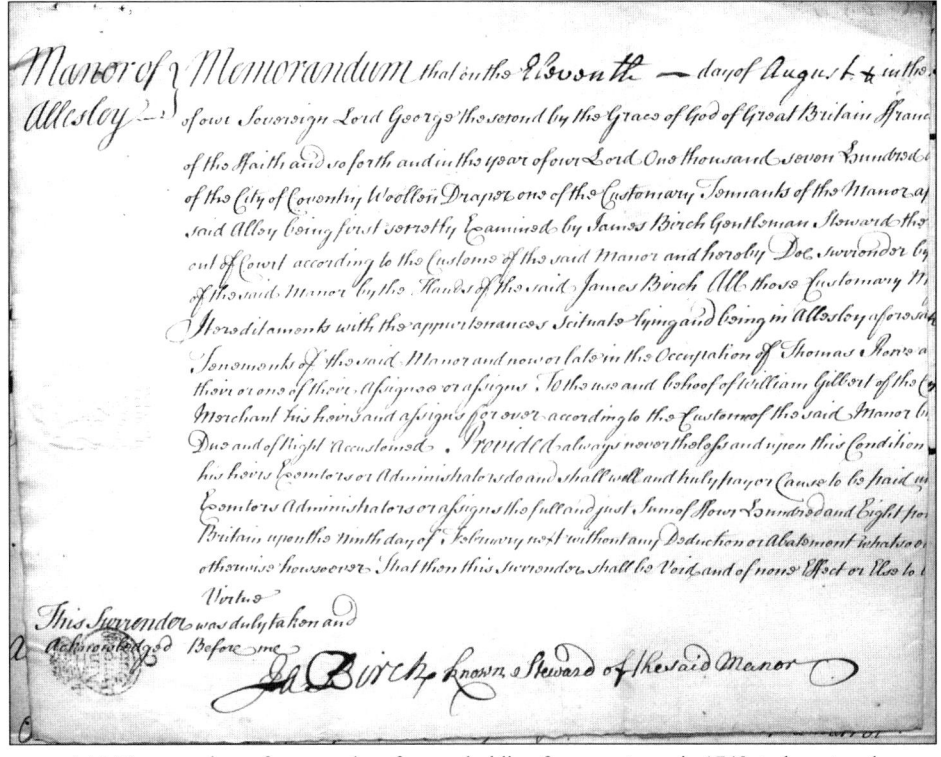

4.14 Memorandum of a surrender of a copyholding for a mortgage in 1749, to be entered on the court roll of the manor of Allesley, Warwickshire. For text, see p. 183. (WCRO, CR623/box2)

It was even possible to carry out a Common Recovery in the manor court, so that copyhold property which had been included in a family settlement could be sold or re-settled. The steward would certainly have needed very careful guidance on just how this was done, as shown in Illus. 4.15.

Manorial Customs

Some items in the court rolls relate directly to the customs of the manor. The tenant of a copyholding might not always be allowed to sub-lease the property, because the sub-tenant would not have the same responsibility towards the other tenants as the copyholder himself; he would therefore need 'liberty of licence' to sub-lease, and would agree that the lord could distrain on the tenement if the rents and services due were not paid as required.

The widow of a copyholder was permitted to continue to hold the tenement after his death, as her 'Free Bench' (as with Mary Beck, above), until her death or remarriage. Much more rarely, a widower might have free bench in the tenement his wife had held in her own right.[37] The custom of free bench was sometimes turned to the tenant's advantage on manors where copyhold land was not automatically inherited. An elderly tenant would marry a young woman, who might retain the holding for many years after his death. She would be in an excellent position to bargain for a renewal of the copyhold on advantageous terms, for the benefit of her husband's children. Of course, such schemes might misfire – in one case in 1620, the tenant was rejuvenated by his marriage and survived for another fifteen years![38] Surprisingly, the customs of the manor might also relate to morals and behaviour, though this was normally only the concern of the church courts. In 1633, in Temple Balsall, Warwickshire, it was recorded that Margery Findern who was with child before her marriage with Henry Essex had forfeited all right in her copyhold lands according to the custom of the manor, but she was able to redeem these by bringing in a purse worth 1d. (*unum crumenam*

APPENDIX.

The Form of suffering a Recovery in a Manor Court, ought to be in the following manner:—

A. B. is the tenant in tail, and defirous of barring the entail by a recovery. In this cafe *C. D.* muft be made tenant to the plaint, or tenant to the precipe; and *E. F.* as demandant, is to bring his action againft *C. D.* for the lands. *A. B.* then comes in as vouchee, to vouch over *R. M.* the common voucher of the court. The copyholds muft in the firft place be furrendered to the ufe of *C. D.:* to make him tenant to the plaint, and he muft be admitted in the ufual manner; the fteward then addreffing himfelf to *E. F.* the demandant: " You being now in court, in
" your own proper perfon, complain againft
" *C. D.* tenant to the plaint, of a plea of land
" to wit, one meffuage, one curtilage, &c. holden of this manor by copy of court-roll, at
" the will of the lord; and therefore you pray
" procefs to be awarded againft him; but you
" the faid *C. D.* voluntarily appear to anfwer
" to the faid *E. F.* and thereupon you, the faid
" *E. F.* demand againft the faid *C. D.* the tenements aforefaid, with the appurtenances, as
" your right and inheritance, and fay that you
" were feifed of the fame, in your demefne, as
" of fee and right, according to the cuftom of
" this manor, at the will of the lord, and into
" which the faid *C. D.* has not entry but after
" the

APPENDIX.

" the diffeifin of one *Hugh Hunt*; whereupon you *C. D.* come and defend your right to
" the tenements aforefaid, with the appurtenances, and vouch over to warranty *A. B.*
" to which you *A. B.* appear. And thereupon you *E. F.* make the like demand againft
" the faid *A. B.* as againft the faid *C. D.* and
" fay that you were feifed of the tenements aforefaid, with the appurtenances, in your demefne, as of fee and right, according to the
" cuftom of this manor, at the will of the lord,
" and into which the faid *A B.* has not entry,
" but after the diffeifin of the faid *Hugh Hunt*;
" whereupon you *A. B.* come and defend this
" right of the faid *C. D.* to the tenement aforefaid, with the appurtenances, and further call
" to warranty *Ralph May*; and thereupon, you
" *E. F.* make the like demand againft the
" faid *Ralph May* as againft the faid *A. B.*
" and fay that you was feifed of the tenements
" aforefaid, with the appurtenances in your
" demefne, as of fee and right, according to the
" cuftom of the manor, at the will of the lord;
" and into which the faid *Ralph May* has not
" entry, but after the diffeifin of the faid
" *Hugh Hunt*; whereupon you, *Ralph May*,
" come and defend the right of the faid *C. D.*
" and fay, that the faid *Hugh Hunt* did not
" diffeife the faid *E. F.* of the tenement aforefaid, as the faid *E. F.* does by his plaint above
" pretend and allege; and thereupon you,

4.15 Instructions for a manor court steward to carry out a Common Recovery of copyhold land, from Richard Fisher, *A Practical Treatise on Copyhold Tenure* (London, 1803), pp. 228–9. The instructions continue on the following pages with the leave to imparle, the failure of Ralph May, the common vouchee, to return, the judgement for E. F., and the precept of the court to the bailiff to deliver seisin to E. F. (see pp. 124–5 for more details of the procedure). This is followed by the seven-page text of the recovery, as it is to be entered on the court roll.

ad valenciam unius denarius) and 5s. in money, and was readmitted (WCRO, CR112/432).

MEDIEVAL COPIES OF COURT ROLL

Medieval copies of court roll are very rare but when encountered are particularly valuable, since the corresponding court roll may well not survive.[39] It seems that copies began to be given to tenants in about 1300, but the reasons why only some manors produced them have yet to be explored. Copies are mentioned in the court rolls of St Albans in 1311, and Wakefield, Yorkshire in 1315, and a very few actual copies have been discovered dating from before 1350.[40] Rather more exist for the second half of the fourteenth century, and they become more frequent from the fifteenth century onwards, which is when the systematic development of copyhold tenure into its full post-medieval form took place.[41] By the sixteenth century, the entries on the court rolls and in copies were following the standard later forms. Illus. 4.16 shows a fifteenth-century copy from Audley, Staffordshire (Audeley in the document); see the text and translation on p. 184).

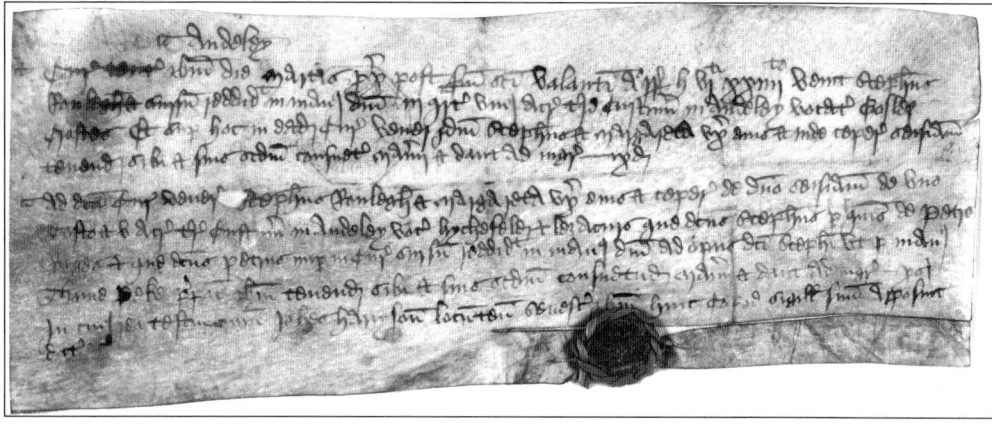

4.16 A medieval copy of court roll, for the manor of Audeley, Staffordshire, dated Tuesday after St Valentine, 24 Hen. VI (1435). It includes two admissions for Stephen Roulegh and Margaret his wife to a croft (first) and a toft and 6 acres (second). For text, see p. 184. (TNA, C 146/11065)

This and other early examples show the same key features as later copies, including the 'surrender to uses' for the benefit of a named person, the payment of a standard fine, and even the examination of a wife separate from her husband.[42] Medieval copies often have side-seal tags, though it is rare for them actually to carry seals, as this one does.

It is also worth noting that medieval court rolls can give information about freeholdings, because manorial custom often required a 'relief' (e.g. 5s.) to be paid when a freeholding was transferred, and the payment of (or failure to pay) these reliefs would be recorded in the court rolls. This has been used effectively, for example, in the manor of Wrotham, Kent, to show that the builders of its handsome late medieval timber-framed houses were often butchers, tanners or others involved in the London meat trade.[43] Thus, even on non-copyhold manors, the medieval court rolls (if they survive) can give invaluable information about tenants and landowners and their property.

Notes

1. These cases were generally pursued in the Court of Chancery, whose records are at TNA. The majority of the sixteenth–nineteenth-century finding aids to these cases are now online in Discovery; sometimes these provide only the names of the first plaintiff and defendant, so considerable searching may be needed. However, success can be rewarded by very interesting information. A useful guide to the sources for tracing particular cases is Henry Horowitz, *Chancery Equity Records and Proceedings, 1600–1800: a guide to the documents in the Public Record Office* (HMSO, 1996).
2. C.R. Cheney and Michael Jones (eds), *A Handbook of Dates For Students of British History* (Royal Historical Society Guides and Handbooks, Cambridge, 2000).
3. You have to be particularly careful in identifying the correct year for Commonwealth deeds dated between 1 January and 24 March, because they have no regnal year to use as a check.
4. Although the collection from which this example comes contains a considerable number of these forms, I have never seen one used for an actual deed. It may be that they were intended for producing drafts of deeds, which were then copied onto parchment for signature.
5. Alcock, 'Fields and Farms in an East Devon Parish', 93 (see p. 42, n. 9).

6. A technical distinction was made between a simple life lease, which had no definite end, and a lease for three lives or ninety-nine years. The former legally transferred the freehold and therefore by law needed to be conveyed as freehold, e.g. by feoffment. In reality, of course, the property leased for lives would revert to the original owner in due course.

7. See R. Stanes, 'Conversion from Three-life Leases to Leases for Years', in W. Minchinton (ed.), *Agricultural Improvement: Medieval and Modern* (University of Exeter, 1981).

8. Covenants are discussed with special reference to those concerning building work by K.T. Ward, 'Covenants in conveyancing instruments: a note for the vernacular architectural historian', *Vernacular Architecture*, 25 (1994), 16–19.

9. In this early example (TNA, E 44/450-3), most significantly, both the lease for a year and the release survive as duplicate counterparts; the rent in the lease is given as 'one penny at the feast of St Andrew the apostle now next insuing if it be demanded', rather than a peppercorn, and it lacks the standard phrase about the purpose of the lease, 'to the intent that the said [purchaser] may be enabled to take and accepte of a release' (see text of Illus. 4.4, p. 175). D. Smith (formerly of Gloucester Record Office) informs me that he has seen an example of 1530; there may have been some special reason for using the lease and release form in this early example.

10. It was decided that if the principal and interest were paid, even belatedly, the mortgagee had obtained what he expected, the return of his money with interest, so that he had no right to take over the property.

11. In such recitals, either in mortgage assignments or in sales, if there had been very numerous assignments all of them might not be recited, but the deeds contain a statement on the lines of 'and by divers mesne [intermediate] assignments became vested in [the current mortgagee]'.

12. Cited from the 1602 will of John Lillye of Heaton Norris (formerly Lancashire, now Greater Manchester (http://debrettancestry.co.uk/docs/6340A.pdf, accessed 19 February 2017).

13. See English and Saville, *Strict Settlement*.

14. E.g. from Google searches, the wills of Edmond Reynell of Sherford, Devon, 1729 and Ann King of Poughill, Cornwall, 1843.

15. Nat Alcock and Joan Lane, 'A Widow's Adornment and Estate', *Warwickshire History*, 12 (3) (Summer 2003), 107–19. For the settlement itself, see WCRO, CR611/748/1.

16. These certificates were abolished by the Married Women's Property Act of 1882.

17. Readers should know that my dislike of these documents is not universally felt. A paper by F.G. Emmison in *The Local Historian* of September 1981 (no. 411) suggests that the acreages given are useful and fairly accurate and that the names of the parties can also be helpful. W.G. Hoskins, *The Midland Peasant* (Leicester University Press, 1961), p. 99f. uses a series of fines from 1586–7 to document the selling off of a substantial Leicestershire property to sixteen freeholders.

18. Feet of fines for the Palatinates of Chester, Durham and Lancaster are in TNA, CHES 31, DURH 12 and PL 17 respectively.

19. I have once only encountered what appears to be a *Portmanteau deed to lead the uses of a recovery*, similar to the *Portmanteau fine*, covering two unrelated groups of people jointly carrying out the recovery – again, presumably to reduce the costs (WCRO, CR228/10/13).

20. The volumes up to 1582 are published by TNA or HMSO, the later ones by the List and Index Society.

21. The record of its proof in the church court that made the will legally valid. The original will with the grant of probate endorsed was retained among the diocesan records.

22. For Devon and Somerset almost all the wills were destroyed in 1942, so the copies in deed bundles may be unique. Originals of early wills may also not survive. Occasionally, the executors of wills did not bother to prove them in the church courts, in which case the only copy is that in the deed bundle.

23. See, for example, N.W. Alcock, *People at Home* (Phillimore, 1993) for a study of inventory evidence related to individual property holdings, though these were mostly located through estate maps and rentals rather than title deeds.

24. See C.A.F. Meekings and P. Shearman (eds), 'Fitznells Cartulary', *Surrey Record Society*, Vol. 26, cxl, for a survey of the changing patterns found in medieval deeds, illustrated from a Surrey archive.

25. For an example of dating in this way, see P.R. Coss (ed.), *The early records of Medieval Coventry* (British Academy, 1986), pp. 65–6.

26. Care is needed because several saints of the same name may exist, while many major saints have several feast days. Here, the most important, St Martin (of Tours), can be assumed; his feast day was known as Martinmas.

27. A recent study of seals is Elizabeth A. New, *Seals and Sealing Practices* (British Records Association, Archives and the User, 11, 2010). See Further Resources for other books on seals.

28. In this context, the furlongs are the subdivisions of a village's open field, each containing a group of aligned strips.

29. See J.H. Hodson, 'Medieval charters: the last witness', *J. Soc. Archivists*, Vol. 5 (2) (1974), 71–89.

30. For examples, see L.F. Salzman, *Building in England down to 1540* (Oxford, 1967).

31. Jonathan Kissock, 'Medieval feet of fines: a study of their uses with a catalogue of published sources', *Local Historian*, May 1994, 66–82 gives a list of published medieval fines and examines their use. See also E.L.C. Mullins, *Texts and Calendars*, Vols 1 and 2 (Royal Historical Society, 1958 and 1983); updated publication lists (society-by-society) can be downloaded from http://royalhistsoc.org/publications/national-regional-history/.

32. P.D.A. Harvey, *Manorial Records* (British Records Association, rev. edn, 1999) gives an excellent general survey of manorial documents, but has very little to say about copies of court roll and does not deal with their interpretation as property deeds.

33. Establishing compensation for the value of the copyhold was under the charge of the Ministry of Agriculture. TNA classes MAF 9 and MAF 20 contain records of enfranchisement for many manors; they also include deeds, court rolls and evidence of ownership of manorial rights.

34. Http://discovery.nationalarchives.gov.uk/manor-search.

35. Mary Ellis, *Using Manorial Records* (Public Record Office, 1994) discusses in detail the location of manorial records, although it was written before the MDR was put online. In theory, though not always in practice, manorial records must be kept in an approved repository (e.g. a county record office) and may not be exported without the permission of the Master of the Rolls (which has never been given).

36. This and most of the following items are quoted from the manor court rolls and papers which provide a good range of examples of the court business. For each item, a copy of court roll would also have been prepared, but most of these have not survived.

37. For example, in Temple Balsall, Warwickshire in 1655 (WCRO, CR112/412).

38. See J.H. Betty, 'Manorial customs and widows' estate', *Archives*, 19 (1987), 208–16.

39. The survival of early copies of court roll is being examined by Dr C. Currie, who is compiling a list of those dating from before 1400; he has kindly shared this information with me.

40. Harvey, *Manorial Records*, p. 44. Among manors for which I have encountered fourteenth-century copies are Harringey, Middlesex (PRO Descriptive Catalogue of Ancient Deeds, Vol. 6 (HMSO, 1915), indexed under 'manor courts'); Sedgley, Staffordshire (Staffordshire Record Office) and Wakefield, West Yorkshire (in West Yorkshire Record Office); the oldest yet identified is for Sherborne, Dorset, of 1306 (Dorset Record Office, D/SHA/M1A).

41. See Mark Bailey, 'The transformation of customary tenures in southern England, c.1350 to c.1500', *Agricultural History Review*, 62 (II) (2014), 201–30; see also E.B. Fryde and N. Fryde, in Edward Miller (ed.), *Ag. Hist. III: 1348–1500* (Cambridge, 1991), p. 813f. Professor C. Dyer has noted surrenders in early fourteenth-century rolls of Blickling Hall manors for the use of a named person, with the condition that they would be void unless specified sums of money were paid; these probably represent deferred purchase payments rather than loans of money (personal communication) and it is not clear if copies of the entries were being provided.

42. TNA, C 146/11060 (a rather damaged copy of court roll of 1384) is the surrender of William Benne of Worksop and Agnes his wife of premises in Mansfield, Nottinghamshire for the use of John Lavston. It reads (towards the end) '*predicte Agnet' examinata et iurata fuit in absencia viri sui que tactis sacrosanctis*' (the said Agnes was examined and sworn in the absence of her husband, touching the sacred [objects]). A similar example from 1355, where the wife was questioned by the steward, and asked if she was being coerced by her husband, is recorded in the court rolls for Romsley, Worcestershire (Birmingham Archives and Heritage, Hagley Hall muniments, Ms. 346814 r; information from Professor C. Dyer).

43. Unpublished study by Jayne Semple.

Appendix 1

FLOWCHART TO IDENTIFY DEED TYPES

Based on a model created by Manuscripts and Special Collections, The University of Nottingham.
See http://www.nottingham.ac.uk/manuscriptsandspecial collections/researchguidance/deedsindepth/introduction.aspx.

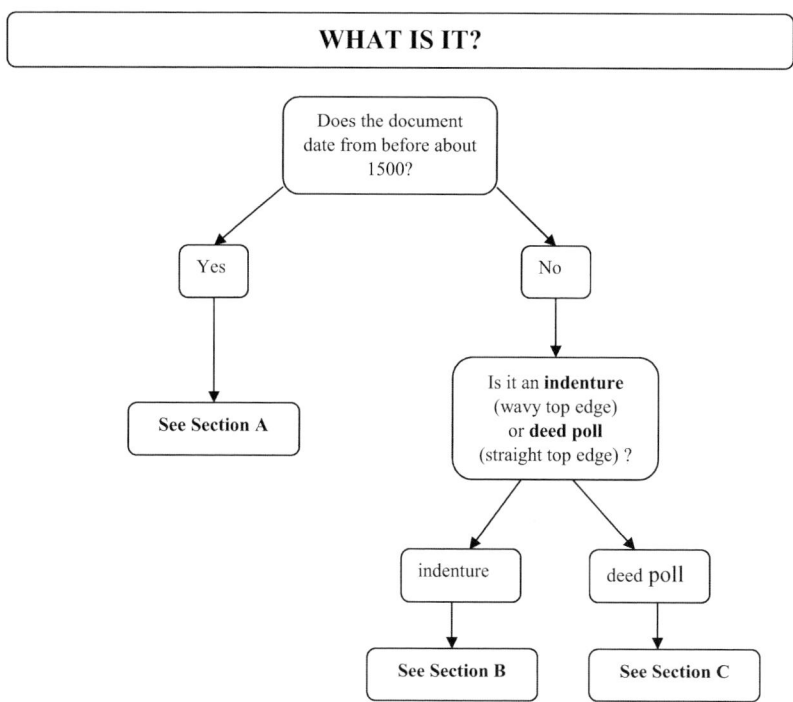

Tracing History Through Title Deeds

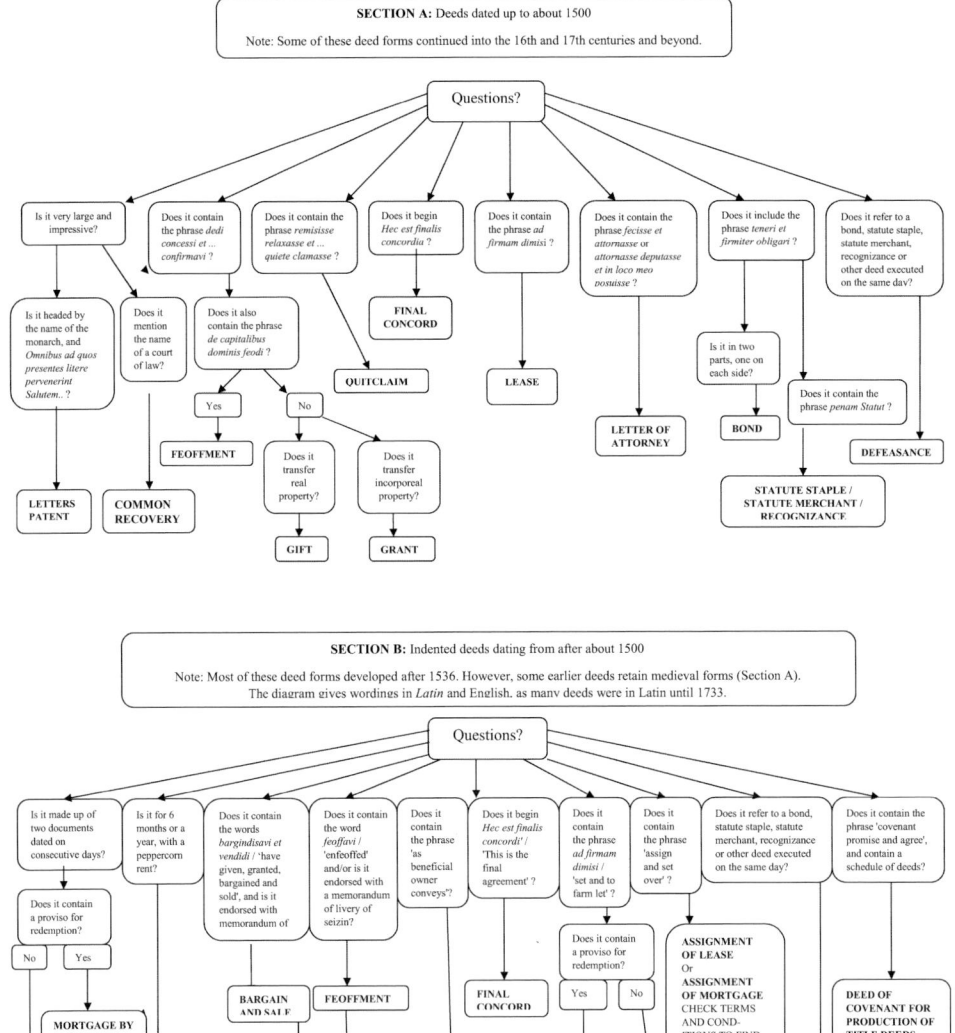

Appendix 1

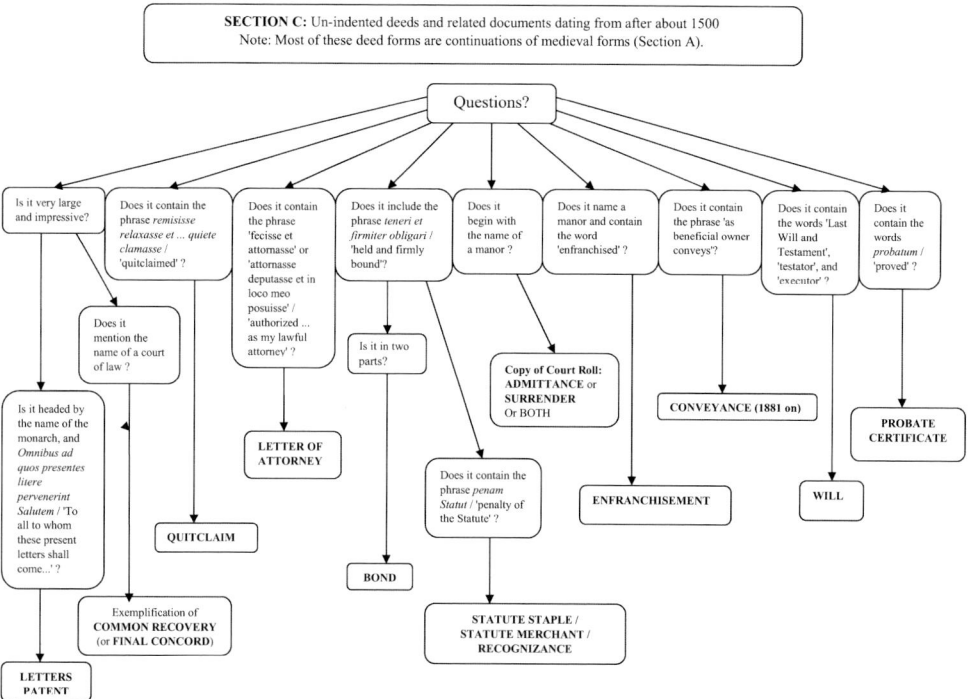

Appendix 2

SAMPLE DEED RECORD SHEET

These headings should be copied onto an A4 sheet, suitably spaced out and omitting the comments in italics. They should cover the most important aspects that need to be recorded for post-medieval deeds. Continue any fields on the back of the sheet if necessary.

Document Reference: Abstractor: Abstract No: Indexed:
The later headings assume this is part of a collaborative project, and that indexes are being compiled.

Document Type (ring): Lease, Assignment, Lease and Release, Feoffment, Mortgage, Mortgage Assignment, Fine, Recovery, Settlement, other (state what)
You may only be able to identify this after working through the document.

Date (a) as in document: (b) modern style

Names of parties, occupations, abodes, relationships (surnames as spelt, Christian names may be modernised):
1) *More parties as needed (Leave a largish space)*
2)

Nature of transaction (e.g. conveyance by (1) to (3) (4) as dower trustee, (2) holds mortgage, assigned to (5) to attend inheritance)

Recitals (dates; details if not already known) (Refer to abstract sheets for earlier deeds as appropriate.)

Appendix 2

Consideration:

Property, including abuttals and all details given:
(Leave a largish space)

Term (years/lives/for ever):
Rent:

Tenure and Uses:

Covenants or Conditions:

Endorsements:

Appendix 3

POST-MEDIEVAL LETTER FORMS

Alphabet of post-medieval letter forms from A. Wright, *Court Hand Restored,* plates 18–19 (8th edn, 1867, online at https://archive.org/details/courthandrestore00wrigrich). See also H.E. Grieve, *Examples of English Handwriting, 1150–1750* (Essex Record Office, 1954, 7th impression, 2004).

Appendix 4

TEXTS OF TYPICAL DEEDS

1. TEXTS OF ILLUSTRATED DEEDS

Punctuation and capitalisation has been modernised. A / indicates the end of the line in the original Latin texts. Note how words are sometimes split between lines, often without any indication that the word continues.

1.2 Thirteenth-century Lease of a House in Coventry (p. 5)

Sciant presentes et futuri quod ego Robertus de Feug's tradidi ad firmam Galfridi de Wilnhall, domum meam inter pontes in Covintr' / in qua manere consuevi, scilicet domum illam propinquior aque, cum pertinentiis suis, habendam et tenendam de me et de heredibus meis / sibi et heredibus suis libere et quiete et honorifice, a Nativitate Sancti Johannis Baptiste tercia post translationem Beati Thome / martiris, usque ad decem annos sequentes completos, pro quattuor marcis argenti, quas ipse Galfridi michi dedit, scilicet totam firmam / decem annorum pre manibus. Et ego Robertus et heredes mei warantizabimus predicto Galfrido et heredibus suis predictam domum / cum pertinentiis suis per decem annos contra omnes homines et omnes feminas. Et totum servitium quod debetur capitalibus / dominis de domo illa singulis annis adquietabimus. Completis vero decem annis predicta domus cum pertinentiis suis rema/nebit michi et heredibus meis sola et quieta ab ipso Galfrido et ab omnibus suis sine omni contradictione. Hanc autem con/ventionem legaliter et sine dolo tenendam utrimque affidavimus. In cuius rei testimonium presenti scripto sigillum / meum apposui. Hiis testibus Willelmo filio Umfredi, Johanne filio eius, Swano parcario, Vincentio filio eius, Henrico filio Edredi, / Willelmo de Franketon, Thoma tinctore, Hamone filio Jordani, Roger de Cornl', Roberto Blundo, Michaele tinctore, et aliis.

TRANSLATION:

Know all men present and future that I Robert de Feugers [a name known from other documents] have leased at farm [for a money rent] to Geoffrey de Willenhall, my house between the bridges [in a street later called Burges] in Coventry, in which I have been accustomed to dwell, to wit that house beside the water, with its appurtenances, to have and to hold of me and of my heirs, to him and his heirs freely, both quietly and honorably, from the [feast of the] Birth of Saint John the Baptist [24 June], the third after the Translation of the Blessed Thomas [à Becket] martyr [as the translation took place on 7 July 1220, the date indicated is 24 June 1223] for ten years following to be completed, for four marks of silver, which the same Geoffrey gave me, to wit the whole farm of ten years in advance. And I, Robert, and my heirs warrant to the said Geoffrey and his heirs, the said house with its appurtenances for ten years against all men and all women. And all service which is owed to the chief lord from that house for every single year we will acquit. Indeed, on completion of the ten years the said house with its appurtenances shall remain to me and my heirs solely and quietly from the said Geoffrey and from all of his [heirs] without any gainsaying. Moreover, we pledge ourselves to hold this agreement legally and without fraud. In witness whereof I have affixed my seal to this present charter. These being witnesses: William son of Humphrey, John his son, Swain the parker, Vincent his son, Henry son of Edred, William de Franketon, Thomas the dyer, Hamon son of Jordan, Roger de Corley, Robert Blund, Michael the dyer, and others.

2.10. Fourteenth-century Lease of a House in Coventry, with Building Details (p. 35)

Noverint universis quod ego Galfridus de Hulle, tannator de Coventre, concessi, tradidi ac dimisi Johannem del Doune tannatori de / Coventre unum mesuagium cum solario suprasito iuxta domum operacionis mee ex parte una, et stabulum meum ex parte altera in latitudine, et in longitudine / sicut se plenarie proportat. Concessi eciam predictum Johannem del Doune unam placeam terre ad superedificand et unam domum pro thorale cum cilicio et unum barkestoke / cum suis pertinenciis ex opposito predictum mesuagium, iacentes in venella que vocatur Wymundeslane de Coventre, inter tenementum Willelmi de Overton, clerici ex parte una et/ quondam palicum ibido stantem ex parte altera in latitudine, et extendit se predictam placea terre cum domo pro thorale et ceteris pertinentiis suis a venella predicta / usque ad aquam currentem, sicut se plenarie proportat per metas et divisas ibidem factas. Habendum et tenendum predictum mesuagium cum solario suprasito et predictam placeam / terre ad superedificand cum domo pro thorale et cilicio [reading *cilicerio*] et barkstoke cum suis pertinencis, de me et heredibus meis prefato Johanni et heredibus et assignatis suis a festo annun/ciationis beate virginis Marie anno regni regis Edwardi tercii post conquestum quartodecimo usque ad finum decem annorum proxime sequente plenarum completorum. Red/dendo inde annuatim me et heredibus meis nonem solidis et sex denariis argenti per equales porciones ad quatuor anni terminos usuales in Coventre. Ita quod ego / dictus Galfridus et heredes mei predictum mesuagium cum solario et domum pro thorale sumptibus nostris proprii contra ventum et pluviam competenter emendabimus ac erigemus. / Et si contingat predictum Johannem, heredes seu assignatos suos aliquod edificium seu necessarium super dictam placeam terre de novo construere seu reparare / quod extunc liceat bene dicti Johanni heredibus seu assignatis suis ad finem dictorum decem annorum illud asportare sine contradictione aliquam nisi per visum ac consi/deracionum proborum et legalium vicinorum inde allocatione seu satisfactione faciverint competente. Et ego vero predictus Galfridus et heredes mei predictum mesuagium cum solario / suprafacto et predictam placeam terre cum domo pro thorale et cilicio et barkstoke cum suis pertinentiis usque ad finem dictorum decem annorum prefatis Johannis et heredibus suis / seu assignatis secundum formam predictam contra omnes gentes warantizabimus et defendemus. In cui reis testimonum his scriptis indentatis tam sigillum meam / quam sigillum dicti Johannis alternatis sicut appensa. Hiis testibus Johnanne le Chaundeler, Roberto de Hampton, Nicholo le Deyster, Ricardo De Herberbury, Thome de Audeleye et aliis

[This is probably the counterpart lease as the document comes from the records of the Catesby family who acquired Geoffrey's property, so the defaced seal is that of John del Doune.]

TRANSLATION:
Know everyone that I Geoffrey de Hulle, tanner of Coventry, have granted, delivered and leased to John del Doune, tanner of Coventry, one messuage [probably meaning hall] and the solar above, beside my workshop on one side and my stable on the other side in breadth and in length as it plainly appears. I also grant to the said John del Doune one plot of building land, one [malt] kiln with a hair-cloth, and one barkhouse, with their appurtenances, opposite the said messuage, lying in the lane called Wymundeslane of Coventry, between the holding of William de Overton, clerk on one side and a certain palisade standing there on the other side in breadth, and extending from the aforesaid lane to the running water, as it plainly appears by the metes and bounds there made. Having and holding the said messuage with solar above it and the said building plot, with the kiln and barkhouse with their appurtenances, from me and my heirs, to the said John and his heirs and assigns, from the feast of the Annunciation of the blessed

Virgin Mary in the year of the reign of King Edward the third after the conquest, the fourteenth [25 March 1340] up to the end of the ten years next following, to be fully completed. Rendering from it annually to me and my heirs nine shillings and six pence of silver by equal portions at the four annual terms usual in Coventry. So that I, the said Geoffrey and my heirs, shall keep in competent repair against wind and rain the said messuage and solar and kiln at our own expense. And if it happens that the said John, his heirs or assigns, constructs or repairs any building or privy on the said plot of land, then the said John, his heirs or assigns, at the end of the said ten years, may take them away without any prohibition, unless competent allowance or satisfaction is made by the view and consideration of trustworthy and lawful neighbours. And I truly, the said Geoffrey and my heirs do warrant and defend the said messuage [etc.] to the end of the said ten years, to the said John and his heirs or assigns according to the aforesaid form against all people. In witness of which things [to] this indented writing [I] have as much my seal as the seal of the said John alternately attached. These are witnesses [names]

4.4. Seventeenth-century Lease (of a Lease and Release) for a House in Derby (p. 99)

This indenture made the twentieth day of May in the fourthe yeare of the raigne of our Soveraigne Lord and Lady William and Mary by the grace of God of England, Scotland, France and Ireland, king and queen, defenders of the faith, etc., annoque domini 1692: BETWEENE John Jackson of Derby in the county of Derby, cordwainer, of the one parte and Roberte Brookhouse of Derby aforesaid in the said county, feltmaker, of the other parte WITNESSETH that the said John Jackson for and in consideracion of the sume of five shillings of lawfull English money to him in hand paid att and befor the ensealeinge and delivery hereof, the receipt whereof hee the said John Jackson doth hereby acknowledge and confesse HATH demised, leased, bargained and sold and by these presents doth demise, lease, bargaine and sell unto the said Roberte Brookhouse his executors, administrators and assignes ALL that his messuage burgage or tenement with a garden and backside to the same belonging situate and being in the parish of St Peter in the borough of Derby aforesaid and now in the possession of him the said John Jackson his assignee or assignes, tenants or undertenants, the house of Joseph Shilton now in the possession of Thomas Brookhouse being on the south thereof and the house of William Wragge being on the North thereof, together with all houses, outhouses, edifices, buildings, barnes, stables, orchards, gardens, yards, backsides, ways, waters, easements, priviledges, profitts, commons, comodytyes, advantages, hereditaments and appurtenances whatsoever to the said messuage, burgage or tenement and all other the premises above demised with their and every of their appurtenances and to every or any parte thereof belonging or in anywise apperteininge, TO HAVE AND TO HOLD the said messuage, burgage or tenement and all other the premises above demised with their and every of their appurtenances unto the said Roberte Brookhouse his executors, administrators and assignes from the day of the date hereof unto the full end and terme of one whole year from thence next ensueinge and fully to be compleate and ended YEILDINGE and payinge therefore dureinge the said terme unto the said John Jackson his heires or assignes the rent of one peppercorne upon the feast of St Michaell the Archangell if the same bee lawfully demanded, to the intent that by virtue hereof and of the statute for transferringe of uses into possession hee the said Roberte Brookhouse may bee in the actuall possession of the said premises and may bee enabled to accept of and take a grant and release of the revercion and inheritance thereof to him and his heires for ever IN WITNESSE whereof the parties above named to these present indentures have interchangeably putt their hands and seales the day and yeare first above written. [Signed and sealed by] John Jackson

4.5. Seventeenth-century Terrier of Open-field Land in Thurlaston, Warwickshire, Attached to a Deed of 1616 (p. 106)

A trewe and perfecte Terrur containeinge the dwellinge howse, with thappurtennces, and all the landes, leyes, meadowe and pasture of one Henrie Bromfeild of Thurleston in the countie of Warr' yeoman, belongeinge unto or occupied with the said dwelling howse, and all comons for beasse, sheepe and horses accordinge to the scale and stinte of the same lande examined and allowed by the steward and homage theire att the courte then holden the seventh daie of October in the yeare of the raigne of our soveraigne lorde James the kinges majestie that now ys of England the seventh and of Scotland the xliiith 1609.

Inprimis the foresaid dwellinge howse, one yard land, threescore sheepe common, eight beasse comons, foure horses or mares & one breeder, one closse, one orchard, one garden adioyninge to the said howse next the comon of Thurleston of thone side and one Thomas Smyth of thother side

The East Feylde or Breach Feylde

Item one Roode lyeinge one [on] Breach Furlonge buttinge into London Waie and to Cawson Hedge betwene the land in the occupacion of Roberte Atkins on the east side & the land in the occupacion of Elizabeth Bucknoll, widdowe on the west side.

Item one other lande lyeinge on the same furlonge buttinge into London Waye betwene Thomas Smyth of the easte side and the land in the occupacion of Richard Sale of the west side

Item five roodes lyeinge on Crosse Furlonge buttinge into London waye betwene Thomas Smyth of the east side and the land in the occupacion of Richard Sale of the west side

Item one other land lyeinge on the same furlonge buttinge into London waie betwen the land in the occupacion of John Guppill of the easte side and the land in the occupacion of Elizabeth Bucknoll of the weste side

Item one acre on Little Crosse Furlonge lyeinge betwene the lande of Thomas Marris on the south side and the lande in the occupacion of Elizabeth Bucknoll on the [south, erased] north side

4.6. Seventeenth-century Bond for Keeping Covenants in a Deed of the Same Date (p. 113)

[First portion in Latin] Noverint universi per presentes me Thomam Dutton de / Civitatis Londiniensis, corne chandler, teneri et firmiter / obligari Leonardo Dutton senior, (patris mei dictis Thomae) de / Oakley in parochia Chynner in Comitatis Oxon', yeoman, in / sexcentis libris bonae et legalis monetae Angliae, solvendis eidem / Leonardo Dutton aut suo certo attornato executoris administratoris / vel assignis suis, ad quam quidem solucionem bene et fideliter faciendam, / obligo me, heredes, executores et administratores meos firmiter per / presentes sigillo meo sigillati, dato tertio die mensis Decembris / anno regni Guilelmi et Mariae Regis et Reginae Angliae etc. / secundo, annoque domini 1698.

Translation:
Know all by these presents, that I, Thomas Dutton of the City of London, corn chandler, am bound and firmly obliged to Leonard Dutton, senior (father of me the said Thomas) of Oakley in the parish of Chynner in the county of Oxford, yeoman, in six hundred pounds of good and legal money of England, to pay the same Leondard Dutton or his certain attorney, his executors administrators or assignes, to well and faithfully making of which payment, I firmly bind myself, my heirs, executors and administrators by these presents, sealed with my seal, Given the third day of December [etc.] and in the year of our Lord 1688.

[The condition continues in English]
The condition of this obligacion is such that if the above bounden Thomas Dutton, his heires executors administrators and assignes shall and doe well and truly observe performe fullfill and keepe

all and singular the covenants graunts articles clauses sentences & agreements which on his & theire and every of theire parts and behalf are or ought to be observed performed fulfilled kept and don, comprised written and contained in one certaine indenture bearing the same date with these presents and made betweene the said Thomas Dutton of the one part, and the above named Leonard Dutton of the other part, and that in all things according to the effect, purport intent and true meaning of the same indenture, then this obligacion shall be void & of none effect, or els remain in full force and vertue.

Signed, sealed and delivered in the Presence of	Thomas Dutton [written against seal]
James Thompson, William Freer, Leonard Dutton junior	Christian Dutton

4.7. Seventeenth-century Final Concord ('Fine') for a Messuage in Coventry (p. 120)

Hec est finalis concordia facta in curia domini Regis apud Westmonasterium in Octavis Sancti Hilarii Anno Regnorum Jacobi Dei gratia Angli Scotie Francie et / Hibernie Regis fidei defensoris etc, Angli Francie et Hibernie undecimo et Scotie quadragesimo septimo, coram Henrici Hobarte, Petro Warburton, Humfrido Winche / et Augustino Nicolls justiciariis et aliis domino Regis fidelibus tunc ibi presentibus, Inter Willemus Wightwicke querens et Thomam Kildermer et Margeriam / uxorem eius deforciantes de uno mesuagio uno gardino et uno pomario cum pertinentiis in parochia Sancti Michaelis unde placitum convencionis summonitum fuit inter / eos in eadem curia, Scilicet quod predicti Thomas et Margeria recognoverunt predictam tenementam cum pertinentiis esse ius ipsius Willelmi ut illud que idem Willelmus / habebit de dono predictorum Thome et Margerie et illi remiserunt et quietclamaverunt de ipsis Thoma et Margeria et heredibus suis predicto Willelmo et /

heredibus suis in perpetuum, Et preterea iidem Thomas et Margeria concesserunt pro se et heredes ipsius Thome quod ipsi warantizabunt predicto Willelmo et / heredibus suis predictam tenementam cum pertinentiis contra predictos Thomam et Margeriam et heredes ipsius Thome in perpetuum, Et pro hac recognitione remissione / quietclamatione warantia fine et concordia, idem Willelmus dedit predictis Thome et Margerie quadraginta et unam libras sterlingorum.

TRANSLATION:
This is the final agreement made in the court of the lord king at Westminster in the octave of St Hilary [i.e. the spring Law Term, starting on 20 January, a week after the saint's feast] in the year of the reign of James by the grace of God King of England, Scotland, France, and Ireland, defender of the faith, etc., of England France and Ireland the eleventh, and of Scotland the forty seventh [1614], before Henry Hobarte, Peter Warburton, Humphrey Winche, and Augustine Nicolls, justices, and other faithful (subjects) of the lord King there then present, Between William Wightwicke, plaintiff; and Thomas Kildermer and Margery his wife, defendants, of one messuage, one garden, and one orchard with their appurtenances in the parish of St Michael [Coventry], concerning which a plea of covenant was summoned between them in the same court, To wit that the said Thomas and Margery have recognised that the said tenement with its appurtenances is of the right of of the same William, as that which the same William had of the gift of the said Thomas and Margery, and they remise and quitclaim for the same Thomas and Margery and their heirs to the said Williamm and his heirs for ever, And further, the same Thomas and Margery grant for them and the heirs of the same Thomas that they will warrant the said tenement with its appurtenances to the said William and his heirs against the said Thomas and Margery and the heirs of the same Thomas for ever, and for this acknowledgment, remission,

quitclaim, warranty, fine, and agreement, the same William gave the said Thomas and Margery forty-one pounds sterling.

4.10 Endorsement Recording an Enrolment in Chancery (p. 129)

[initial flourish probably for *Irrotulatus*] in dors' claus' cancellar' infrascriptis / domini regis vicesimo secundo die maii anno infrascripto / per Johannem Lewes

TRANSLATION:
Enrolled on the dorse of the close [rolls understood] of the chancery of the within-written lord king on the 22nd day of May, the year within-written, by John Lewes.
[Below: Ex[aminatus?] confirming that the enrolment has been checked; Rex et Tumberlake et al. (the parties to the lease). The various other annotations probably refer to lists of the owners' deeds]

4.11. Medieval Gift (p. 140)

4.12. Fifteenth-century Letter of Attorney (p. 150)

Noverint universi per presentes me dominum Johannem Bewchamp militem attornasse et loco meo apposuisse dilectos mihi in Christo / Johannem Wilde capitale ballivum meum de Alcestr' ac Thomam Freston et Rogerum Smythe sub-ballivos de eadem meos / veros et legittimos attornatos ad deliberandum Thome Madley de Alcestre, bocher, plenam et pacificam pocessionem de et in / una parcella terre condam [*quondam*] vacua et nunc per ipsum Thomam de novo edificata in Colbroke in villa de Alcestr' infra / comitatum Warwick', habendum et tenendum predictam parcellam terre cum pertinenciis predicto Thome, et Agnete uxori eius et heredibus inter / predictos Thomam et Agnetem legittime procreatis iuxta vim formam et effectam quarundam indenturarum inter prefatum dominum et /

dictum Thomam inde confectarum. Ratum habiturum et gratum, quicquid iidem attornati mei aut duo eorum fecerint / in premissis sicut ego prefatus dominus personaliter interessem proviso semper quod dictus capitalis ballivus meus sit / unus illorum duorum. In cuius rei testimonium huic scripto meo atornati sigillum meum aposui. Datum apud / Alcestre predicto, tercio die mencis Septembris anno regni regis Edwardi quarti post conquestum duodecimo.

TRANSLATION:
Know all men by these presents that I Lord John Bewchamp, knight, attourn and in my place appoint the beloved to me in Christ John Wilde, my chief bailiff of Alcester, and Thomas Freston and Roger Smythe, sub-bailiffs of the same, my true and legitimate attorneys to deliver to Thomas Madley of Alcester, butcher, full and peaceable possession of and in one parcel of formerly vacant land, now newly built on by the same Thomas in Colbroke in the town of Alcester within the county of Warwick, to have and to hold the said parcel of land, to the same Thomas, Agnes his wife, and the heirs of the said Thomas and Agnes between them legitimately begotten, following the form and effect of certain indentures between the said lord and the said Thomas, made. And that I will hold as accepted and agreed whatsoever those my attorneys or two of them shall do in this matter as if I the said lord were present in person provided always that my said chief bailiff shall be one of those two. In witness whereof, I have affixed my seal to this my writing of attorney, dated at Alcester aforesaid, the third day of the month of September in the l2th year of the reign of King Edward the fourth after the conquest [1472].

4.13. Eighteenth-century Copy of Court Roll (p. 153)
The Manor of Weston on the Green in the County of Oxford
The view of frank pledge of our lord the King with the court baron of Norreys Bertie esquire, Lord of the manor aforesaid, there

holden on Monday the twelfth day of October 1741, before Robert Launder, general steward of the said manor.

At this court came Stephen Hanks and did take of the lord of the manor aforesaid one messuage and orchard and garden with the appurtenances in Weston on the Green aforesaid, late in the tenure of Henry Cox and thereupon at this court the Lord of the manor aforesaid by his steward aforesaid did grant and deliver to him seisin by the rod TO HAVE AND TO HOLD the aforesaid messuage orchard and garden and premises with the appurtenances to the aforesaid Stephen Hanks and Samuel Hanks his eldest son for the term of their lives and the life of the longest liver of them successively at the will of the lord according to the custom of the said manor, rendering therefore yearly two pence at the times there usuall and ten shillings and sixpence for an herriot when it shall happen and doing suite of court and all other services and customs therefore formerly due and of right accustomed, and gave to the lord for a fine for such his estate and entry twenty pounds, so thereof to be had as between them is agreed and did fealty and was admitted tenant thereof.

A true copy examined with the roll by me Rob Launder, steward of the said manor

4.14. Eighteenth-century Memorandum for Enrolment on the Manor Court Roll of Allesley, Warwickshire (p. 157)

Manor of Allesley. Memorandum that on the eleventh day of August in the twenty third year of the Reign of our Sovereign Lord George the second by the Grace of God of Great Britain, France and Ireland King, Defender of the Faith and so forth and in the year of our Lord One thousand seven hundred and forty nine, Samuel Crichlowe of the City of Coventry, Wollen Draper, one of the Customary Tennants of the Manor aforesaid and Alley his wife (the said Alley being first secretly Examined by James Birch, Gentleman, Steward there and thereto consenting) Did out of Court according to the Custome of the said Manor and hereby

Doe surrender by the Rod into the hands of the Lord of the said Manor by the Hands of the said James Birch, All those Customary Messuages, Lands, Tenements and Hereditaments with the appurtenances scituate, lying and being in Allesley aforesaid, being part of the Copyhold Tenements of the said Manor and now or late in the occupation of Thomas Rowe and Joanna Jefferys or one of them, their or one of their assignee or assigns, To the use and behoof of William Gilbert of the City of Coventry aforesaid, Tammy Merchant, his heirs and assigns for ever according to the custom of the said Manor by the Rents and services therefore Due and of Right accustomed, Provided always nevertheless and upon this condition that if the said Samuel Crichlowe his heirs, executors or administrators do and shall well and truly pay or cause to be paid unto the said William Gilbert, his executors, administrators or assigns, the full and just sum of four hundred and eight pounds of lawfull money of Great Britain upon the nineth day of February next without any Deduction or abatement whatsoever for and on account of Taxes or otherwise howsoever, That then this surrender shall be Void and of none Effect or else to be and remain in full force and Virtue.

[signed] Sam Crichlowe

This surrender was duly taken and Alley Crichlowe acknowledged before me [signed] Ja Birch known & Steward of the said Manor

4.16. Fifteenth-century Copy of Court Roll from the Manor of Audley, Staffordshire (p. 160)

Audeley

Curiam tentam ibidem die martis proxime post festum Sancti Valantini anno regno regis Henrici sexti xxiiij^{to}, venit Stephanus / Roulegh et sursum reddidit in manis domini iij quarter unius acram terre customarii in Audeley vocatus Goslez / Croftes. Et super hoc in eadem curia venerunt idem Stephanus et Margareta uxor eius et inde ceperunt seisinam / tenendum sibi et suis secundum consuetudinem manerii et dant ad ingressum ixd

Ad dictam curiam venerunt Stephanus / Roulegh et Margareta uxor eius et ceperunt de domino seisinam de uno / tofto et v acris terre custumare in Audeley vocato Hychefeld et lez acris que dictus Stephanus perquisit de Petro Riges et que dictus Petrus nuper in curia sursum reddidit in manis domini ad opus dictum Stephanum, ut per manis / Thome Peke prepositum ibidem, tenendum sibi et suis secundum consuetudinem manerii et dant ad ingressum xs. In cuius rei testimonium Johannes Harryson, locum tenens senescalli ibidem huic copia sigillum suis apposuit / dat' etc.

TRANSLATION:
Audeley
Court held there on Tuesday next after the feast of St Valentine, the year of the reign of King Henry VI, 24th, came Stephen Roulegh and surrendered into the hands of the lord three quarters of an acre of customary land in Audeley called Goslez Croftes. And above this, in the same court came the same Stephen and Margaret his wife and then took seisin, to hold to him and his according to the custom of the manor and gave for admission 9d.

At the same court came Stephen Roulegh and Margaret his wife and took from the lord seisin of one toft and 5 acres of customary land in Audeley, called Hychefeld, the acres which the said Stephen purchased from Peter Riges and which the said Peter formerly surrendered in to the hands of the lord to the use of the said Stephen, as by the hands of Thomas Peke, reeve there, to hold to him and his according to the custom of the manor and gave for admission 10s. In witness of which things, John Harryson holding the place of the steward there to this copy has placed his seal, dated, etc. [With seal on a side tag]

2. EXAMPLE OF A RELEASE
Seventeenth-century Release (of a Lease and Release)
[Introduction and date] This indenture made the sixteenth day of

March in the thirtyeth yeare of the raigne of our Sovereign Lord Charles the Second by the grace of God, of England, Scotland, France and Ireland, Kinge, defender of the faith, etc. annoque domini 1677

[Parties] BETWEENE Samuell Hope of the Citty of Coventry in the county of the same city, tayler, Richard Palmer of the Citty of Coventry aforesaid, tayler, and Mary his wife, and Hanna Hope of the Citty of Coventry aforesaid, spinster, sisters of the said Samuell Hope of the one part, and Michael Mann of Tamworth in the county of Warwicke, clothworker, of the other part WITNESSETH that they the said Samuell Hope, Richard Palmer and Mary his wife, and Hannah Hope [Consideration] for and in consideration of the summe of seaven and twenty pounds of good and lawfull money of England, to them or one of them well and truely in hand paid by the said Michaell Mann before the ensealinge and delivery of these presents

[Action] HAVE and every of them hath graunted, bargained, sold, alyened, released, and confirmed, and by these presents doe and every of them doth graunte, bargaine, sell, alyen, releas, and confirm unto the said Michaell Mann, his heires and assigns

[Property: The detailed property clause of this deed is given on p. 67; it continues as follows] With all houses, edifices, buildings, shopps, entryes, watercourses, profitts, and commodities whatsoever thereunto belonging or appurteyninge, and the revercion and revercions, remainder and remainders, of all and singuler the premisses, and all the estate, right, tytle, use, interest, possession, clayme, and demaunde whatsoever of them the said Samuell Hope, Richard Palmer and Mary his wife, and the said Hanna Hope and of every and either of them, of, in, and to the same premisses and every part thereof with the appurtenances

[Recital of the preceding lease] all which said premisses with the appurtenances were by them the said Samuell Hope, Richard Palmer and Mary his wife, and the said Hanna Hope for the better

Appendix 4

execution of these presents by their indenture of lease by them duely executed and beareinge date the day next before the day of the date of these presents for the considerations therein mentioned, graunted, bargained and sold unto the said Michaell Mann, his executors, administrators, and assigns for the term of six months from thence next ensueing and followinge fully to bee compleate and ended att and under the rent of one peppercorne only payable att or upon the feast of St Michaell the Archangell next ensueinge the date thereof, as in and by the said recited indenture relacion beinge thereunto had, itt may more att large appeare

[Term, uses and tenure] TO HAVE AND TO HOLD the said messuage or tenement and premisses hereby graunted and released with theire and every of theire appurtenances unto the said Michaell Mann, his heires and assignes for ever, to the only proper and absolute use and behoofe of the said Michaell Mann and of his heires and assigns for ever, To be held of the cheife Lord or Lords of the fee or fees of the aforesaid premises by the rents and services therefore heretofore due and of right accustomed

[Covenant of good title] AND the said Samuell Hope for himselfe, his heires and assignes and every of them doth covenaunte and graunt to and with the said Michaell Mann, his heires and assignes and every of them by these presents, that hee the said Samuell Hope att the time of the ensealeinge and delivery of these presents for and notwithstandinge any act or thinge by him the saide Samuell Hope or by the said Thomas Hope, father of the said Samuell Hope (party to these presents) or either of them doth to the contrary hereafter, hee the said Samuell Hope now is and standeth lawfully rightfully and absolutely seized of and in the aforesaid messuage or tenement and premisses with theire and every of their appurtenances and of and in every part and parcell thereof, of a good, sure, perfect, lawfull, absolute and indefeizable estate of inheritance in fee simple or fee tayle generall, without any manner of condicion, mortgage, or limitation of use or uses, or other matter or thinge whatsoever to alter, change, charge, incumber, determine, or make void the same estate

[Of authority to make the grant] And that he the said Samuell Hope att the time of the ensealinge and delivery of these presents for and notwithstandinge any act, matter or thinge, charge or incumbrance whatsoever by him the said Samuell Hope or by the said Thomas Hope done to the contrary hereof, hee the said Samuell Hope hath good right, full power, and lawfull authority in his owne righte to graunt, bargaine, sell, releas, and confirm the hereinbefore graunted and released premisses with theire and every of theire appurtenances, unto the said Michael Mann, his heires and assignes for ever

[Of quiet enjoyment] And that he the said Michaell Mann his heires and assigns shall and may from time to time and att all times hereafter have, hold, use, occupy, possesse, and enjoy the said messuage or tenement and premisses with theire and every of theire appurtenances, and receive and take the rents, issues, and profitts thereof and of every part thereof, free and cleere and freely and cleerely acquitted, exonerated and discharged, or from time to time and att all times hereafter upon reasonable request well and sufficiently to bee saved, kept harmelesse, and indempnified by he said Samuell Hope, his heires and assignes off and from all and all manner of former and other guifts, graunts, bargaines, sales, leases, estates, joyntures, dower, tytles, and tytle of dower, uses, wills, intayles, rents charge, rents secke, arrearages of rent and rents, Statutes Merchant and of the Staple, recognizances, fines, issues, amerciamentes, seizures, judgments, executions, and of and from all other charges, tytles, troubles, incumbrances and demands whatsoever, had, made, committed, done or suffered to bee done or hereafter to bee had, made, committed, done or sufferred to bee done by him the said Samuell Hope, his heires or assignes or by the said Thomas Hope, his heires or assignes or any of them, or by any other person claymeing by from or under theire or either of their right tytles or interests

Appendix 4

[To levy a fine] AND they the said Samuell Hope, Richard Palmer [Mary Palmer's name was erased here], and the said Hannah Hope for themselves, theire heires and assignes and every of them jointly and severally do convenaunte, promise and graunt to and with the said Michaell Mann his heires and assignes and every of them by these presents, That they the said Samuell Hope, Richard Palmer and Mary his wife, and the said Hanna Hope shall and wilt before the end of Easter Terme next ensueing the date hereof acknowledge and levy unto the said Michaell Mann his heires and assignes in due forme of law one Fine *sur Cognizance de Droit come ceo*, etc. with proclamations to be thereupon had according to the forme of the Statute in that case made and provided, Of the said messuage or tenement and all and singuler ther the premisses with the appurtenances as by the said Michaell Mann, his heires or assigns or his or theire councell learned in the law shall be reasonably devised or advised and required and att the proper costs and charges in the law of the said Michael Mann, his heires or assignes, Which said fine soe as aforesaid intended to bee levyed of the aforesaid premises shall bee and enure and shalbe adjudged, deemed, consstrained and taken to bee and to enure to the only proper and absolute and behoofe of the said Michaell Mann, his heires and assignes for ever, and to or for noe other use, intent or purpose whatsoever

[Witness] IN WITNESS whereof the parties first above named to these present indentures have interchangeably sett their hands and seales the day and yeare first above written.

    Samuell Hope
    The mark of Richard Palmer
    The mark of Mary Palmer
    The marke of Hanna Hope

[Endorsed with a receipt for the purchase price and with two notes witnessing the signing and sealing] [Deed in private ownership]

FURTHER RESOURCES AND SELECT BIBLIOGRAPHY

Website addresses are correct at the time of writing, but they frequently change and, if they fail to work, you will need to search for the site.

GUIDES TO DEEDS

Cornwall, J., *An Introduction to Reading Old Title Deeds* (Federation of Family History Societies, 1997).

Dibben, A.A. (ed. Clive H. Knowles), *Title Deeds, 13th–19th Centuries* (Historical Association, 1990).

Foster, A., 'Conveyancing Practice from Local Records', *Thoresby Society*, Vol. 12 (1948), 197.

Kaye, J.M., *Medieval English Conveyances* (Cambridge University Press, 2009).

Meekings, C.A.F. and P. Shearman (eds), 'Fitznell's Cartulary', *Surrey Record Society*, Vol. 26 (1968).

Pugh, R.B. (ed.), 'A Calendar of Antrobus Deeds to 1624', *Wiltshire Record Society*, Vol. 3 (1947).

Wormleighton, Tim, *Title Deeds for Family Historians* (Family History Partnership, 2012).

PROPERTY LAW AND LEGAL HISTORY

Davidson, Charles, *Concise Precedents in Conveyancing* (1845) (e-book: https://books.google.co.uk/books?id=51EaAAAAYAAJ)

Holdsworth, W.S., *An Historical Introduction to the Land Law* (Oxford University Press, 1935) (e-book, 1927 edn: https://catalog.hathi trust. org/Record/001323726).

Horsman, Gilbert, *Precedents in Conveyancing* (3rd edn, 1768).

Jacob, G., *New Law Dictionary* (1729 and later edns) (e-book: https://archive.org/details/newlawdictionar00jacouoft).

Jones, F.C., *Attorney's Pocket Book* (1841).
Pollock, F., *The Land Laws* (Macmillan, 1883 and later edns).

PALAEOGRAPHY
Grieve, H.E., *Examples of English Handwriting, 1150–1750* (Essex Record Office, 1954 and later edns).
Hector, L.C., *The Handwriting of English Documents* (2nd edn, 1980).
Ison, Alf, *A Secretary Hand ABC Book* (Family History Partnership, 1982). The best short guide to Tudor and Stuart handwriting.
Jenkinson, H., *The Later Court Hands in England from the 15th to the 17th Century* (Cambridge University Press, 1927).
Johnson, C. and H. Jenkinson, *English Court Hand, A.D. 1066–1500* (Cambridge University Press, 1915).
Marshall, Hilary, *Palaeography for Family and Local Historians* (Phillimore, 2010).
Newton, K.C., *Medieval Local Records: A Reading Aid* (Historical Association, 1971).
'Palaeography: Reading Old Handwriting, 1500–1800, A Practical Online Tutorial', http://www.nationalarchives.gov.uk/palaeography/.

LATIN AND LATIN TEXT INTERPRETATION
Gooder, E.A., *Latin for Local History* (Longmans, 1978).
Latham, R.E. (ed.), *Revised Medieval Latin Word List* (Oxford University Press, 1983).
Martin, C.T., *The Record Interpreter* (repr. Phillimore & Co., 1982).
Morris, Janet, *A Latin Glossary for Local and Family Historians* (Family History Partnership, 2009).
Stuart, Denis, *Latin for Local and Family Historians* (Phillimore & Co., 1995). Includes a chapter on translating deed texts.
Westcott, Brooke, *Making Sense of Latin Documents for Family & Local Historians* (Family History Partnership, 2014).

DATING
Cheney, C.R. (rev. by Michael Jones), *A Handbook of Dates For Students of British History* (Royal Historical Society Guides and Handbooks, Cambridge University Press, 2000).

SEALS
Harvey, P.D.A. and Andrew McGuinness, *A Guide to British Medieval Seals* (British Library and Public Record Office, 1996).

Jenkinson, H., *Guide to Seals in the Public Record Office* (HMSO, 1968).

McEwan, John and Elizabeth New, *Seals in Context: Medieval Wales and the Welsh Marches* (CAA Aberystwyth University, 2012).

New, Elizabeth A., *Seals and Sealing Practices* (British Records Association, Archives and the User, 11, 2010).

Williams, D.H., *Welsh History through Seals* (National Museum of Wales, 1982).

MANORIAL RECORDS
Ellis, Mary, *Using Manorial Records* (Public Record Office, 1994).

Harvey, P.D.A., *Manorial Records* (British Records Association, rev. edn 1999).

Palgrave-Moore, Patrick, *How to Locate and Use Manorial Records* (Elvery Dowers, 1985).

Park, Peter B., *My Ancestors were Manorial Tenants* (Society of Genealogists, 1994).

Stuart, Denis, *Manorial Records: an Introduction to their Transcription and Translation* (Phillimore, 1992). Little information on copyhold.

BACKGROUND TO DEEDS AND ASPECTS OF THEM
Clanchy, M.T., *From Memory to Written Record* (2nd edn, Blackwell, 1993).

Clay, C., 'Landlords and Estate Management', in J. Thirsk (ed.), *The Agrarian History of England and Wales: Vol. 5, 1640–1750* (Cambridge University Press, 1985), Part II, pp. 119–251.

English, B. and J. Saville, *Strict Settlement: A Guide for Historians* (University of Hull, 1983).

Hoskins, W.G., *The Midland Peasant* (Leicester University Press, 1965).

Keene, D., 'The Medieval Urban Environment in Documentary Records', *Archives*, 16 (1983), 137–44.

Further Resources and Select Bibliography

NATIONAL ORGANISATIONS (AND THEIR ONLINE MANUSCRIPT CATALOGUES)

Bodleian Library, Oxford OX1 3BG (an incomplete catalogue: http://www.bodley.ox.ac.uk/dept/scwmss/wmss/online/online.htm).

British Library, Department of Manuscripts, 96 Euston Road, London NW1 2DB (http://searcharchives.bl.uk).

Cambridge University Library, West Road, Cambridge CB3 9DR (http://www.lib.cam.ac.uk/deptserv/manuscripts/collections.html. https://janus.lib.cam.ac.uk/ provides a search over many Cambridge archives including the University Special Collections).

The National Archives, Ruskin Avenue, Kew, Richmond, Surrey TW9 4DU includes: Discovery: http://discovery.nationalarchives.gov.uk/advanced-search; Manorial Documents Register: http://discovery.nationalarchives.gov.uk/manor-search. The National Register of Archives is part of TNA. For information about its holdings, search Discovery under 'Record Creators'.

National Library of Wales, Aberystwyth, Dyfed SY23 3BU (https://archives.library.wales).

RECORD OFFICES

See under National Organisations: The National Archives, National Register of Archives. For record office addresses, etc. use TNA's 'Find an Archive': http://discovery.nationalarchives.gov.uk/find-an-archive.

Folger Shakespeare Library: *Catalogue of Manuscripts* (G.K. Hall, 1971).

Foster, J. and J. Sheppard, *British Archives* (Macmillan, 1982 and later edns).

Guide to British Historical Manuscripts in the Huntington Library (Huntington Library, San Marino, 1982).

Harvard University Law Library: http://www.law.harvard.edu/library/special/collections/manuscripts/deeds/index.htm.

University of Nottingham: The Manuscripts and Special Collections Department have produced a particularly useful guide to title deeds: http://www.nottingham.ac.uk/manuscriptsandspecialcollections/researchguidance/deeds/introduction.aspx.

OTHER ORGANISATIONS AND RESOURCES

Canal and River Trust: For deeds relating to canal property, contact in the first instance their archives, at The National Waterways Museum, South Pier Road, Ellesmere Port, CH65 4FW (http://collections.canalrivertrust.org.uk/home).

Network Rail: Freedom of Information Requests: Network Rail, Freedom of Information Team, 1st Floor Willen, The Quadrant, Elder Gate, Milton Keynes MK9 1EN (FOI@networkrail.co.uk), https://www.networkrail.co.uk/who-we-are/transparency-and-ethics/freedom-information-foi/.

The Society of Genealogists, 14 Charterhouse Buildings, Goswell Road, London EC1M 7BA.

Web source: Notes on Medieval English Genealogy: Medieval Source Material on the Internet: charters
http://www.medievalgenealogy.org.uk/sources/charters.shtml
(includes links to various lists and abstracts of deeds).

GLOSSARY OF DEED TERMS

Abstract of Title Summary of prior ownership, prepared when a property was about to be sold.

Abuttal Names of owners or tenants of property adjoining that involved in a deed, recorded as an aid to identification.

Assignment Transfer of a right, usually a lease, or a mortgage; **assignment to attend the inheritance**: assignment of the residue of a mortgage term to a trustee, after the mortgage has been paid off.

Attorney See **Letter of Attorney**

Bargain and Sale Deed (usually sixteenth-century) transferring property, rendered valid by **Enrolment**. Also used in the action clause of a **Lease for a Year**.

Bond (also **Recognisance**) Agreement to pay a financial penalty if specified conditions are not met. A **Recognisance in the nature of a Statute Staple** or **Statute Merchant** was a strong form of bond that was normally cancelled by a separate deed, the **Defeasance of a Recognisance**.

Burgage Tenure Type of tenure in a borough, similar in its rights to **Freehold**, often involving the payment of a uniform burgage rent for each plot.

Cartulary Volume containing copies of deeds (often with other material), most often compiled by a monastery.

Consideration The purchase money for a property.

Copy of Court Roll Copy of entry on roll of manor court proceedings, recording admission of a **Copyhold** tenant to his holding, and serving as a title deed.

Copyhold Property held by copy of court roll.

Counterpart The second half of an indenture, precisely matching the first part; usually used for the second copy of a lease, signed by the tenant and retained by the grantor.

Covenant An agreement entered into by one of the parties to a deed; a **covenant for production of title deeds** is an agreement to produce deeds not being handed over to a purchaser.

Coverture The legal status of a married woman, by which all her property was held by her husband.

Curtilage Yard or court associated with a dwelling house.

Defeasance See **Bond**.

Dower The right of a widow to a third of her late husband's property; a dower trustee might hold it on his behalf to prevent a claim for dower.

Dowry A woman's marriage portion.

Endorsement The writing on the back (*dorse*) of a deed.

Enrolment The copy of a deed on a roll kept by a court as a permanent record.

Entail The settlement of property so that it must descend to the owner's heirs in a specified fashion, and not be sold or otherwise disposed of. The current owner of entailed property is the **tenant for life** and his next heir is the **tenant in tail**.

Equity of Redemption The right of a mortgagor to redeem the property he has mortgaged, even if the due time for repayment has passed; this right could be granted to someone else.

Executor The person appointed to carry out the provisions of a will.

Exemplification Formal copy of a court record issued with the court's seal. The most common exemplifications are those of **Recoveries** (See **Recovery**) but **Exemplifications of Fines** are sometimes found, as are exemplifications of Chancery decrees or proceedings.

Fee-farm See **Rent**.

Feoffee See **Trustee**.

Feoffment A simple grant of property.

Fine (a) Entry Fine: sum of money paid for the granting of a lease or for admission to a copyhold tenement; (b) Final Concord: record of a collusive court case in the Court of Common Pleas, provided as two matching copies (Left- and Right-hand Indentures of Fine); the Foot of Fine is the third copy of the record, kept by the Court; **Deed to Lead the Uses of a Fine**: agreement to levy a fine, declaring the uses for which the property is held.

Glossary of Deed Terms

Freehold Tenure **in fee simple**, i.e. absolute and unlimited, though possibly paying a fixed rent (a chief rent or fee-farm rent).

Gift Any transfer of real property in the medieval period is described as a gift, in contrast to a grant of rights, such as tithes.

Grant See **Gift, Reversion**.

Heriot A fine paid on the death of a tenant holding by copy or by a lease for more than one life in succession (e.g. a three-life lease). The heriot was either a sum of money (often a year's chief rent) or the best beast or best possession. For a freeholder, the similar payment was known as a **Relief** (q.v.).

Indenture Deeds with the top indented, in principle prepared in two or more identical copies, one for each party; see **Counterpart**.

Knight Service The feudal tenure of a manor, by providing the service of a knight or part of one (or in the post-medieval period, by a payment in lieu of this).

Lease Grant of property to a tenant for a specified period, usually a term of years; types of lease include **life lease**: lease for the life of the tenant; **three-life lease**: lease until the deaths have occurred of three named people (with an upper limit of ninety-nine years); **'perpetual' lease**: intended to continue indefinitely, granted for a very long period, e.g. 1,000 years; **building lease**: generally a ninety-nine year lease including an agreement for the tenant to build a house. See **Reversion**; **Counterpart**.

Lease and Release Post-medieval transfer of property by granting a **Lease for a year** (sometimes six months), and then a **Release** of the grantor's rights the following day; the **Release** contains the detailed information about the transaction.

Leasehold Tenure by lease.

Letter of Attorney Deed establishing a substitute to act for one of the parties in a transaction, in the medieval period usually to grant or receive **Seisin**. Often recorded in manor court rolls when the local solicitor might surrender or be admitted to property on behalf of the owner.

Letters Patent (always in the plural) Royal grant, enrolled on the Patent Rolls.

Licence to Alienate Royal permission, by letters patent, to sell or dispose of a property held from the Crown by knight service.

Messuage Standard term for a property including a dwelling house.

Moiety Half of a property, often **undivided moiety**, when the shares of the two owners have not been separated or physically divided.

Partition Division of a property between two or more interested parties.

Portmanteau Fine (or Recovery) A Final Concord in which two or more unrelated parties are involved. Recognisable from the **Deed to lead the uses of a fine**, in which the various properties conveyed to the trustee are held to the use of the different parties; also (rare) a similar recovery.

Precipe See **Recovery**.

Probate The establishment of the validity of a will in a church court, recorded in the **grant of probate**.

Quitclaim Deed renouncing any possible right to a property.

Recital Rehearsal of prior event and deeds affecting a property being transferred.

Recognisance See **Bond**.

Recovery Collusive law suit in the Court of Common Pleas, normally used to destroy (bar) or alter an entail; its result are recorded in an **Exemplification** of a (Common) Recovery; **The Deed to make a Tenant to the Precipe** precedes a Recovery, transferring the property involved to a trustee and declaring the uses for which it is held.

Regnal Year The current year of a king's reign, counting from his accession, used as the means of dating deeds until the mid-seventeenth century.

Release See **Lease and Release**.

Relief Manorial payment from a freeholding required for the heir to inherit or for the property to be sold.

Rent Payment due for use of property; **chief rent** or **quit rent**; a fixed rent due from a freehold property. A **fee-farm** or **reserved rent** is similar, set up on the sale of property by a grant in fee farm. A **rack rent** may be either a very high, extortionate, rent, or a rent corresponding to the full market value.

Glossary of Deed Terms

Reversion The return of leased property to the original owner on expiry of a lease. A **Grant** (or **Lease**) **in reversion** starts after the termination of a previous lease, or sometimes after some other specified time or event.

Seisin (also **seizin**) The possession of freehold property; **livery of seisin** is the ceremony of taking possession by physical transfer of a turf, key, etc. recorded on the dorse of a feoffment, with the witnesses' names.

Settlement Transfer of property to trustees, for a particular purpose; **marriage settlement**: settlement preceding (**pre-nuptial**) or occasionally following a marriage (**post-nuptial**), involving property held for the benefit of husband, wife and children; **family settlement**: settlement of property to descend to the owner's heir(s) and other children, i.e. establishing an **entail**.

Statute Staple See **Bond**.

Surrender The return of property held by lease or by copyhold to the lessor or the lord of the manor.

Tenant for Life and **Tenant in Tail** See **Entail**.

Tenement A formal description of any type of property, but particularly property including a building.

Tenure The form of right by which property is held. See **Burgage tenure**; **Copyhold**; **Freehold**; **Knight Service**; **Leasehold**.

Trustee Person holding property on behalf of another, for specified uses. See also **Dower**. A **feoffee** holds property similarly, but without specification of the uses.

Uses The purposes for which property is held by a trustee, in a marriage or family **Settlement**, etc.

Virgate See **Yardland**.

Warranty An undertaking by a grantor to support a new owner's title to a property.

Yardland or **Virgate** A measure of the amount of land (usually applying to open fields), conventionally of 32 acres, but in reality varying very much from place to place; holdings were often described by the number of yardlands they contained. Grazing rights in the common fields were often proportional to the number of yardlands held.

INDEX OF SUBJECTS

A2A, *see* Access to Archives
abstract of title, 36–7, 76, 92–3, 133, 194
abuttals, 24, 107, 144–5, 194; urban, 26; variation in, 18
Access to Archives, 77–8
Acre, Cornish, 144; medieval, 144
Acts of Parliament by Fines and Recoveries Act (1833), 118; Married Women's Property Acts (1872, 1882, 1893), 117, 162; private, 116; *Quia Emptores* (1290), 144; Real Property Act (1845), 100; 'Release' (1841), 100; Statute of Enrolments (1536), 128; Statute of Uses (1535), 127
agreement, building, 148; maintenance, 148; medieval, 138–9, 150–1; to purchase, 103
agriculture, 24
AIM25, record catalogue, 77
alienation, royal licence, 126
Ancient Deeds, *see* TNA, Ancient Deeds
annuity, 7
archives, of estates, 49
Archives Hub, 77
articles of agreement, 94, 132

assignment, *see* lease; mortgage
Attorney, Letter of, *see* Letter of Attorney
auction, in foreclosing a mortgage, 110; posters, 134
Augmentations, Court of, *see* Court, of Augmentations

bankruptcy, 36, 64; schedules of debts and creditors, 103
bargain and sale, 127, 166, 194; counterpart, 129; enrolled, 65, 128–9; summary, 94
bills, from solicitors, 134
Bodleian Library, *see* libraries
bond, 89, 94, 112, 166–7, 194; appearance, 112; condition, 112; for quiet enjoyment, 114; medieval, 138–9; penal sum, 114; text, 178–9; to keep covenants, 113–14
Borough English, 19, 154, 156
boundaries, of urban tenements, 26
brewery companies, deed holdings of, 70
Bride Cart, 115
British Library, *see* libraries
building contract, *see* contract, building

200

Index of Subjects

building dates, 36
building lease, *see* lease, building
building societies, 30; deed holdings of, 72
burgages, 36
business partners, 21

Cambridge University Library, *see* libraries
Canal and River Trust (former Canal Companies), deed holdings of, 71
Cartae Miscellanae, 52, 58
cartularies, 66, 136
catalogues, Collection level, 46; Item level, 45; online, 45, 47, 76
certificates, baptism, marriage, burial, 134; in deed bundles, 13; of acknowledgement by married woman, 118, 134
Chancery, Court of, *see* Court, of Chancery
charters, Anglo-Saxon, 135; forged, 136
chief rent, *see* rent, chief rent
chimneys, 35
chirograph, *see* indenture, medieval
Colleges, Oxford and Cambridge, deed holdings, 70
Common Recovery, *see* recovery
community, structure, 24
computers and deeds, applications, 40; ChartEx project, 41; correspondence analysis, 42; data capture, 40; dating undated deeds, 42; DEEDS project, 41; feasibility, 40; seriation analysis, 44; statistical analysis, 41
confiscated estates, deeds from, 58
Congreve, William, *The Way of the World*, 118
consideration, 195
contract, building, etc., 94, 132, 134
conveyance, 166–7
copy of court roll, *see* court roll, copy of
copyhold, 22, 151; admission fine, 160; family settlement, 156; mortgage, 156; recovery, 158–9; tracing house history of, 34
copyhold property, 22
copyhold surrender, 154, 199; by married woman, 118; conditional, 156–7; illustration, 157; medieval, surrender to uses, 161; to use of purchaser, 155; to use of will, 156
cottage, 105; *see also* houses
counterpart, *see* lease, counterpart
court, borough, 149; manor, 22; of Augmentations, 52, 58; of

Chancery, 110, 124, 161; of Common Pleas, 119, 122, 149; of Hustings, London, 65; of Record, 65; of Wards and Liveries, 54, 59

court books, 152; indexes, 152

Court of Wards and Liveries, *see* Court, of Wards and Liveries

court roll, 22, 151–2, 194; medieval, 18; memorandum for enrolment in, text, 183–4; orders in, 22

court roll, copy of, 2, 89, 131, 151; illustration, 153; text, 153, 182

court roll, copy of, medieval, 18, 160; illustration, 160; text, 184–5

court, suit of, to manor court, 97

covenant, 195; agricultural, 25; to produce title deeds, 75, 166, 196

coverture, 196

curtilage, 196

customs, manorial, 151, 158; free bench, 158; morals, 158

databases, searchable, 46

dating, by regnal year, 87, 137, 142; by saint's day or church feast, 137, 142; Commonwealth period, 87–8; medieval, 136–7; of deeds, 87; of undated deeds, 136–7;
Old/New Style, 87; tree-ring, 34

deed, disentailing, 124; texts, 171; to lead the uses of a fine, 196

deed boxes, 9

deed poll, 165

deed record sheet, 92, 168

deed registries, 65; indexes to, 66; Memorials in, 66; Middlesex, 69; Yorkshire, 69

deeds, bundles, 7, 83, 92 dating, 3–5; dispersed, 71; endorsements, 83–6; enrolled, 64; family relationships, 11, 14; for communities, 10; for descriptions of buildings, 32; for factories, 36–9; for history of land ownership and use, 24; for local history, 10; for marriages, 10; for migration, 10; for people, 10; for places, 10; for places and houses, 24; for property, 10; for property values, 29; for social networks, 10; for the age of houses, 31–2; for the names of builders, 32; for urban history, 24, 26; in catalogues, 75; in private hands, 69; initial phrases of, 89; interpreting, 81; Irish, 2; location of, 45; miscellaneous, 132; objects attached to, 6; occupiers in, 108; of sixteenth-century

Index of Subjects

hospital, 25; offered for sale, 72–3; overseas, 73; parties to, 20; plans, 26, 108; retained by sellers, 75; schedules of, 104; Scottish, 2, 9; shapes, 88–9; significance, 6; types, 89, 94; urban, 2

deeds, location of, *see* National Register of Archives

deeds, medieval, 2, 135; clauses, 138; scribe of, 146; shapes of, 137–8; types, 143

deeds, post-medieval, 2, 11, 83; *see also* bargain and sale; charters; court roll, copy of; feoffment; mortgage

deeds, registered, *see* deed registries

defeasance, 166–7, 167, 195; of recognisance, 133; *see also* Statute Staple

deforciant (defendant in fine), 119

dendrochronology, 34

descent of property, 11

development, 36; financing, 36

dower, 19, 196

dower trustee, 92

dowry, 196

emigration, 15

enclosure awards, 79

endorsement, 196; in secret writing, 85; of covenant to produce deed, 86; of enrolment, text, 129, 181; of production in lawsuits, 86; receipts and witnesses, 86; with second deed, 86

enfranchisement of copyhold, 57, 132, 152, 167

enrolled deeds, 64

enrolment, 100, 196

Enrolments, Statute of (1536), 65

entail, 116, 196; docking and barring, after 1833, 124

entry fine, 196

equity of redemption, 110, 112, 196

examination, of married woman, 155, 164

exchange, deed of, 132

executors, 102, 196

exemplification, 167; of fine, 119, 196; of recovery, 122, 196

factory, development of, 37, 39

family, relationships of, medieval, 17

family tree, 13; from court rolls, 22–3

farm size, 24

fee farm, grant in, 132; rent, 56–7

fee simple, 197

Feet of Fine, 119–20

feoffment, 89, 127–9, 166, 196; summary, 94

203

Final Concord (Fine), 60, 89, 94, 118, 139, 148, 166, 196; covenant to levy, 104; deed to declare the uses of, 121; deed to lead the uses of, 121; exemplification, 119; Feet of, 148; illustration of, 120; indenture of, 119–20; medieval, 119, 138; portmanteau, 121, 198; text, 179–80
fine, entry, 97
fine and recovery, script of, 119
Free Bench, 158
freehold, *see* tenure

gardens, conversion to houses, 36–8
gavelkind, 19
gift or grant, deed of, 138; medieval, 19, 138–9, 143, 166, 197; clauses, 140–2; illustration, 140; in fee farm, 131; in pure alms, 143; in pure widowhood, 143; rent and service, 145; royal, 125; text, 140
glass, stained, 32
government departments, deed holdings of, 70

hamlets, 46
heriot, 97, 151, 155, 197
houses, back-to-back, 36; building costs, 29; converted from farm buildings, 32; converted from yards and gardens, 32; cottages, urban, 26; courtyard, 33; division, 35; medieval, 32, 35; new-built, 32; plans, 33; rooms in, 35
housing, industrial, 9
Hustings, Court of, *see* Court, of Hustings

indenture, 88–9, 165, 197; action, 90; clauses of, 90; consideration, 90; date, 90; introduction, 90; lordship, 90; medieval (chirograph), 138; parties, 90; period, 90; property, 90; recital, 90; rent, 90; seals, 90; signatures, 90; tenure, 90; uses, 90; witnesses, 90
indexes, person, 45; place, 45; to out-county records, 48
industry, debentures and partnership agreements, 36; factory plans, 36–40; prosperity and depression of, 36
inheritance rules, 11, 19
inquisition post mortem, 17
insurance policies, 134
interest, mortgage, 110
intestacy, 11
inventories, probate, 29, 133

kiln, malt, 36

Index of Subjects

knight service, *see* tenure

labour services, 25
land, drainage, 24
land ownership, 25
Land Registry, 66–9; tracing deeds through, 67–9
Land Tax assessments, 24
Latin, use of, 81, 135
law, conveyancing, 3; Roman, 3
lease, 88, 95, 166, 197; action, 96; assignment, 95, 98, 166, 194; building, 95, 98; building, 36, 166; conditions: carriage, husbandry, social, 98; consideration, 96, 196; counterpart, 88, 95, 138; covenants, 98; in reversion, 95; life, 96; medieval, 138–9, 147, 171–4; conditions, 148; for life, 148, of lease and release, 175–6; parties, 96; period, 96; perpetual, 95, 130, 197; property, 96; rent, 97; reversion, 96, 199; sub-letting, 95; summary, 94; surrender, 95, 97; three-life, 20, 96, 152, 162, 197; 'to add one life to two', 96; under-lease, 95
lease and release, 91, 95, 166, 197; function, 99; summary, 94; *see also* release
lease for year, 99, 197; clauses of, 100

leasehold, *see* tenure
letter forms, *see* palaeography
Letter of Attorney, 138–9, 149, 166–7, 194, 197; illustration, 150; text, 181–2
Letters Patent, 89, 125, 166–7, 197; illustration of, 126
libraries, Bodleian Library, 49–50; British Library, 49–51; Cambridge University Library, 49–50; Cardiff, 50; Folger Shakespeare Library, 74; Harvard Law Library, 74; Huntington Library, 73; Library of Birmingham, 48; Library of Congress, 74; National Library of Wales, 49–50, 53; overseas, 45; Shakespeare Centre, 48; University of Chicago, 74; University of Kansas, 74
Licence to Alienate, 126, 198
livery (clothing), 98
livery of seisin, *see* seisin

malt kiln, 36
manor court rolls/books, 31
manorial customs, *see* customs, manorial
Manorial Documents Register, 152
map regression, 26
marriage settlement, *see* settlement, marriage

messuage, 105, 198
migration, 15; individual, 16–18
mill, fulling, 32
moiety, 198
mortgage, 29, 36, 109; assignment, 110–11, 166, 194; assignment to attend the inheritance, 94, 112; assignment, summary, 94; by demise, 109, 166; by fine, 110; foreclosure, 110; in fee, 110, 166; interest, 110; reconveyance, 86; second, 110, 110; sixteenth-century, 30; summary, 94; types, 109; variation by place, 30
mortgagees, 20, 29, 102, 109–10; local people, 30; 'professional classes', 30; occupations of, 30
mortgagors, 20–1, 30, 102, 109–10

National Archives, *see* TNA
National Library of Wales, *see* libraries
National Register of Archives, 74, 80; *see also* TNA, Discovery, 'Record Creators'
Network Rail, deed holdings of, 71
Norman French, use of, 135

obit (prayers for a soul), 32

occupiers, of property, 20; sequence of, 31
open-field systems, 24
opinions, by counsel, 134
option to purchase, 36
owner, beneficial, 101
owners, joint, 101
ownership, by married women, 117; divided, 11–12; joint, 16, 101; sequence, 31

palaeography, 81, 170; abbreviations in, 135; guides to, 135; letter forms, 170; medieval, 135
parish registers, 10, 14; *see also* certificates
parishes, 46
parties to deeds, 20
partition, 198; deed of, 132
pedigree, 13, 134; medieval, 13, 18
plague, 25
plans on deeds, *see* deeds, plans
population, 36
probate, 198; grant of, 133; inventories, 133
probate certificate, 167
property, bequests of, 14; purchase of, 20

Quarter Sessions, rolls of, 65
querent (plaintiff in fine), 119
quitclaim, 19, 89, 130, 166, 198; medieval, 138–9, 147;

Index of Subjects

summary, 94

rack rent, *see* rent, rack rent
rates, church and poor, 24
recital, 92, 103, 198
Recognisance, 166–7, 194; Statute Staple, 194
reconveyance, *see* mortgage
record offices, county, 48; location of, 48; Nottinghamshire, 48; out-county material in, 48; Warwickshire, 48; West Midlands, 48
recovery, 60–1, 89, 94, 118, 122, 166, 198; conveyance to make a tenant to the precipe, 124; exemplification of, 122; illustration, 123; procedure, 125–6
regnal year, 198
relationships, from deeds, 21; network diagram, 21
release, 99, 197; clauses of, 100, 104; covenants, 104; parties, 101; property clauses, examples, 104; text, 185–9; *see also* lease and release
relief, 161, 198
rent, 198; chief rent, 198; fee farm, 146, 198; in kind, 25, 97, 145; rack rent, 97, 198
reservation, of space in house, 148
reversion, *see* lease, in reversion

sale particulars, 134
schedules, of building fixtures and fittings, 32, 34; of debts, 86; of furniture, 86; of open-field strips, 86; of ownership, 86; of shop fittings, 32
Seal, Great, 125
seals, 53, 142
searching, for family history, 47; for local history, 46; for places, 47
seisin, 143, 154, 199; livery of, 100, 128–9
settlement, 114, 199; family, 9, 14, 20, 114, 116, 199; marriage, 12, 14, 20, 114, 166, 199; pre-nuptial or post-nuptial, 115; on trustees for married women, 117–18; trustees of, 114; uses, 115;
skippet, 9, 123
slums, 20
socage, *see* tenure, free socage
social links, 19, 22; network, 21
solskifte (sun-sequence) in open-fields, 24
status, gentry, 17; manorial, 17; social, 19
Statute Staple, 133, 166–7; defeasance of recognisance, 133; recognisance in the nature of, 133
statutes, *see* Acts of Parliament
statutory declaration, 134

surnames, variability, 18, 41
surrender, *see* copyhold; lease

tanner, 36
tenancy, agreement, 166
tenant, for life, 116, 196; in tail, 116, 196
tenants, in common, 101; in survivorship, 101
tenement, 18, 26, 28, 37, 105, 107, 145, 158, 196, 199
tenure, 82, 199; at will, 95, 151; burgage, 18, 82, 194; by knight service, 197; copyhold, 18, 82, 131, 151, 194; free socage, 82; freehold, 18, 82, 197; in manorial records, 161; from Crown, 126; in chief, 126; in free socage, 126; leasehold, 82, 197; life, 95; medieval, 144; sub-infeudation, 144; substitution, 144; villein, 18
terrier, 24; of open-field strips, 105–6, 177
TNA (The National Archives), Ancient Deeds series, 51, 58; bankrupt property, enrolled, 64; Chancery deeds, 52, 58; Chancery Masters' Exhibits, 54, 59; Close Rolls, 60, 63–4; Court of Wards and Liveries, 54, 59; Crown Estate deeds, 59; deed holdings of, 51; Discovery, 48; 'Find an Archive', 48; 'Record Creators', 49; Duchess of Norfolk's deeds, 59; Enrolled deeds, 59–64; Exhibits in law suits, 59; Feet of Fine, 63; fines and recoveries, 119; grants to charities, enrolled, 63; Greenwich Hospital deeds, 59; Land Revenue series, 53; Manorial Documents Register, 152; Miscellaneous Deed series, 55–7; Modern Deeds series, 53, 59; Particulars for Grant, 127; Patent Rolls, 127; Plea Rolls, 63; rentals and surveys, indexes, 127

towns, location of occupiers in, 27; slums in, 20; social character, 29; trades in, 27
Treasury Solicitor, deed holdings of, 70
trustees, 20–1, 199; dower, 102, 199; for married women, 117; in bankruptcy, 102; of family settlements, as mortgagees, 31; of settlements, 101, 114

under-lease, 95
unregistered property, 69
urban history, *see* towns
uses, in settlements, 199
usury, 30

virgate, *see* Yardland

Index of Subjects

vouchee, common, in recovery, 125

warranty, 199; medieval, 146, 148
waste, impeachment of, 109
widow's rights, 19
widows, in deeds, 19
wills, 10, 20, 34, 89, 167; bequests to emigrants, 17; probate copies, 133; unproved, 134
witness, 20; final, 20; medieval, 146; to seisin, 128
wives, in deeds, 20
workshops, 36

yardland (or virgate), 24, 34, 104–5, 115, 199
yards, conversion to houses, 36–8

INDEX OF PEOPLE AND PLACES

Abbey, Henry, 156; Joyce, 156; Thomas, 156
Acle, Norfolk, 54
Agborow, Edward, 14
Alcester, Warwickshire, 150, 182
Allesley, Warwickshire, 154, 156–7, 183
Alrewas, Staffordshire, 54
Anstye, John, 108
Arbury, Warwickshire, 15, 58
Aston, Treaford, Staffordshire, 16
Aston, Warwickshire, 58
Atherstone, Warwickshire, 26, 37
Atkins, Robert, 177
Attleborough, Warwickshire, 15
Auckland, Turua, New Zealand, 17
Audley, Staffordshire, 160, 185
Austin, Geoffrey, 19, 36; Joan, 19; William, 19

Bacon, family, 74
Bagge, John, 142
Bainbridge, Elizabeth, 12
Barker, Edward, 12; Letitia, née Hill, 12
Baron, Edward, 107
Barston, Warwickshire, 23

Basnett, Mr, 85
Batell, John, 140
Bath, 95
Battle Abbey, Sussex, 73
Baxter, Robert, 125
Beake, R., 21
Beauchamp (Bewchamp), Lord John, 182
Beck, George, 154; John, 154; Mary, 154, 158; William, 154
Becket, Thomas à, Archbishop of Canterbury, 4–5
Bedfordshire, 49
Berkswell, Warwickshire, 84, 153
Bertie, Norreys, 182
Bezeley, Anthony, 16
Billers, Joseph, 21; Julius, 21
Birch, James, 183
Birmingham, Warwickshire, 58
Blickling Hall, Norfolk, 164
Blithfield, Staffordshire, 74
Blund, Robert, 172
Bolter, John, 140; William, 142
Bond, Abraham, 16; Ann, 16; Catherine, 16; John, 16; Joseph, 16; Mary, 16; Richard, 16; Sarah, 16; Thomas, 16; William, 16
Bonhomme, Joan, 19, 36; John,

210

Index of People and Places

18, 19; Robert, 18, 19;
William, called le Galeys, 19
Bradney, E., 21
Breconshire, 76
Brett, Walter, 156
Bright, family, 80
Brockhurst, B., 21
Bromell, Mr, 85
Bromfeild, Henry, 177
Brooke, J., 21
Brookhouse, Robert, 175;
Thomas, 176
Brownell, J., 21
Buckingham, Dukes of, 73
Bucknoll, Elizabeth, 177
Bulbek, William, 140
Burnes, T., 21
Burton Dassett, Warwickshire, 7, 13
Burton Hastings, Warwickshire, 115
Buxted, Sheperdshill, Sussex, 16

Cambridge, 70
Candeler, John, 142
Canterbury Cathedral, 5
Capell, C., 21; H., 21; Hugh, 25
Cater, Joseph, 154
Catesby, Anne, 34; family, 174; Robert, 58
Charles II, King, 88
Chatham, Kent, 55
Cheadle, Staffordshire, 23
Chelsea, 15

Cheltenham, Gloucestershire, 23
Cheshire, 53, 62, 163
Chesterfield, Earl of, 78
Chilvers Coton, Warwickshire, 15
Chinnor, Oxfordshire, 178
Chiswell, T., 21
Clarke, Jeremiah, 101; John, 101; Samuel, 108
Clifford Chambers, Warwickshire, 98
Coki (Cokus), Robert, 18, 145
Coles, Mary, 108
Collins, J., 21
Congreve, William, 118
Conway, Lord Seymour, 8; Marquess of Hertford, 9
Cooke, H., 21
Cooling Castle, Kent, 6
Cooper, Elizabeth, 155; Robert, 34; William, 155
Corley, Roger de, 172
Cornwall, 50, 58
Coundon, Warwickshire, 108
Courte, John, 128
Coventry, 3–4, 9, 13, 19, 21, 25–6, 30, 32, 35, 37, 102, 120, 174, 180, 186; Bonhomme Lane, 18; Broadgate, 27–8; Burges, 4, 39, 172; Greyfriar Lane, 85; Much Park Street, 108; Parkside, 39; St John's Street, 12, 38; Tolbooth, 107; Wymond Lane, 18, 36, 174
Cox, Henry, 183

Crichlowe, Alley, 183; Samuel, 183–4
Crofts, Robert, 104
Crowell, Oxfordshire, 113
Crynes, J., 21

Dadley, T., 21
Daffern, Catherine, née Bond, 16; John, 16
de Mandeville, Geoffrey, 4
Denny, Robert, 125
Derby, 99; St Peter's Abbey, 176
Derbyshire, 55, 76
Derwentwater, Earl of, 55
Dester, Sarah, née Tallis, 34; William, 34
Devon, 30, 49, 65, 163
Dougan, Alexander, 128
Doune, John del, 174
Dugdale, Sir J., 21
Dunton Bassett, Leicestershire, 115
Durham, 53, 62, 163
Dutton, Christian, 179; Leonard, 178; Thomas, 178

Eburne, J., 21
Edwards, Ann, 13; Anthony, 108; Mary, née Smith, 13; William, 13
Elizabeth I, Queen of England, 37
Ellesmere, Cheshire, 73
Erdington, Warwickshire, 58

Essex, 41, 65
Essex, Henry, 158
Ettington, Warwickshire, 101

Faccombe, Hampshire, 86
Feake, Revd S., 21
Fenn, grocer, 34
Fens, The, 79
Ferrers, family, 74
Feugers, Robert de, 172
Findern, Margery, 158
Fisher, Ann, 23; Elizabeth, née Evetts, 23; George, 23; Margaret, 23; Mary, 23; Thomas, 23
Flint, M., 21
Forest of Dean, Gloucestershire, 56
Forth, William, 141
Fox, J., 21
Franketon, William de, 172
Freer, William, 179
Freston, Thomas, 182
Frome, Somerset, 9

Gamage, Joan, 35
Geoffrey, Earl, 4
George I, King of England, 87
Gilbert, W., 21; William, 184
Gleddall, Ann, née Bond, 16; Charles, 16
Gloucester, St Peter's Abbey, 54
Goolde, Thomas, 142
Gravenor, H., 21

Index of People and Places

Greenoway, Elizabeth, 104; John, 105
Grenville, family, 67; William de, 41
Greville, Fulke, 126
Guppill, John, 177

Hamon, son of Jordan, 172
Hands, Richard, 39
Hanks, Samuel, 183; Stephen, 183
Harringey, Middlesex, 164
Harris, Elizabeth, 12; Mary, 117; Richard, 117
Harryman, F.C., 21; N., 21
Harryson, John, 185
Harwich, Essex, 55
Hathershaw Moor, Lancashire, 55
Hawten, Thomas, 142
Hayward, R., 21; S., 21
Heaton Norris, Greater Manchester, formerly Lancashire, 162
Henry, son of Edred, 172
Hent, Thomas, 140
Hertford, Marquess of, 8
Hill, Warwickshire, 19
Hill Morton, Warwickshire, 12
Hill, Hannah, née Woodcock, 12; John, 107, 128; Letitia, 12; Mary, 12; Samuel, 12
Hitch, Sarah, 115
Hobbins, Henry, 98
Hobyndone, Thomas, 140

Holloway, John, 107
Holme Lacy, Herefordshire, 7–8
Hoo, Suffolk, 98
Hope, Hanna, 186; Samuel, 107, 186; Thomas, 107, 187
Hopwood, Lancashire, 55
Horsman, Gilbert, 3
Howard, Sir Charles, 16
Howson, grocer, 34
Hubert, Michael, 117; Susannah, 117
Hulle, Geoffrey de, 36, 174
Hunt, S., 21

Ireland, 65, 79
Ireland, John, 17

Jackson, John, 175
Jefferys, Joanna, 184
Jersey, 79
John, son of William, 172
Jones, F.C., 3; John, 155

Kaye, family, 80
Kemsey, John, 128
Kenilworth, Robert de, 18, 145
Kenilworth, Warwickshire, 17
Kennon, T., 21
Kent, 55
Keu, Alice le, 145; Robert le, 18, 145
Kildermer, Margery, 180; Thomas, 180
Kilsby, J., 21

King, Ann, 162; Gilbert, 106; T., 21
Kingsbury, Warwickshire, 15–16
Kirtling, Cambridgeshire, 74
Knibb, John, 37
Knightley (alias Wightwick), John, 153, 180
Knowle, Warwickshire, Dial House, 34; Springfield Hall, 23
Knutsford, Cheshire, 16

Lancashire, 53, 55, 62, 163
Lander, R., 21
Lanvigan, Breconshire, 16
Lapworth, Warwickshire, 9
Latymer, Cowcroft, Buckinghamshire, 80
Launder, Robert, 182
Lawrence, T., 21
Lea, Edward, 102
Leamington Spa, Warwickshire, 32, 36, 71; Clarendon Crescent, 29
Leeds, 36
Leeson, Elizabeth, 12
Leicestershire, 76, 162
Lewes, John, 181
Lewes, Sussex, 155
Lillye, John, 162
Lincolnshire, 76
Little Aston, Staffordshire, 16
Littlemore, Oxfordshire, 35
Llantony Priory, Breconshire, 59
London, 65, 95, 178; Botolph Lane, 32–3; Chancery Lane, 57; East Greenwich, 126; Greenwich Hospital, 55, 59; Savoy Hospital, 55; Tower of, 129
London, Robert de, 18, 145
Long Marston, Warwickshire (formerly Gloucestershire), 34
Love, E., 21; J., 21
Lucas, S., 21
Luke, John, 145

Madley, Agnes, 182; Thomas, 182
Madox, Thomas, 52
Makepeace, family, 9
Malling, South, Sussex, 156
Man, Isle of, 79
Manchester, 16
Mann, Michael, 186
Marris, Thomas, 177
Martin, Francis, 125
Michael the dyer, 172
Middlesex, 65–6, 69
Mills, John, 16; Sarah, née Bond, 16
Mint Spring, Virginia, USA, 17
Moland, Anna Maria, 23; Lucy Margaret, 23; Mary, née Fisher, 23; Richard, 23
Monks Kirby, Warwickshire, 58

Napton on the Hill, Warwickshire, 104
Neale, family, 9

Index of People and Places

Needham, Humphrey, 12; Joseph, 12
New Zealand, Auckland, Turua, 17
Newdigate, Sir Richard, 15
Norfolk, Duchess of, 54, 59
North, family, 74
Northampton, Hospital of St John, 141
Northamptonshire, 58
Norwich, Norfolk, 65, 70
Nottinghamshire, 48, 76
Nuneaton, Warwickshire, 16, 98

Oadham, Catesby, 34; Matthew, 34
Olds, Joseph, 21; Julius, 21
Olney, Buckinghamshire, 140
Overton, William de, 174
Owen, A., 21; C., 21; Christopher, 85; E., 21
Oxford, 26, 70
Oxhill, Warwickshire, 14

Paget, family, 74
Paglesham, Essex, 56
Paignton, Devon, 106
Palmer, Mary, née Hope, 186; Richard, 186
Parker, Ann, 15; Richard, 15; William, 14, 15
Peasnall, Stephen, 37
Peke, Thomas, 185
Perry, John, 15
Phillips, R., 21

Polesworth, Warwickshire, 16
Porter, Richard, 108
Poughill, Cornwall, 162
Pyne, Agnes, 96; Leonard, 96; Thomas, 96

Ramsey Abbey, 4
Ramsgate, Kent, 57
Ravenstun, Buckinghamshire, 140
Raynsford, Henry, 98
Reskymer, family, 58, 78
Reynell, Edmond, 162
Richards, L., 21
Riges, Peter, 185
Riley, William, 17
Rokeby, Juliana, 35
Romsley, Worcestershire, 164
Rothersfield, Hampshire, 74
Roulegh, Margaret, 160, 185; Stephen, 160, 185
Rowe, Thomas, 184
Rowington, Warwickshire, 13
Rugby, Warwickshire, 71

St Albans, Hertfordshire, 160
Sale, Richard, 177
Sandes, Mary, née Hill, 12; William, 12; William Henry, 12
Savage, John, 156
Sawyer, D., 21
Scotland, 2, 9, 67, 79
Scudamore, family (Duchess of Norfolk), 54, 59
Sedgley, Staffordshire, 164

Seymour, *see* Conway Marquesses of
Shakespeare, Mary, 13, 42; William, 13
Sharratt, Elizabeth, 107
Shed, John, 124; Thomas, 125
Sherborne, Dorset, 164
Sherborne, River, Coventry, 39
Sherborne, Warwickshire, 13
Sherford, Devon, 162
Shilton, Joseph, 176
Skutt, Henry, 17; William, 17
Smith, Ann, 13; John, 13; Mary, née Shakespeare, 13, 42; William, 13, 42
Smyth, Thomas, 177
Smythe, Roger, 182
Snell, E., 21; J., 21; S., 21
Somerset, 163
South Kirby, Yorkshire, 16
Sowton, Devon, 96
Spyer, John, 115
Squire, Stafford, 125
Staffordshire, 55, 104
Stevenson, grocer, 34
Stoke Gabriel, Devon, 105
Stoneleigh, Warwickshire, 14, 32, 117; Stoneleigh Abbey, 32, 58, 98
Stowe, Buckinghamshire, 73
Stratford-upon-Avon, Warwickshire, 14, 16
Sutton-under-Brailes, Warwickshire, 25
Swain the parker, 172

Tallis, Edward, 34; Sarah, 34
Tamworth, Staffordshire and Warwickshire, 74, 186; Glascote, 16
Tanworth-in-Arden, Warwickshire, 42
Tebowde, William, 140, 142
Temple Balsall, Warwickshire, 23, 158, 164
Thomas the dyer, 172
Thompson, James, 179
Thurlaston, Warwickshire, 106, 177
Tole, Richard, 145
Tompson, J., 21
Townsend, William, 102
Troughton, S., 21
Trowbridge, 70
Tully, Gilbert, 106; Odes, 106
Tumberlake, 181
Turner, Susan, 12
Tylney, family, 74

Vincent, son of Swain, 172
Virginia, USA, Mint Spring, 17

Wakefield, Yorkshire, 160, 164
Walden, I., 21
Waldron, Possingworth, Sussex, 16
Wales, 30, 50, 53, 55, 62
Wallingford, Oxfordshire, 65
Warden, J., 21
Warwick, 3, 48–9, 58, 65, 75, 104; Warwick Castle, 126;

Index of People and Places

Chapel Street, 37, 93; St James's Hill, 107; St Nicholas, 123
Washfield, Devon, 74
Webb, Thomas, 108
Webster, W., 21
Wedon, John de, 145
West Midlands, 48
Weston on the Green, Oxfordshire, 153, 182
Weston Underwood, Buckinghamshire, 140–2
Whateley, Thomas, 16, 42
Whateley, Warwickshire, 16
Wheatley, Thomas, 42
White, Bartholomew, 15; Elizabeth, 15; Leonard, 15; Thomas, 15; William, 15
Wightman, W., 21
Wightwick, Wightwicke (alias Knightley), John, 153; 180
Wigston Magna, Leicestershire, 25
Wilde, John, 182
Willenhall, Geoffrey de, 172
William I, King of England, 82
William, son of Humphrey, 172
Wilnecote, Warwickshire, 16
Wolston, Warwickshire, 117
Woodcock, family, 12; Ann, 12; Benjamin, 12; Elizabeth, 12; Hannah, 12; James, 12; John, 12; John Thomas, 12; Mary, 12; Thomas, 12
Woolrich, J., 21
Wootton Underwood, Buckinghamshire, 35, 41–2, 67
Worcester Cathedral, 5
Worth, family, 74
Wragge, William, 176
Wright, T., 21
Wrotham, Kent, 161
Wymond, Agnes, 19; Emma, 19; John, 19; William, 18, 19
Wynchester, Thomas, 157
Wyse, Thomas, 128

Yerrow, William, 13
York, 41
Yorkshire, 65–6, 69